Seeds of Change

Seeds of Change

The International Vegan Rights Alliance and the Vegan Rights Revolution

Jeanette Rowley

LEXINGTON BOOKS
Lanham • Boulder • New York • London

Published by Lexington Books
An imprint of The Rowman & Littlefield Publishing Group, Inc.
4501 Forbes Boulevard, Suite 200, Lanham, Maryland 20706
www.rowman.com

86-90 Paul Street, London EC2A 4NE

British Library Cataloguing in Publication Information Available

Library of Congress Cataloging-in-Publication Data

Names: Rowley, Jeanette, 1962- author.
Title: Seeds of change : the international vegan rights alliance and the vegan rights revolution / Jeanette Rowley.
Description: Lanham : Lexington, 2024. Includes bibliographical references and index. | Summary: "This book explains the rights of vegans as supporting the animal protection movement. It explores some of the issues vegans face, the principles that ground their legal rights, and how legal provisions have been used to adapt policies that support compassionate living and a future, compassionate, inclusive, system of justice"— Provided by publisher.
Identifiers: LCCN 2024028449 (print) | LCCN 2024028450 (ebook) | ISBN 9781666951530 (cloth) | ISBN 9781666951547 (ebook)
Subjects: LCSH: Vegans—Legal status, laws, etc. | Veganism—Political aspects. | Human rights—Philosophy. | Food law and legislation—Philosphy. | Food sovereignty. | Animal welfare—Law and legislation. | Animal rights. | Human-animal relationships. |Vegetarianism.
Classification: LCC K3253 .R687 2024 (print) | LCC K3253 (ebook) | DDC 344.04/232—dc23/eng/20240624
LC record available at https://lccn.loc.gov/2024028449
LC ebook record available at https://lccn.loc.gov/20240284

∞™ The paper used in this publication meets the minimum requirements of American National Standard for Information Sciences—Permanence of Paper for Printed Library Materials, ANSI/NISO Z39.48-1992.

As always, my work is dedicated to other animals, to the animal protection movement and to those asserting and defending their right to live with compassion.

Contents

Acknowledgments ix
List of Abbreviations xi
Foreword xiii
Introduction 1
1 Issues Faced by Vegans 17
2 The Campaign for Legal Protection for Vegans and the International Vegan Rights Alliance 49
3 Research Validating and Supporting Rights for Vegans 75
4 How Research, Law, and Guidance Apply to the Issues Faced by Vegans 107
5 The Successes, Additional Inroads, Still Listening 145
Conclusion 185
Appendix A: Table of Cases 197
Bibliography 199
Index 215
About the Author 221

Acknowledgments

This book would not exist but for the hundreds of vegans who have pushed the movement for vegan rights forward by registering their complaints, raising formal grievances, and in some instances, escalating their cases to be heard by a tribunal. The book is testament to your convictions, strength, and tenacity. The knowledge I am able to share with the vegan community has developed in the course of supporting you through the issues you have faced. I know firsthand the difficulties and hurdles you have dealt with, and I hope I have done you justice!

I am eternally grateful for the support of so many friends, associates, and supporters who have shared and contributed to my journey through legal research and a vegan rights-based approach to vegan advocacy over the last thirteen years: Ralf Müller-Amenitsch, Dr Carlo Prisco, Greg McFarlane, Camille Labchuk, Marcelo Daidone Chalita, Alexandra Cantarelli, Angela Radich, Edie Bowles, Jess Swallow, Sean McHale, Jonathan Dennis, Ruby Sandhu, Dina Aherne, Dr Gabor T. Fodor, Professor Gary Francione, Alex Monaco, Sara Dent, Dr Maureen O'Sullivan, Kadri Sikk, Mari-Liis Sepper, Nuno Alvim MSc, Marie Laffineur-Pauchet, Matthew Overton, Dr Richard Twine, Dr Joe Wills, Anoushavan Sarukhanyan, Adam Karp, and many others have been great sources of strength, inspiration, and at times, motivation.

Making things happen involves a great number of people, and it is impossible to mention them all by name. I am grateful for all the wonderful support, collaboration, and insights from acquaintances, old and new, including Petr, Jonathan, Laura, Heather, Chantal, Andrea, George, Kat, Louise, Lulu, Mark, Rich, Sam, AC, Vicky, Ruth, Ellie, Jordi, Elisa, Ronja, Francisco, Violeta, Alex, Lorna, Emma, Brittany, Hayley, Lynda, and Nicholas—and not forgetting Adam, Astrid, Alexander, Olivier, Jane, and Emily! Heartfelt thanks to everyone who has given their time, support, or expertise so generously. You know who you are.

Thank you to The Vegan Society, Vegan Australia, and PETA Germany for early positive engagement with the campaign for vegan rights. Thank you to the Hungarian Vegan Association for honorary membership. Thank you to the vegan societies of Finland, Estonia, and everyone else involved in raising awareness around the world. Thank you to Christina Rees MP and convenors of the APPG for inviting me to speak at the first meeting in 2016.

Special thanks to Adam Knauff for a valuable firsthand account of their lived experience in employment and in accessing justice in Canada.

Thank you to Sara, Emily, and Anna at Lexington Books for their first-class support and another wonderful drafting and publishing experience and, as always, thank you to Dr Karen Atkinson for professional attention to my draft manuscript. Any errors remaining in the text are my sole responsibility.

List of Abbreviations

ACAS	Advisory, Conciliation and Arbitration Service
AHDB	Agriculture and Horticulture Development Board
APPG	All-Party Parliamentary Group
BTEC	Business and Technology Education Council
CLOtC	Council for Learning Outside the Classroom
CPD	Continuing Professional Development
ECHR	European Convention on Human Rights
ECtHR	European Court of Human Rights
EDI	Equality, Diversity and Inclusion
EU	European Union
EYFS	Early Years Foundation Stage
HMP	His Majesty's Prison
HRTO	Human Rights Tribunal of Ontario
ICCPR	International Covenant on Civil and Political Rights
IMB	Independent Monitoring Board
IVRA	International Vegan Rights Alliance
MOD	Ministry of Defence
MSP	Member of the Scottish Parliament
NHS	National Health Service
OT	Occupational Therapist
PPC	Provision, Practice, or Criterion
PPE	Personal, Protective Equipment
PSED	Public Sector Equality Duty
QC	Queen's Counsel
UDHR	Universal Declaration of Human Rights
UNESCO	United Nations Educational, Scientific and Cultural Organization
VEND	Vegan Equality-Non-Discrimination

Foreword

My dream was always to be an animal rights lawyer, yet human rights for vegans were one of the first issues on which I cut my legal teeth. It occurs to me as I sit down to write this foreword that my own career path may have been very different without the work of Jeanette and others to develop this area of law.

I became aware of the novel idea of human rights protections for vegans as a law student. I was lucky enough to spend the summer working at Animal Justice. The Canadian animal law organization had just helped a vegan veterinary student with an outrageous case: she was told that after undertaking a spay operation on a dog, she would be required to euthanize the animal. If she refused, she would not graduate. The school initially denied her request for a non-lethal alternative but finally backed down once our lawyers got involved and raised the specter of a human rights lawsuit. Her eleven-month-old beagle patient, Rainbow, was adopted by a loving family, and the school ended the routine killing of healthy dogs, promising that the canines would be adopted out in the future.[1]

Encouraged by the victory, I got involved in an Ontario Human Rights Commission consultation aimed at modernizing a decades-old policy on "creed"—a protected ground in Ontario, but one that had historically been considered mostly synonymous with religion. We saw an opportunity to expand the definition of creed to include secular belief systems, like ethical veganism. I participated in a legal workshop, presenting on the harm done to ethical vegans when the law fails to protect their beliefs. We saw more success—the Commission's new creed policy recognized that secular beliefs mattered. The potential for legally enshrined protections for ethical vegans in Ontario was within reach, and the new policy made international headlines.[2]

I first met Jeanette a few weeks later when she reached out to extend an invitation to attend an upcoming legal symposium in Berlin hosted by the International Vegan Rights Alliance (now known as the International Rights Network). What a revelation to learn that lawyers around the world were organizing and theorizing about the fight for vegan rights! It was remarkable to connect and collaborate with others in this global movement, and the community quickly became a valuable resource.

But perhaps most importantly, it is also through Jeanette that I first met and worked with Adam Knauff—a vegan firefighter who eventually filed the first case seeking a legal ruling on whether ethical veganism was, in fact, a protected creed in Ontario.[3] Adam's case is discussed extensively in chapter 5. Not only was he denied vegan food while fighting forest fires, but he was mocked, punished, and suspended simply for trying to assert his rights. Jeanette's expert evidence at his hearing was invaluable, and although Adam's claim was recently rejected at first instance, efforts are underway to seek review by a higher court. This setback is a reminder that shepherding the adoption of a novel rights framework is not easy.

As Jeanette details in this book, vegan rights have been making slow progress for decades, with many favorable court decisions and settlements recognizing and rejecting discrimination against those with vegan belief systems. Yet, this has not stopped governments, service providers, and employers from engaging in bad behavior directed at vegans. In fact, it would be a surprise to meet a vegan from anywhere in the world who hasn't faced discrimination or marginalization from the non-vegan majority.

I am struck by the familiar themes in the case studies Jeanette describes in chapter 2. Many members of the International Rights Network have engaged with the parents who are told their vegan toddler can't have non-dairy milk at pre-school (even though a child with a dairy allergy would be fed an alternative); with one-sided promotion in the school system of animal farming (e.g., hatching an egg as a class project) or zoos (e.g., a class field trip); with the employee who is never offered vegan food at work events; or with the military member who is told they will face discipline if they object to wearing leather boots.

Anti-vegan harassment, marginalization, and exclusion can touch nearly every area of the lives of vegans, and this shows how difficult it can be to challenge social norms in a non-vegan world. To me, it feels like anti-vegan bias is one of the last bastions of socially acceptable discrimination. Despite growing public awareness and concern over how animals suffer in farming and elsewhere at human hands, social bias against those who opt out of these systems remains painfully real—one study showed that only drug addicts were evaluated more negatively than vegetarians and vegans.[4] Anti-vegan bias has also been demonstrated in the media[5] and in social science literature.[6] The mere existence of vegans challenges the dominant view that eating animals is normal, natural, and necessary, and this can be perceived as an identity threat to non-vegans. People are almost universally opposed to animal cruelty, and it provokes cognitive dissonance to consider that one's actions might be misaligned with one's values. It is tempting to defensively judge vegans rather than engage with the discomfort or take a hit to one's self-image and identity.[7]

Yet, if we are to take seriously our mission to liberate animals from the confinement, suffering, and killing they endure, then we need more people to consider being vegan. This requires veganism to be further normalized and its broader adoption to be encouraged. If anti-vegan discrimination becomes legally difficult, less normalized, and less common, we can help remove barriers to people going vegan and staying vegan, and we can grow veganism as a social movement. Vegan rights should thus be seen as a stepping stone along the pathway to animal liberation. With this book, Jeanette lays down a further stone on this path, offering a succinct legal theory and narrative grounded in international human rights law, freedom of conscience and belief, and equality.

Jeanette and others in the International Rights Network have given countless vegans the space and tools to come forward, seek representation, and be heard and accommodated. The impact in my own country is already clear—the publicity surrounding vegan rights has led many lawyers to proactively advise about the risks of failing to accommodate ethical vegans. The international campaign for vegan rights is making progress, and with this book as an important new resource for lawyers, advocates, and vegans everywhere, we will undoubtedly see more in the years ahead.

Camille Labchuk, 2024
Executive Director, Animal Justice

NOTES

1. Animal Justice, "Students No Longer Required to Kill Dogs, Says Vet Dean," Animal Justice, 2010, accessed February 18, 2024, https://animaljustice.ca/media-releases/students-no-longer-required-to-kill-dogs-says-vet-dean.

2. Camille Labchuk, "Veganism Is One Step Closer to Becoming a Human Right in Ontario," Animal Justice, January 12, 2016, accessed February 18, 2024, https://animaljustice.ca/blog/veganism-is-one-step-closer-to-becoming-a-human-right-in-ontario.

3. Animal Justice, "Vegan Firefighter Claims Discrimination in Groundbreaking Case," Animal Justice, May 21, 2019, accessed February 18, 2024, https://

animaljustice.ca/media-releases/vegan-firefighter-claims-discrimination-in-ground-breaking-case

4. Cara C. MacInnis and Gordon Hodson, "It Ain't Easy Eating Greens: Evidence of Bias Toward Vegetarians and Vegans from Both Source and Target," *Group Processes & Intergroup Relations*, 20 no. 6(2017), 1–24.

5. Matthew Cole and Karen Morgan, "Vegaphobia: Derogatory Discourses of Veganism and the Reproduction of Speciesism in UK National Newspapers," The British Journal of Sociology 62, no. 1 (March 2011), 134–53.

6. Matthew Cole, "Asceticism and Hedonism in Research Discourses of Veg*anism," *British Food Journal* 110, no. 7, (January 1, 2008), 706–16.

7. Emily Moran Barwick, "The Science of Why People Hate Vegans," The Bite Size Vegan, August 30, 2023, accessed February 18, 2024, https://bitesizevegan.org/the-science-of-why-people-hate-vegans/.

Introduction

This book documents and celebrates the history and success (in the UK and Europe) of the dedicated campaign for vegan rights, launched publicly in 2012. It frames the success of the campaign for rights for vegans in terms of "seeds of change" and as facilitating a "vegan rights revolution" for two reasons. First, the global vegan community has access to, is now aware of, and is able to articulate vegan ethical convictions in terms of fundamental human rights principles and equality law. Second, members of the vegan community, vegan advocates, academics, and lawyers around the world are now using the information, research, and knowledge about useful legal principles and provisions disseminated by the vegan rights campaign to challenge policies and dominant practices that restrict the practice of veganism.

My idea to develop a campaign to use law to advance veganism and protect vegans as a strategy to support the liberation of nonhuman animals is set in the context of many decades of animal rights campaigning but has specific origins in the UK in 2010. At this time, new consolidated equality law, in the form of the Equality Act 2010, was about to come into force. Accompanying the Equality Act was draft guidance, published by the Equality and Human Rights Commission, that contained examples of how employers could accommodate the needs of vegans. One of the purposes of the guidance was to explain how to avoid discriminating against those with a qualifying "philosophical belief".

Veganism is a philosophy that raises important questions about our relationship with other animals, our ethical responsibilities, prejudice, suffering, and violence. It offers a perspective on what it means to be human, and on inclusive justice. Vegans hold strong moral convictions about the status and our treatment of nonhuman animals and endeavor to avoid participating in animal exploitation in their daily lives. The inclusion of vegans in the draft guidance was reasonable and appropriate, and was groundbreaking, but was mocked by some of the popular press.

Following the consultation period, the examples referring to vegans to illustrate compliance with forthcoming legislation were removed. The removal of these examples was unexplained and detrimental to the vegan community, and was the impetus for my embarking on several campaign activities: researching, documenting views from the vegan community about their ability to practice veganism on a daily basis in different contexts, establishing the IVRA, and unexpectedly embarking on a career promoting vegan rights and supporting individual vegans with their complaints of unfair treatment and discrimination.

In 2010, what was not well-known, utilized, promoted, or considered valuable within the vegan community was that in 1993, the European Court of Human Rights (ECtHR) had found the convictions of vegans to be within the legal meaning of the human right to freedom of belief, as guaranteed by Article 9 of the European Convention on Human Rights (ECHR). The relevant case involving a vegan that had been presented to the court lay quietly gathering dust for seventeen years before the campaign for vegan rights brought it into the light and used it to ground a movement for change; a movement that intended to make full use of the human right to freedom of belief to prevent discrimination against vegans and ensure vegan convictions were respected and accommodated in employment, education, and in the provision of goods and services.

The mission of the dedicated campaign for vegan rights was to undertake research, share information about fundamental human rights, and empower the vegan community to contribute, in a powerful way, to "shifting the balance"[1] of power in which vegans struggle for respect and accommodation of their needs in a dominant non-vegan majority, and in the context of unexamined unfair and discriminatory policies that are propped up by, and perpetuate, speciesist prejudice.

It is fair to say that the campaign has been successful. It has brought about what can be described as a vegan rights revolution in that vegans are now informed and ready to challenge breaches of their rights, discrimination, and unfair treatment. Since the start of the campaign, veganism has been recognized in law in Germany, Italy, and Denmark, under British equality law, and vegans around the world, in Canada,[2] Peru[3] and the Basque Country,[4] for example, are defending their legal rights. This new era offers seeds of change that contribute to our combined efforts to dismantle speciesism and change the dreadful conditions we, collectively, have created for the nonhuman animals of Earth's community.

Legal protection for vegans stems from the international human right to freedom of thought, conscience, and religion (commonly shortened to freedom of belief), which guarantees protection for religious, non-religious, and philosophical beliefs. The human right to freedom of belief is considered to be a *primary* human right. The right to be free to work out and believe in our own moral orientation is absolute, and there are very strict limits to lawful interference with our right to practically manifest our religious or moral values and convictions.

Under this human rights principle, interference with our practice of veganism will only be lawful if there is a law that is required in a democracy for an important reason, such as public health, public order, or public safety, or to protect the rights of other people. This has been confirmed under the European system of human rights. The law relied on must support a legitimate aim, and any interference with an individual's right to freedom of belief must be proportionate to meeting the specified legitimate aim. In addition, everyone (including vegans) benefits from the human right to equality, which underlies and is enshrined in human rights and anti-discrimination law.

Legal support for veganism is, however, notoriously inconsistent. Gains have been hard-fought, and individual successes have been achieved in the context of a confused social, political, and legal landscape regarding our relationship with nonhuman animals, the wider natural environment, and an entrenched anthropocentric culture of exploitation and prejudice against other animals, which is represented and reflected in our human system of justice. In this context, veganism is misunderstood, and the convictions of vegans are often dismissed, trivialized, and ridiculed. Through a widespread lack of knowledge and understanding of the scope of the human right to freedom of belief and how it should be interpreted and represented in equality law, veganism has not enjoyed as much institutional support as other belief systems, and vegans struggle to access justice. While vegans can be protected in the legal systems of Germany, Italy, Denmark, and the UK, an adjudicator's decision in a case presented to the Ontario Human Rights Tribunal in Canada is that veganism does not meet all the elements of the criteria for protected status under its Code.[5]

At this point, it might be helpful to remind the reader that vegans aim to avoid causing harm to nonhuman animals. It might also be useful to offer a short overview of the social and political context for veganism.

THE SOCIAL AND POLITICAL CONTEXT FOR THE PROTECTION OF VEGANS

Socially, anti-vegan attitudes are so prevalent that there is a specific and growing body of academic literature dedicated to examining and analyzing them.[6] Researchers observe that the topic of veganism is so polarizing that there are online anti-vegan communities who are publicly and vehemently against veganism, and that there is other literature that refers to vegans as uneducated, ill-informed, and obstinate.

In 2020, hostility toward vegans was so remarkable that the BBC published an in-depth overview of "veganophobia," highlighting that research has shown that only drug addicts face the same degree of stigma, and that the least popular vegans of all are those who cite animal suffering (ethical veganism) as the reason for their moral convictions.[7]

Historically, veganism has not enjoyed widespread support from people in power, and, furthermore, people in power have referred to veganism and vegans in ways that encourage and perpetuate ridicule, unfair treatment, and discrimination.[8] Veganism has been mentioned in the UK Parliament on a number of occasions but not as a matter for serious political engagement. Rather, references to it evidence a long-standing culture of disrespect for veganism. In 1987, in a debate on complimentary medicine, Lord Rea registered their support for approved training programmes for complimentary practitioners and spoke about the dangers to clients from the possibility of being treated by a "bizarre vegan diet".[9] In 1996, Conservative Parliamentarian Mr John Marshall participated in a debate on Creutzfeldt-Jakob Disease (CJD). During the debate, Mr Marshall raised a question seeking confirmation on international incidences of CJD and "that there was no correlation between the incidence of CJD and behavioral patterns, such as whether one eats beef or meat or is merely a stupid vegan".[10] In 2017, Scottish Conservative MSP Murdo Fraser was reprimanded in the Scottish Parliament because they referred to the Scottish Greens as "lentil-munching sandal-wearing watermelons".[11] In 2018, during a tenth sitting debate on an Agricultural Bill, Kerry McCarthy MP was so astounded and frustrated by irrelevant but frequent references to veganism by their (professional) peers that they finally commented "I seem to be here to provide light entertainment, basically by giving the lads over there the chance to do a little bit of vegan bashing in the afternoon".[12] This was decades after veganism had been recognized at the ECtHR, and eight years after the Equality Act 2010 came into force and the Equality and Human Rights Commission had referred to veganism as relevant to the protected characteristic "religion or philosophical belief" in its Draft Code of Practice.

During a debate preceding the Equality Bill, in March 2010, Baroness Warsi sought clarity on what was included under the protected characteristic of religion or belief. The Baroness understood that "beliefs" can be capable of qualifying for legal protection but that they must attain a certain level of cogency, seriousness, cohesion, and importance, be worthy of respect in a democratic society, and not be incompatible with human dignity or conflict with the fundamental rights of others. She also understood that qualifying beliefs must be grounded in weighty and substantial aspects of human life and behavior and not on mere opinions. The Baroness wanted to emphasize that the protected category was not intended to include cults or other similar belief systems and expressed dismay that vegans might be protected under the new equality law. Disappointed by the guidance provided by the Equality Commission, that the beliefs and ethical convictions of vegans would likely be covered by the Bill, Baroness Warsi remarked that prior debates had confirmed that only serious and important beliefs would be included as religious or philosophical beliefs for the purposes of the law, and to include cults and other lifestyle choices such as veganism would make something of a farce of those debates.

The Baroness also registered surprise that the Government Equalities Office had endorsed the codes of practice.[13] Fortunately, more informed comment on the relationship of philosophical belief to the internationally agreed principles on the human right to freedom of belief immediately followed Baroness Warsi's contribution to the debate.

On January 3, 2020, a decade since the draft guidance was published by the UK Equality and Human Rights Commission and since the start of a dedicated campaign to promote the validity of veganism in law, a UK employment tribunal confirmed that veganism was a protected characteristic for the purposes of the Equality Act 2010.[14] Shortly after, on January 8, 2020, Lord Blencathra expressed their frustration about the decision in a debate in Parliament. They described the tribunal as "idiotic" and called for the government to reverse the "crazy" judgment at the earliest opportunity. Their concern was that the tribunal had "changed" the law (which it had not), and it was also stated that if "we do not get rid of this nonsense," police officers might be required to run around investigating "vegan hate crimes from those who claim they could not get a Greggs vegan sausage roll".[15]

Since the tribunal decision of 2020, vegans have been referred to in the UK Parliament as "vegan extremists"[16] and "vegan militias"[17] (although references to vegans in anti-terror legislation have rightly raised questions[18]). Vegan diets have been referred to as sometimes "very damaging to the climate because the materials are sometimes grown where rainforests used to be"[19] (although veganism has also been cited as relevant to the national food strategy and net-zero targets[20]).

Vegan police staff networks have also been criticized in Parliament because of the potential for a blurring of the boundaries between policing and politics,[21] while the force hosts a wide range of other staff networks including the Christian Police Association (est. 1883), the British Association for Women in Policing (est. 1987), the National Black Police Association (est. 1998), the Jewish Police Association (est. 2001), the National Association of Muslim Police (est. 2007), the Police Pagan Association (est. 2009), the Disabled

Police Association (est. 2012), the Gypsy Roma Traveller Police Association (est. 2014), the National Police Autism Association (est. 2015), the National LGBT+ Police Network (est. 2015), and the National Sikh Police Association (est. 2019). The UK's leading "think tank," *Policy Exchange*, states the following about a vegan staff network:

> While most of the Staff Networks are based on self-selected specific characteristics, such as religion, ethnicity, gender, sexuality or disability there are a number which stray beyond these boundaries. Two examples are the Cleveland Police Vegan Network and the West Yorkshire Green Police Network.[22]

It is in this social and political context that vegans have struggled for validation, to have their legitimate voice heard, defend their rights, and bring their convictions as legitimate issues for consideration in our democracy.

This social and political context for veganism is not specific to the UK. In 2016, Italian politician Elvira Savino was concerned about the increasing interest in veganism as a potential "ideological excess" and proposed the "Savino Law" to prosecute parents who fed their children inadequate, restrictive, and damaging diets. Custodial sentences for parents whose children became sick or injured as a result of malnutrition ranged from two-and-a-half years to four years, and in the event of child fatalities, parents could be imprisoned for four to six years. While attention to child nutrition is, of course, important, stigmatizing veganism in this way is prejudicial, unfair, and unnecessary.[23]

Prior to establishing a campaign to explain the experiences of vegans as examples of violations of the human right to freedom of belief, vegans themselves typically endured negative experiences because their moral outlook is focused on the suffering of other animals rather than on themselves as legitimate entities within the system of human justice.

The dedicated campaign for vegan rights aimed to disseminate information about law and legal protection within the vegan community and explains that by claiming our rights as vegans, we can positively impact the development of policy and practice to support veganism and vegans, and can thus contribute to the development of a social, political, and legal infrastructure that supports animal rights.

WHAT THIS BOOK IS ABOUT

In this book, I explore some of the difficulties vegans face in their daily practice of veganism and why it is important to defend the rights of vegans. I discuss the conception and development of the campaign to use law to protect vegans and advance veganism as a strategy to support the animal protection movement. I explain the origins, rationale, and history of the campaign for vegan rights, and the work, challenges, and development of the IVRA. I discuss the legal research undertaken to inform the campaign and how relevant guidance, principles, and law have been applied to support vegans and help safeguard their daily practice of veganism. Importantly, I document some of the beneficial changes to policies and practices in public and private sector organizations that not only protect vegans but also contribute to sustaining and advancing veganism and, arguably, help bring about a more compassionate society that better supports the campaign for animal rights.

LIMITATIONS

A lot of information about veganism can easily be found online and in various publications, along with dynamic discussions and debates on a diverse range of issues relating to veganism itself, the reasons for adopting veganism, and ideas on how best to advance veganism. Other than presenting a very brief overview of the social and political conditions for veganism and vegans (above), I do not explore the wide-ranging issues on the subject of veganism itself nor discuss and debate the various views and issues presented by different organizations or individuals.

The book is also limited to utilizing a specific definition of veganism. Many readers may already be aware that there is more than one definition of veganism, and that veganism can be explained in different ways. My intention is not to set one definition against the other or undermine the importance and significance of different or evolving definitions.[24] The reason for the limitation in this book is that the definition promoted by The Vegan Society has been helpful in legal cases involving vegans and is, therefore, key to my discussion.[25] This definition is referred to in the book where necessary, but readers might find it helpful to introduce or refamiliarize themselves with it at this point. The definition provided by The Vegan Society states that:

> Veganism is a philosophy and way of living which seeks to exclude—as far as is possible and practicable—all forms of exploitation of, and cruelty to, animals for food, clothing or any other purpose; and by extension, promotes the development and use of animal-free alternatives for the benefit of animals, humans and the environment. In dietary terms it denotes the practice of dispensing with all products derived wholly or partly from animals.[26]

Vegans around the world experience discrimination. However, a further limitation to the scope of this book is that I do not discuss a wide range of issues and legal cases involving vegans in different parts of the world. While I do explain the international legal framework for the worldwide protection of vegans, the international work of the IVRA and its members, and note a limited number of cases in other jurisdictions in chapter 5, legal professionals in different countries have specialist knowledge about their domestic legislation and are, thus, more able to discuss cases in their own regions. Therefore, the book does not provide a comprehensive discussion about discrimination against vegans and the legal systems and legislation of multiple jurisdictions, or words and concepts in specific languages that potentially have important legal meanings. In addition, the reach of the idea of rights for vegans has grown independently of the ongoing campaign and complaints raised by vegans often now no longer involve the campaign's founders, long-standing or new members, and supporters. Subsequently, information about legal challenges may not be publicly available until cases have already been heard. Therefore, the book focuses on the situation in the UK as things stand in 2024, with chapter 5 providing some references to and examples of the use of law to protect vegans and advance veganism in other countries.

In addition, the scope of the book does not allow for an in-depth discussion of the potential for protection from unlawful interference and discrimination for vegans who adopt the vegan diet for health reasons, in the interests of a healthy global climate, for environmental reasons, or for any other reason. This is because, currently, protection for vegans revolves around the conviction that it is morally wrong to exploit nonhuman animals for human gain. The legal principles applicable to possible protection for other potential philosophical beliefs and convictions are outlined in chapter 3.

WHY NOW?

There are a number of reasons for publishing this new volume now. Much has happened in the thirteen years since I embarked on the vegan rights campaign, and these developments deserve to be documented and shared. In this regard, the book aims to be an informative historical record of the difficulties vegans face in their daily lives as matters of justice, of the research and insights of the campaign, and of how it has been able to support vegans and help change policy and practice. The global campaign for vegan rights is a new movement that has been promoted over the last decade or so as functioning to defend the vegan way of life and support a paradigm shift from prejudice to compassion. The campaign and its message have been successful, and the practice of using law to protect vegans and advance veganism is now gathering pace independently of the original IVRA. This is a good time to document the formative beginnings and share more information and the knowledge and insights gained.

My early work on vegan rights introduced the human rights principles that were applicable to vegans and the vegan community. It provided vegans around the world with an understanding of their legal status as individuals whose convictions were within the legal meaning of the human right to freedom of belief.

In the beginning, encouraging vegans to consider the utility of legal provisions protecting them from discrimination was a sensitive issue. Many vegans did not agree with describing veganism as a "belief," so strong were their identity-forming convictions: how could such life-directing and identity-defining convictions be described as, what felt to some, a *mere* "belief"? Animal rights activists were rightly suspicious of the idea too. It was important to me, and critical for the campaign for vegan rights, that using law to protect vegans and advance veganism was acceptable to the animal rights community. However, it was not comfortable or easy to face groups of activists at events to give a presentation on the legal protection for "belief" in law, to explain how the beliefs and convictions of vegans could be protected, and to share my views about how subsequent changes to policy and practice could contribute to dismantling prejudice against other animals. Sharing more helpful information now aims to support the movement further, especially those challenging resistant legal systems.

There are also three anniversaries that are significant to me. The first is that at the time of drafting the outline for this book in 2023, it had been thirty years since the former Commission of the European Court of Human Rights found that veganism comes within the scope of Article 9 of the European Convention on Human Rights.[27] As noted above, until 2010, when the campaign for vegan rights was conceived, this groundbreaking legal case (and discussion about additional useful measures to protect vegans) lay dormant and was unremarked-on in the vegan and animal protection movements. Its value had not been discussed and it had not been utilized to advance legal rights for vegans. This case, the underpinning human rights principles, related legal cases, and guidance are the backdrop to the strength of the vegan rights campaign, without which the inroads made since would likely have proven to be considerably more challenging, if at all possible.

The second and third anniversaries are personal. In 2024, it has been ten years since the campaign book *Vegan Rights: Questions and Answers* was made available, and ten years since I completed the first-ever vegan equality survey.[28] Ten years ago, when the legal principles and laws that could be used to defend and protect vegans were not widely discussed or known about within the vegan community, a survey on "vegan equality" raised more than a few eyebrows and piqued the interest of only a small number of vegans. A few years into the campaign, this minimal response to the idea of vegan rights changed significantly.

Vegan Rights: Questions and Answers explained the relationship of human rights law to the relevant provisions of British equality law under which vegans could claim their right to practice veganism free from discrimination. The first survey on "vegan equality" documented the vulnerability of vegans and their negative experiences in different contexts, and highlighted veganism as an issue for and in law. My hope was to instil a different and important kind of confidence and solidarity in the vegan and animal rights communities.

Since those early days, three further vegan equality surveys have been undertaken by campaign groups in Scotland and Canada, and one by employment lawyers in the UK. All attracted many more participants than my original survey as a result of sharing and spreading information about the law that supports vegan rights. All the subsequent surveys also evidenced prejudicial views against veganism and the unfair practices vegans endured. Sharing and disseminating the knowledge and experience I have acquired over the years of campaigning for vegan rights and supporting vegans are my ways of marking these personal anniversaries.

Explaining and sharing knowledge with the vegan community has been transformative. It has inspired international discussion, grabbed the attention of vegan organizations and groups, inspired and motivated undergraduate and postgraduate research projects, been the subject of legal commentary and publications on vegan rights and discrimination, and inspired lawyers to get on board, present, and argue for the convictions of vegans. Through this valuable and novel work, the vegan community has come to understand its legitimacy and validity as a community of people with beliefs about compassion for nonhuman animals that are relevant to and can be protected by law.

An important aim from the outset of the campaign for vegan rights was to defend individual vegans to help safeguard their daily practice of veganism and ensure they were able to practice their veganism free from unlawful discrimination and interference. This would be achieved by providing information and support to individual vegans complaining about unfair treatment and help them bring about changes in specific policies and practices, whether in employment, education, health care, or consumer services, and, by doing so, help make veganism more sustainable and the adoption of veganism easier for everyone.

Another important aim for me was to help achieve legal protection for veganism in domestic legal systems around the world and help secure the normalization of living with compassion as a legitimate issue in law.

Over the years, there have been significant achievements that have contributed to fulfilling the aims of the campaign. These achievements have done much more than facilitating a positive impact on the lived experience of individual vegans or bringing tangible benefits to them. I like to think of these achievements as, arguably, representing the real potential for a positive shift in the balance of human and nonhuman relations. These small achievements are seeds of a change toward law recognizing, supporting, and entrenching living with compassion, encouraging the normalization of a human desire to live with compassion and the collective ethical duty to respond to suffering and reject oppression and exploitation in all their forms.

I believe that the campaign for vegan rights has a place in this process of change because it demands that we be granted the ability to live free from being required to participate in the exploitation and oppression of nonhuman animals. When policies and practices are changed to accommodate the needs of vegans, veganism is more easily adopted and sustained. With this in mind, the campaign for vegan rights can be represented as contributing seeds of change that support our combined effort to bring about a transformation away from the entrenched prejudice against other animals and toward the socio-politico-legal validation of veganism and formal assistance to live with respect and compassion.

Sharing the information in this book at this point in time is a way of celebrating a new awakening within the vegan community. We have come to understand that a policy that supports vegans is surely a socio-political statement that our moral concern for other animals is valid and respected. This work celebrates the community's acceptance and validation of the campaign dedicated to vegan rights, the normalization of the use of the legal meaning of "belief," and the success of this in legal cases.

THE TITLE OF THE BOOK

This title of the book, *Seeds of Change: The International Vegan Rights Alliance and the Vegan Rights Revolution*, is intended to be compelling and convey important messages. Through this title, I recognize as revolutionary the vegan community's new understanding of validity and legitimacy in law but also want to suggest a narrative of growth, change, and progress in the ongoing struggle to protect other animals and the transformation aimed for in our relationship with them. Regarding this transformation, the title chosen alludes to the function of ethical beliefs and values in the development of social practices and policies. The use of "revolution" in the title is intended to convey the dynamic climate for the potential for change, as well as the urgency of addressing the issue of our treatment of nonhuman animals.

Seeds of Change . . . is informed by personal views, experiences, and opinions, and also reflects a personal journey. I like to think of the campaign for vegan rights as a kind of disruptive legal activism, through which I stand with other animals in their struggle to be seen, respected, heard, recognized, loved . . . *in community*, and to be represented as such in our democracy. Our mission is urgent; there is much work to be done to dismantle prejudice toward other animals, and my hope is that readers feel that the work I present offers a small but important, contribution to our overall mission. It celebrates the articulation of the status of veganism in law and the campaign for vegan rights, but never loses sight of the fact that nonhuman animals are the center of our mission.

The narrative of the vegan rights campaign utilizes the human rights principle of human dignity and the legal framework for the protection of belief. But this narrative looks to ethical principles that extend far beyond protection for human individuals. The vegan rights narrative is not about achieving tangible individual human gains but is a comment on justice that questions the anthropocentric orientation of the exclusive human rights project. Its mission is to entrench a duty to respond appropriately to all suffering, and it is valid only insofar as it helps disrupt the machinery of prejudice.

In recognition of the diversity of activism, our shared desire to eliminate animal exploitation, and our efforts to facilitate anti-oppressive activism and discourse—and in good faith—I offer *Seeds of Change* . . . I like to think that there are reasons to be optimistic, inspired, and motivated.

THE STRUCTURE OF THE BOOK

The book is structured as follows: In chapter 1, I explain some of the issues vegans have reported to give readers an insight into the range of difficulties for the practice of veganism in both public and private contexts, in employment, education, and in the provision of goods and services, such as health care. Many of the difficulties faced by vegans reveal the extent of hidden prejudice toward nonhuman animals and the subsequent difficulties faced by vegans on a daily basis as they try to navigate the non-vegan, sometimes *anti-vegan*, world. Chapter 1 explains both the practical difficulties that some vegans face, the potential impact of unfairness, exclusion, and discrimination on the individual well-being of vegans, and points to the need for the vegan community to be informed about their status in law and their legal rights.

In chapter 2, I discuss how the campaign for vegan rights was established. I explain the origins of the campaign and the early presentation of the idea to utilize rights for vegans. I discuss the direction of early research, the establishment of the IVRA, its aims and objectives, its first symposium, the development of the Alliance's *Declaration,* its conferences and themes under discussion, and collaborative projects. I also share in chapter 2 information about the inspiring and motivating statistical records that reveal the growth of global interest in the idea of rights for vegans.

Chapter 3 shares some of the research undertaken in the course of the campaign for rights for vegans. It explains why protection for vegans is relevant to the protection of other animals, as well as the legal framework for the protection of vegans themselves. I explain that vegans are legitimate beneficiaries of international legal provisions that can be and have been applied successfully to defend the practice of compassion for other animals, and that they can be used to protect vegans from unlawful interference and discrimination. That said, I do not avoid the issues and limits relevant to the use of vegan law to support animal rights: the rights applicable to safeguarding the practice of veganism free from discrimination do not recognize the moral imperative to live with compassion for other animals, and the application of law requires balance. Nevertheless, in chapter 3 I hope to present a convincing argument that explains why we should advocate for the protection of vegans as a valid element in our effort to protect other animals.

Chapter 4 returns to some of the issues faced by vegans presented in chapter 1 to explain how research undertaken during the campaign for vegan rights has supported complaints made by vegans and helped develop *no choice* adaptations to practices and policies in public and private contexts, in employment, education, health care, and the provision of goods and services. I illustrate that when important legal principles are applied, despite the sometimes hostile social and political landscapes, they can function to sustain and advance veganism and can bring about useful discussions about the suffering of nonhuman animals.

Chapter 5 reflects on the success of the IVRA, examines the current scope of legal protection for vegans in the UK, and highlights legal cases involving vegans in other countries. In this chapter, I present the personal experience of Canadian litigant Adam Knauff, a vegan firefighter whose claim of discrimination was heard by the Ontario Human Rights Tribunal. Mr Knauff's personal experience highlights the prevailing context of prejudice toward vegans, the ongoing difficulties experienced by some vegans in resolving problems, and in terms of access to justice.

The book concludes on the issues addressed and comments on pressing matters for future research and the application of law.

It is hoped that this book will capture the interest of a wide range of readers; not only those who stand with other animals in their struggle for the right to live free from prejudice and exploitation, but also those with a general interest in veganism, human rights, social justice, and ethical issues.

DISCLAIMER

Nothing written in this book constitutes legal advice. The author is not responsible or liable for losses as a result of actions taken in relation to the content in this book. If you believe you have been treated unfairly because you are vegan and need advice, you should discuss your specific circumstances with an appropriately qualified lawyer.

The general information provided in this book includes the author's opinions, but nothing in this book represents the views or opinions of any members of the former International Vegan Rights Alliance, the current International Rights Network, other individuals, The Vegan Society, or other organizations.

Information in this book gives the author's views, experience, and opinions as of 2024. The author's views and opinions do not necessarily reflect those of any of the contributors to this book.

PRIVACY

The author has taken steps to comply with the General Data Protection Regulations and general principles of privacy. As such, where necessary, the names of individual vegans, and information about their circumstances, have been changed. Some example cases have been created from multiple instances of similar circumstances and are necessarily analogous and fictitious. Any similarities between the information provided and individuals involved in past, current, or future events are entirely coincidental.

NOTES

1. "Shifting the balance" was the strapline of the International Vegan Rights Alliance. See chapter 2.
2. *Knauff v. Ontario* (Natural Resources and Forestry), 2023 HRTO 1729.
3. Diego Casimiro, "Alumnos de San Marcos piden en tribunales que se sirva comida vegana y rectora responde: Es un absurdo," *infobae*, April 12, 2024, accessed May 7, 2024, https://www.infobae.com/peru/2024/04/12/pj-admite-demanda-para-que-el-comedor-de-la-unmsm-cuente-con-una-opcion-vegana/, and Jazmine Angulo, "Alumnos de San Marcos piden en tribunales que se sirva comida vegana y rectora responde: "Es un absurdo," *infobae,* May 1, 2024, accessed May 7, 2024, https://www.infobae.com/peru/2024/05/01/alumnos-de-san-marcos-piden-en-tribunales-que-se-sirva-comida-vegana-y-rectora-responde-es-un-absurdo/.
4. See FEUMVE, "Lawsuit for Infringement of Rights. The Demand," accessed May 7, 2024, https://www.feumve.com/feumve/juicio-por-vulneracion-de-derechos-la-demanda/.

5. See chapter 5.

6. See, for example, Rebecca Gregson, Jared Piazza, and Ryan L. Boyd, "'Against the Cult of Veganism': Unpacking the Social Psychology and Ideology of Anti-Veganism," *Appetite*, 178 (2022), https://www.sciencedirect.com/science/article/pii/S0195666322002343.

7. Zaria Gorvett, "The Hidden Biases that Drive Anti-Vegan Hatred," *BBC,* February 4, 2020, accessed September 1, 2023, https://www.bbc.com/future/article/20200203-the-hidden-biases-that-drive-anti-vegan-hatred. See also historical research by Matthew Cole and Karen Morgan, "Vegaphobia: Derogatory Discourses of Veganism and the Reproduction of Speciesism in UK National Newspapers," *British Journal of Sociology* 62, no. 1 (2011), and Cara C. MacInnis and Gordon Hodson, "It Ain't Easy Eating Greens: Evidence of Bias Toward Vegetarians and Vegans from Both Source and Target," *SAGE Group Processes & Intergroup Relations* 1–24 (2015), DOI: 10.1177/1368430215618253.

8. For example, Ed Balls commented on the YouGov survey asking the public whether the Chancellor was suited to the job of Prime Minister. A small number of respondents said the Chancellor was suitable, and Ed Balls commented that some of those "must be vegan." See "Jobs and Growth," *Hansard*, HC Deb., vol 545, col. 722 (May 17, 2012). Mr Jackson MP for Peterborough remarked about "tofu-eating, *Guardian*-reading, sandal-wearing people" which was taken to refer to vegan people. See Cathy Jamieson, "Finance (No. 2) Bill," *Hansard,* HC Deb., vol. 579, col. 330 (April 9, 2014). Michael Gove also remarked: "I am not sure that Labour Members would agree with the suggestion that I have become a sandal-wearing, muesli-*munching,* vegan vaguester." ("Topical Questions," *Hansard*, HC Deb., vol. 605, col. 149 [January 26, 2016]).

9. Lord Rea, "Complementary Medicine,"*Hansard,*HL Deb., vol. 489, col. 1395 (November 11, 1987.)

10. Mr. John Marshall, "Creutzfeldt-Jakob Disease," *Hansard*, HC Deb., vol. 279, col. 674 (June 18, 1996).

11. Murdo Fraser, "Budget (Scotland) Bill: Stage 1," Meeting of the Parliament, Chamber and Committees, February 2, 2017.

12. Kerry McCarthy, "Agricultural Bill (Tenth Sitting)," *Hansard,* HC Deb., col. 354 (November 13, 2018).

13. Baroness Warsi, "Equality Bill," *Hansard*, HL Deb., vol. 718, col. 852–854 (March 23, 2010),

14. *Casamitjana Costa v. The League Against Cruel Sports* [2020] UK ET 3331129/2018.

15. Lord Blencathra, "Queen's Speech," *Hansard,* HL Deb., vol. 801, col. 277 (January 8, 2020).

16. Baroness Buscombe, "Online Safety Bill," *Hansard,* HL Deb., vol 831, col. 405 (June 22, 2023).

17. Alicia Kearns, "Business of the House," *Hansard*, HC Deb., vol. 705, col. 1173 (December 16, 2021).

18. Diane Abbott, "Prevent Programme," *Hansard*, HC Deb., vol. 670, col. 304 (January 22, 2020).

19. Lord Benyon, "The Food Strategy White Paper," *Hansard*, HL Deb., vol. 823, col. 1076 (July 7, 2022).

20. The Lord Bishop of Manchester, "The Food Strategy White Paper," *Hansard*, HL Deb., vol. 823, col. 1076 (July 7, 2022).

21. Lord Bellingham, "Metropolitan Police: Criminality," *Hansard*. HL Deb., vol. 827, col. 663 (February 1, 2023).

22. David Spencer, Chris Donaldson, and Paul Stott, "Blurred Lines: Police Staff Networks – Politics or Policing?" foreword by Rt Hon. Priti Patel MP, Policy Exchange, 2023, accessed December 4, 2023, https://policyexchange.org.uk/wp-content/uploads/2023/01/Blurred-Lines.pdf.

23. Elle Hunt, "Parents who Feed Children Vegan Diet Face Prosecution Under Proposed Italian Law," *The Guardian*, August 10, 2016, accessed October 1, 2023, https://www.theguardian.com/lifeandstyle/2016/aug/10/parents-children-vegan-diet-prosecuted-italian-law.

24. It is critical that veganism as a philosophy continues to be articulated and developed. My personal view from lived experience and communicating with vegans on a daily basis is that veganism is identity-forming on the basis of an ethical awareness of, connection with, and respect for nonhuman animals. It can be a catalyst for a wide range of views and practices relating to becoming aware that our anthropocentric tradition has blinded us to appreciating the intersectional nature of our existence on our planet and acting with responsibility, and appropriately, in community with nonhuman animals and nature. The conditions we have created for nonhuman animals and the suffering they endure are frequently cited as a motivating force.

25. The definition features in the case of *Casamitjana* and the Canadian case of Adam Knauff.

26. "Definition of Veganism," The Vegan Society, accessed July 3, 2023, https://www.vegansociety.com/go-vegan/definition-veganism.

27. See Jeanette Rowley, "Celebrating 30 Years of Legal Recognition for Veganism," The Vegan Society, 2023, accessed October 2, 2023, https://www.vegansociety.com/get-involved/research/research-news/celebrating-30-years-legal-recognition-veganism.

28. Jeanette Rowley, "Veganism and Equality Research (2013–2014)," Lancaster University Research Directory (2015), accessed July 20, 2023, https://www.research.lancs.ac.uk/portal/en/publications/veganism-and-equality-research(f7c7c455-d6b6-49a2-9766-863fc7a92213).html.

Chapter 1

Issues Faced by Vegans

Veganism is life-directing. Vegan people proactively live their lives according to the moral principle that the suffering of other animals matters, and they make conscious decisions in their daily lives to avoid participating in the exploitation of nonhuman animals. Vegans aim to live their lives with compassion and choose to eat a diet that does not contain any products derived from other animals, including derivatives and food additives such as "whey powder," which is made from cow's milk, and "carmine," which is a red pigment created by crushing female cochineal beetles.[1] Vegans choose not to wear the skin and hair of other animals, which means that they seek out alternatives to footwear made from skin (leather), and don't buy jumpers, coats, or other clothing made from the hair of sheep and other animals (wool).[2]

There are a wide range of derivatives and additives created from animal exploitation, and vegans will typically read labels on food products, clothing, cosmetics, toiletries, and cleaning products and will avoid participating in animal exploitation as far as is possible and practicable. This means that vegans make choices every day of their lives, in all social contexts, to sustain their ethical practice.

Vegans wish to avoid making mistakes as far as possible and sometimes need to request information and support—for example, when being prescribed medication. A vegan will want to find out if there is a vegan version of a given medication and whether it is suitable for them. Vegans in a wide range of consumer contexts, in education, and in employment will, at some time in their lives, be faced with an issue that they will need to discuss and navigate to maintain their ethical practice.

In some situations, vegans will be affected by circumstances outside of their control, such as finding out that they need to take a course of medication for which there is no vegan alternative. Circumstances such as these are emotionally and psychologically challenging for vegans. Accepting a course of medication or other health intervention on medical advice that conflicts with vegan convictions does not mean that the vegan involved is no longer vegan. Veganism is an ethical orientation that adherents follow as far as is possible in specific circumstances in the non-vegan world. This does not mean that the prevailing social conditions in which veganism exists, or the views and norms of the dominant non-vegan majority, justify dismissing and ignoring the concerns and needs of vegans. In fact, it is precisely because vegans are a minority that their voice must be heard and their needs considered, whether as consumers of goods and services or in the context of education or employment. In all of these contexts, however, vegans have historically experienced ridicule, bullying, harassment, marginalization, unfair treatment, and discrimination.

Since the first vegan equality survey in 2013,[3] many examples of alleged unfair treatment of and discrimination against vegans have been documented. Prior to the dedicated campaign to explain the experiences of vegans as examples of unfairness or discrimination under the human right to freedom of belief and related equality law, it was common for vegans themselves to simply endure their negative experiences because their moral outlook focuses on the suffering of other animals rather than on themselves as valid and legitimate individuals in our system of human justice. Historically, however, those involved in the animal protection movement have always known that vegans reported feeling disrespected, distressed, and mocked, struggling with "banter," putting up with unfairness, feeling ignored and dismissed, and having their ethical convictions trivialized. Some have framed their experience in terms of having their dignity compromised.

Although there are many situations in which vegans report feeling unfairly treated, most are not discussed publicly. This is often because a vegan involved in distressing circumstances typically wants only to deal with the situation and move on and does not want to see their name and details of their circumstances published as (often misreported and sensationalized) news.

Everyone is legally entitled to privacy and confidentiality, and information given in this chapter complies with the legal duty to avoid disclosing any personal or identifying information. Unless information is already in the public domain, the case studies discussed necessarily recreate example situations in which some vegans have reported feeling unfairly treated or discriminated against when navigating the non-vegan, sometimes anti-vegan, world. The method adopted in the case selection process ensured that there were multiple occurrences of the issue under consideration and that names, locations, and so on were changed to leave only the substance of the complaint. Despite the need to create some analogous but fictitious case studies for the purpose of strict compliance with confidentiality and privacy obligations, insights are given into a range of real lived experiences of vegans, in both public and private contexts, as consumers of goods, facilities, and services, in education, employment, health care, prison, and when accessing justice.

At this point, I want to acknowledge the thousands of vegans who have contacted me over the years, and the tenacity and courage they have shown in their efforts to deal with the unfair and discriminatory experiences they have endured. Since the start of the campaign for vegan rights over a decade ago, many vegans have raised complaints about policies and practices in a wide variety of situations that disadvantage them. They have stood against ridicule, prejudice, and, sometimes, exclusion, and have claimed their right for their convictions to be heard, represented, included, and accommodated as a matter of justice for other animals. They have defended their right to live as vegans, free from unlawful interference and, in many cases, to also be assisted to live with compassion. The campaign for rights for vegans as a seed of change that supports the liberation of nonhuman animals would have amounted to nothing without community participation. The rights and equality claims of vegans everywhere are the concrete in the foundation of the campaign's progress.

The case studies below explore issues reported by vegans in Britain, some of which are then revisited in chapter four to explain the application of relevant research, law, and guidance to each specific issue. A number of escalated complaints made by vegans in other countries are presented in a discussion in chapter five on the scope of legal protection for vegans.

VEGANS AS CONSUMERS OF GOODS, FACILITIES, AND SERVICES

It was clear from the survey in 2013 that some vegans, as consumers of goods and services, did not feel respected or supported. Under British equality law, the provision of a service includes the provision of goods, facilities, and services, and guidance specifies that "refusing to provide or not providing a service includes providing a person with a service of different quality, or in a different way (for example hostile or less courteous) or on less favourable terms than the service would normally be provided". Thus, the way vegans are treated as consumers is relevant to equality provisions, and less favorable treatment can be grounds for claims of discrimination under equality law.[4]

The terms "goods," "facilities" and "services" are not precisely defined in equality law. They should be understood to be broad in scope in terms of their ordinary meaning and together cover a wide range of consumer contexts.

Consumers in Britain have access to a Citizens Advice service, which provides independent and impartial advice on a wide range of issues. Citizens Advice lists examples relating to the provision of goods, facilities, and services to the public. The list includes:

- pubs, restaurants, and hotels
- shops
- cinemas and theaters
- hospitals and clinics
- estate agents, private landlords, and local authority housing departments
- banks, building societies, insurance, and finance companies
- railway stations, bus stations, and airports
- churches and other places of worship
- charities and voluntary organizations
- government departments, local authorities, courts and tribunals, police officers, and prisons
- welfare services, such as housing advice, day care, or community care.

Vegan Consumer of Financial Services

Case Study 1: NatWest Bank Customer Service

A high-profile case in which a vegan consumer in Britain felt unfairly treated concerns a vegan customer of the NatWest bank.[5] In 2019, the customer called the bank to apply for a loan to help with the costs of a vegan nutrition course and was refused the loan. During the call, the customer service operative told the customer that "all vegans should be punched in the face". The NatWest customer service operative told the customer that they were upset by "vegan" chalk messages they had seen on the pavement near their home, and that they felt vegans were forcing their beliefs onto them. (The BBC news report shows an example of a similar chalk message; it depicts the face of a pig and the words "Animals are friends NOT food".) It was clear to the customer from the operative's tone and behavior that they were not happy to be speaking with them. They naturally felt very uncomfortable in the conversation and unfairly treated because they were vegan.

As is often the case these days, the call to the bank was recorded and, therefore, available to senior staff assessing the customer's complaint. NatWest upheld the customer's complaint, agreeing that the comments made by the operative were wholly inappropriate. The bank offered its apologies for the distress their operative's behavior had caused, offered compensation, and committed to internal staff training.

Vegan Consumers of Holidays and Trips

Case Study 2: Vegans Excluded from Booking an Excursion

Also in 2019, three older vegans, who will be referred to as John, William, and Joseph, decided to join a tour to the beaches, war memorials, and military museums of Normandy, France.[6] When the three vegans made their booking, they were asked about dietary requirements, and when, in response, they requested vegan food, they were informed that the tour operator could not accept bookings from vegans. The reasons given were that there would be no vegan food and that the rest of the people on the tour would not want vegans in the group. They were told that if they were vegetarian, that would be more acceptable, but vegans were not welcome on the trip.

Naturally, John, William, and Joseph were shocked and in disbelief that their vegan identity was the reason for their exclusion. They all felt unfairly treated and discriminated against. Following a formal complaint and difficult, lengthy advocacy discussions, the tour provider agreed to change its "no vegan" policy and offered John, William, and Joseph a discount. However, given the circumstances in which they had found themselves—having to submit a complaint about discrimination and unfair treatment, and feeling the impact of exclusion and prejudice—John, William, and Joseph ultimately chose not to join the trip.

Case Study 3: Failure to Provide Vegan Food

Vegans, who will be referred to as Irene and Dave, were attracted to a two-week all-inclusive water sports activity holiday abroad.[7] The fully catered package was very expensive, and Irene and Dave did not want to take any risks regarding their vegan dietary needs. Sensibly, prior to booking, Irene and Dave spoke with a company representative about their dietary requirements and were assured, both verbally and in writing by email, that their vegan diet would be catered for. In addition, they confirmed with the tour operator the published terms and conditions of the holiday, which stated that all dietary requirements could be accommodated.

As soon as Irene and Dave arrived at the destination, they experienced difficulties obtaining suitable food. They spoke to a company representative, who did their best to help by providing a few portions of fruit but who was unable to provide what could be described as an adequate meal. Irene and Dave continued trying to sort out the problem by phoning the company's head office and speaking with food providers at various activity locations but were unsuccessful. Everyone else in the group was catered for, including vegetarians. As a last resort, on some occasions, Irene and Dave did their best to adapt some vegetarian meals, but many were prepacked, and it proved difficult to separate the cheese and egg from the containers.

Irene and Dave spent a lot of time during the first few days of their holiday communicating with the tour operator, and their entire holiday trying to find suitable food for themselves, feeling exhausted from the programme of activities, and feeling unhappy that they were spending three weeks of a well-planned break in such difficult and disappointing circumstances.

Irene and Dave submitted a formal complaint while on holiday and continued with the complaints process on their return home. Ultimately, they received an apology and a substantial refund, but the complaints process required great tenacity, effort, and time, and they had not benefitted at all from the annual leave they had taken from their employment.

Vegan Consumers of Entertainment

Case Study 4: Vegans Publicly Targeted in a Joke about Being Denied Access to an Entertainment Venue

On January 3, 2023, it was reported that The London Dungeon had announced that for the whole of January, vegans would be banned from entering the venue. January is the month known globally for "Veganuary", an annual celebration of veganism and a month dedicated to providing education and support to people who wish to adopt veganism. The London Dungeon, rebranded Veganuary as "VeBANuary" in a publicity campaign, stated that:

> we've decided to not only ignore Veganuary but launch our very own version, denying entry to any vegan visitor who tries to darken our Dungeon. And the best bit, no need for additional security to help identify the veggie lovers, as we know they will most likely mention it within minutes of stepping foot into the attraction![8]

The advertisement for the promotion of VeBANuary featured a baker holding a sign saying "Vegan Free Zone".

Members of the vegan community registered their complaints about the complete lack of respect shown by The London Dungeon, and six days later, it was reported that The London Dungeon had issued an apology for any upset caused and that everyone was welcome at the venue.[9]

Vegan Consumers of Food

Case Study 5: Poor Quality of Service in Restaurant

A frequent complaint made by vegans in consumer contexts concerns issues related to the provision (or lack of) vegan food. Complaints can be about poor service, lack of knowledge on the part of servers about food ingredients, and even suspicion of malicious contamination of vegan food with non-vegan products.

In 2021, a complaint about service received in a restaurant in Edinburgh hit the news. The vegan customer had asked a member of staff to indicate which dishes on the menu were suitable for vegans and were shocked, angry, upset, insulted, and in disbelief about the way their request was handled.

The member of staff had, apparently, obtained information from a chef, and all vegan options on the menu had been circled. However, a note accompanying the clarified vegan options was also discovered by the customer, which read "[t]he vegan sh**e has been circled".

The customer spoke to the manager about the note. The manager apologized and agreed that the note was not acceptable. It was reported that an assistant manager also spoke with the customer afterward and was "much more understanding about the situation".[10]

Case Study 6: Vegans Denied Service

Post-2020, a group of friends in the southwest of the UK booked a table at a local restaurant to celebrate an anniversary.[11] Four members of the party were vegan, and although the restaurant's website stated that it could cater to all dietary requirements, they sensibly thought it best to send an email to the restaurant a few weeks in advance to inform them of the group booking and to specify that they would require vegan food. The restaurant responded, stating that they did not provide for vegans because veganism isn't an allergy. The vegans explained that they didn't want anything special; they only wanted to be able to dine with the rest of the group to celebrate the anniversary. They also offered to supply the restaurant with some vegan items that were commonly available in any supermarket. The restaurant declined their offer and repeated that they would not cater to vegans. The vegan members of the group were unable to join the party at the restaurant.

Following a lengthy complaints process involving the presentation of information about relevant law, the restaurant agreed that the practice of excluding vegans must be stopped, and they should not unreasonably withhold service from vegans.

Case Study 7: Vegan Given Non-vegan Food

A situation that can cause vegans distress is when they realize that they have unknowingly eaten nonhuman animals. This is typically very upsetting for vegans and invariably generates complaints. It can happen in restaurants, when purchasing takeaway food from various outlets, and when fresh food ordered online is delivered to a vegan's home, but it has also happened when a supermarket product labelled as vegan contains animal products.[12]

Post-2020, a customer of a well-known takeaway shop requested and paid for a vegan pastry. Once outside, they started eating their food, but, to their horror, realized that they had not been given the vegan pastry; the one they were eating contained meat. The impact of the experience seriously affected the vegan's sense of well-being. They reported a range of uncomfortable feelings, including feeling sick, shocked, guilty, and intensely remorseful, and were very upset that they were only offered an apology, refund, and replacement pastry.[13]

Case Study 8: Vegans Suspect Malicious Food Spiking

Post-2020, a group of vegans ordered vegan pizzas online. When the pizzas were delivered, the friends found pieces of chicken and meat in the boxes. The vegans complained, believing that their food had been intentionally contaminated, but reported that their complaints and requests for a refund were ignored.[14]

Case Study 9: Suspected Malicious Food Spiking Reported in News

In 2018, *The Guardian* reported that a head chef and restaurant owner resigned after receiving death threats following a comment on social media about spiking vegan food.[15] The news report explains that a group of diners had booked a table and eaten at the restaurant, and that some hours later, the chef-owner of the restaurant posted to an online group, "[p]ious, judgemental vegan (who I spent all day cooking for) has gone to bed, still believing she's a vegan". When asked by a member of the group whether they were saying that they had done something to the vegan food to make the meal non-vegan on purpose, they replied, "Actually, I should have said 'they're' not a vegan . . . not 'she's'". The restaurant owner was also reported to have posted to the group, "[s]piked a vegan a few hours ago".

The report goes on to explain that "comments were soon shared across social media, causing outrage among both vegans and non-vegans. The restaurant's TripAdvisor and Google pages were flooded with negative reviews, and its Facebook page was taken down after being overwhelmed with complaints".

Case Study 10: Evidence of Routine Adulteration of Vegan Food

In 2019, an employment tribunal in London heard the case of *Mr M. Ali v. Indian Cuisine Limited*.[16] Mr Ali claimed unfair dismissal from a restaurant for making a protected interest disclosure relating to an apparently standard practice of adding chicken stock to various dishes, including dishes advertised on the menu as being suitable for vegans. Mr Ali was very concerned about vegan consumers (and other customers) being misled, the need to provide accurate information about allergens, and the potential breach of legal obligations. The tribunal heard that staff were instructed to continue selling the food as suitable for all dietary requirements and that staff who were unhappy needed to be "phased out".

The claimant was not the only member of staff to raise this issue. The tribunal heard that other staff were unhappy and upset about the practice, including a former member of staff who had resigned for reasons which included the alleged dishonest and deceitful practices. The former member of staff gave evidence showing that they had also raised the issue and argued that it was unacceptable and unethical to disregard the faiths and beliefs of customers.

Vegan Litigant: The Threshold for Evidence of Ethical Veganism

Case Study 11: Vegan Accessing Tribunal Services

In 2023, a preliminary Manchester employment tribunal heard a case brought by a vegan who claimed they were unfairly dismissed and discriminated against on the grounds of veganism.[17] The case concerned a requirement to be vaccinated against COVID-19. It must be emphasized at the outset that the vegan community is not against the use of medicines or vaccines. Evidence shows that 87 percent of vegans in the UK aged 16 and over were vaccinated against COVID-19.[18] Campaigns emerging from the vegan community typically focus on the need to create medicines without exploiting nonhuman animals, and further, they encourage vegans to always act on advice given by healthcare professionals.[19]

It is well known in the animal rights and vegan communities that nonhuman animals are used during the development of most medicines and vaccines, and, unsurprisingly, this is upsetting for vegans. The claimant in this case felt unable to accept vaccination.

The vegan claimant swore an oath and provided evidence that they ate a vegan diet, took their own food into work, wore gloves at work when required to handle non-vegan products, did not wear leather, and did not buy products tested on nonhuman animals. However, the tribunal judge was not happy with the evidence provided and expected more evidence from the claimant to prove that they genuinely believed in ethical veganism, perhaps by way of "photographs of products or specific examples of behaviour".

The tribunal, ultimately, ruled that the claimant's belief in veganism did not qualify for protection under equality law. What is interesting about this case is that the judge compared the vegan applicant to a vegan in a different case, and the following reasons were given as relevant to their conclusion:

> She accepted that she did use products in the respondent's employment that were not vegan, but that she would use gloves. This seems to me to be inconsistent with the extent of the belief as described in Costa.

The tribunal decided that the use of gloves to handle non-vegan products in employment was inconsistent with the extent of the belief on the basis of a prior tribunal (Costa), in which a vegan was found to genuinely hold the belief. However, it is important to note that vegans necessarily must find ways to navigate the non-vegan world, and this is particularly relevant to employment contexts. Not all vegans are lucky enough to work in entirely vegan contexts.

> She gave no examples of ways in which her daily life is structured to adhere to her belief. She gave me no examples of travel, clothing, holidays whether she ate honey or figs, or spoke about her relationships with other people, for example. It was only when it was pointed out to her that she said she did not wear leather, but she did not expand on that and shrugged when she was asked about wool.

The reference to figs in this statement appears to be based on the view of a vegan in the previous case (Costa), who did not eat figs because some varieties of figs are pollinated by wasps, and they may have accidentally eaten wasp larvae.

> The most significant reference to veganism was to her diet, which does not go far enough to establish a belief in ethical veganism (see Costa). She did not explain how she went about ensuring she was following a vegan diet, how she checked her products, what she did if she was around someone else who did not eat vegan food, for example.

Again, the tribunal referred to the prior case, of Costa, without considering that adopting a vegan diet is by far the most common first step taken by those who become aware that they believe in the vegan philosophy, start living with respect for other animals, and continue educating themselves and adapting their practice.

Vegans Accessing HealthCare Services

Case Study 12: Vegan Forced to Handle and Cook Animal Products

Issues reported by vegans in health care contexts include access to food in hospitals and care homes, the attitude of some staff toward vegan people, and access to vegan medications. In 2013, survey participants reported feeling dismissed, stressed, and not properly cared for or given good nutrition; being treated as if they were being awkward; coping with an apparent lack of understanding; and staff apparently having little sympathy toward them in health care contexts. There was also an anecdotal report alleging that healthcare staff conspired to lie to a vegetarian patient with compromised capacity to avoid a fuss about the beef sandwich they had been given to eat.

In October 2019, the All-Party Parliamentary Group (APPG) on Vegetarianism and Veganism launched an inquiry into the extent to which vegan and vegetarian people in care were fed a diet that aligned with their convictions and beliefs and published the report *Respect for Religious and Philosophical Beliefs while Eating in Care* in 2021.[20] The report raised concerns from the evidence presented that the dietary preferences of vegan and vegetarian people have been disrespected and disregarded in some care contexts, describing case studies as "harrowing stories" about the daily challenges faced by older vegetarians and vegans in care settings.[21] The report states that the inquiry "reveals examples of the most basic failings in care homes and hospitals when it comes to protecting the human rights of those receiving care".[22]

One case study in the report describes how a vegan was forced to handle and cook animal products before being allowed to leave a mental health care facility.

> David was in a mental health ward after having a psychotic depressive breakdown. In order to be discharged, David was told he had to be able to cook himself a traditional English breakfast. David and his wife live together, where she does most of the cooking, and they eat a vegan diet. Unfortunately, they would not accept this from David as a reason to forego cooking the breakfast, and said if he wanted to be released, this is what he must do. David had to cook eggs, bacon, sausage, etc. to be able to leave the ward.[23]

The report goes on to make recommendations for better practice regarding catering to the dietary needs of vegans and vegetarians.

Vegans in Detention

Case Study 13: Protecting the Rights of Vegan Prisoners

In 2022, *The Mirror* reported that registered vegan prisoners at HMP Warren Hill had been reduced from thirty to six following the implementation of a monitoring policy that included denying vegan food to registered vegans food if they were found to be wearing leather belts or shoes.[24] The assumption was that prisoners were pretending to be vegan. The Annual Report of the Independent Monitoring Board (IMB) at HMP Warren Hill states that "[r]equests for special diets, especially vegan diets, are carefully monitored, and prisoners who are found to be eating non-vegan food are removed from the list".[25] The Vegan Society registered its concern about this report and published its response, arguing (inter alia) that:

> veganism attracts protection in law as a philosophy and way of living which seeks to exclude—as far as is possible and practicable—all forms of exploitation of, and cruelty to, animals.
>
> In this case, prisoners, who are deprived of their liberty, can experience difficulties regarding what is possible and practicable, and those who are new to veganism often need time to adjust to it. For example, prisoners may not be able to immediately replace their leather shoes or belts and so should not be accused of pretending to adopt veganism.
>
> Under human rights law, every person has an absolute right to adopt a belief of choice and, in this case, 23 prisoners who registered as vegan have been denied their request to be provided with a vegan diet, forced to eat non-vegan food, and thus, denied their rights.[26]

VEGANS IN EDUCATION

In the survey of 2013, there were reports from both parents and pupils about not feeling supported in education. Some parents with very young children reported feeling apprehensive about approaching their child's first school. Pupils reported feeling disrespected in class when talking about veganism and when there was a requirement to use non-vegan products in teaching or assessment.

This section highlights issues faced by some vegans in various educational contexts, including nursery and early years providers, infant schools, primary schools, high schools, colleges, and universities.

Vegan Issues in Nursery

For any parents or guardians, the process of choosing a suitable nursery school or early years provider can induce a range of perfectly understandable emotions. Since the birth of their child, they have been nurturing, teaching, and protecting them, providing for their needs, and raising them in accordance with their values. For parents and guardians, the time of their child starting school is a milestone; a time of "letting go" to some extent, involving a process of transition. They may feel anxious, concerned, or worried at times, but also happy and positive about this new stage in the lives of both themselves and their child. They naturally want their child to be happy, nurtured, stimulated, and well provided for in their new environment, and are likely to aim to develop a cooperative and trusting relationship with the chosen early years provider.

For vegan parents, choosing an early years provider will usually involve initial discussions about whether the childcare or nursery facility can provide appropriate vegan food, milk, and other refreshments. In some cases, the parents or guardians are told that the childcare provider does not accommodate the dietary needs of vegans because it is a lifestyle choice rather than an allergy. In other cases, the provider informs the parents that they are free to self-supply food and refreshments, and the childcare staff will make sure they are given to the child at appropriate times.

These circumstances can be eye-opening for vegan parents because they become aware that they have different needs that are not widely understood or catered for in an education context. Vegan parents soon come to realize that the transition involves a major change in environment: often from a completely vegan environment to one where veganism has minority status at best, or is misunderstood and unsupported at worst.

In 2019, the BBC reported that a Scottish council agreed to provide vegan meals in all its schools, following one vegan mum's complaint and long-running campaign for inclusion.[27] The extent of overt exclusion allegedly included the head of catering telling a nursery to stop providing vegan food when they found out that provision had been made for a young vegan pupil. The mother reported that the head of catering had said: "[y]ou're not allowed to provide for [the vegan pupil]. The mother is not allowed to provide for [the vegan pupil]. And we're not going to provide either".

Case Study 14: Vegan Complaints about the Lack of Vegan Milk in Nursery

Many complaints over the years have been raised by vegan parents who are not provided with a plant-based alternative to cow's milk for their nursery-age children. Vegan parents in England, who will be referred to as Jane and Mike, had discussed their vegan values and convictions with their chosen nursery school and requested plant-based milk for their child.[28] In the UK, children under five in early years settings are entitled to a daily portion of free milk under the Nursery Milk Scheme (the Scheme).[29] Jane and Mike assumed that the nursery would provide a suitable soya alternative for their daughter. They were told, however, that their child was not eligible for free soya milk while at nursery because the free milk provided was cow's milk and the milk scheme did not include soya milk alternatives.

Jane and Mike felt that the policy around the provision of milk was unfair and discriminatory, but agreed with the nursery that they would supply their own cartons of soya milk to be given to their child when the other pupils were given their free issue of cow's milk.

Vegan Issues in Primary School

Case Study 15: School's Cow's Milk or Water-Only Policy

Complaints from vegans about policies relating to the provision of free milk in educational settings are common and increasing. The widely publicized case of Mr Paul Roberts[30] two years later, in 2020, is a case in point.

Mr Roberts wanted to raise his child according to the vegan philosophy, and the child had never drunk cow's milk. As in the case of Jane and Mike above, Mr Roberts had agreed with the nursery school the child attended that they would take their own soya milk to school every day. The child subsequently got into the routine of getting their milk from their bag at "milk time" and drinking it in class with their peers. However, when the child finished nursery and moved to the reception class at the infant school (which included the nursery on the same site), Mr Roberts was horrified to learn that the child, at only four years old, had been instructed to put it back in their bag.

This upsetting event was not the result of a mistake on the part of the teacher. Mr Roberts was informed that under the school's policy, the child was prohibited from bringing their own milk into school. Further, if they were not participating in the school's "Cool Milk" scheme and drinking the supplier's cow's milk at milk time, they would only be allowed to drink water.

The school, thus, imposed a policy under which pupils could only bring water into school, and those who did not subscribe to a subsidized school "Cool Milk" cow's milk scheme would only be allowed to drink water during school hours.

Mr Roberts, quite understandably, felt a range of negative emotions and raised the issues with the school. Little did Mr Roberts know at that point that it was the beginning of a very stressful nine-month-long battle with the school to have the child's needs accommodated.

Mr Roberts tried, initially, to resolve the issues by speaking to the headteacher, but the request was rejected on the grounds of the school's policy. Mr Roberts then submitted a formal grievance which was escalated to the school's governing body but, again, the request to accommodate the child's needs was rejected on the grounds of school policy.

During the many weeks it took to go through the complaints process, Mr Roberts' child missed out on essential nutrition, and Mr Roberts started to suffer from stress, anxiety, and insomnia. Feeling helpless and clearly in great need of appropriate guidance and support, Mr Roberts discussed the case publicly on social media. After making several attempts to resolve the issues, Mr Roberts was eventually signposted to and obtained appropriate and effective support and vegan rights advocacy. Eventually, Mr Roberts achieved a successful outcome to the complaint, as discussed further in chapter 4.

Case Study 16: Vegan Complaints about Educational Resources

Numerous unreported complaints from vegan parents of children in primary schools raise issues about the use of inaccurate and misleading teaching and learning materials that perpetuate the exploitation of other animals and reinforce prejudice against them. Vegan parents object to the use of such resources often on two grounds. The first objection is that the resources they have seen give a false impression of the environmental conditions farmed animals are kept in and that the learning resources, therefore, avoid the truth. The second is that the learning experience does not include the vegan perspective.

In one case, a parent of a three-year-old vegan was horrified and distraught to find that her daughter had been sent home with a "first" reading book about milking cows. The vegan child was likely attracted to the reading material because it was highly appealing to the senses: soft and pleasant to touch, with beautiful, pastel-shaded depictions of young, healthy, sweet-faced cows, with smooth brown fur, lying in sunlit meadows of lush green grass, interspersed with cute buttercups and daisies. The offending images were complete with distant white picket fences and the occasional apple tree. The printed text was large and brief, indicating its simplistic form for younger readers. Complaints made about the reading book referenced farmed animals depicted outdoors in beautiful countryside settings as "happy," and statements along the lines of "she doesn't mind being milked," "it doesn't hurt" and "they graze on lush green grass in summer, dropping cow pats to help plants grow".[31] The pupil had been told to "read it to Mummy and Daddy at home".

Teaching and learning resources such as these are sometimes produced or endorsed by animal farming organizations such as the Agriculture and Horticulture Development Board (AHDB) or The Royal Association of British Dairy Farmers.

Case Study 17: Issues for Vegan Inclusion in Education

In 2018, a vegan mother in Ramsbottom, UK, was told that because her daughter's vegan dietary requirements were a lifestyle choice, rather than based on a religion or allergy, she would not be entitled to a free school meal. The mother, Laura Chepner, explained in a press interview that she was not only disappointed but felt "excluded for being compassionate". Laura, a teacher herself, made a further important point about an educational culture in which "Every Child Matters":

> I'm a teacher myself and I started my training at the same as the Every Child Matters programme was launched. I remember going into teaching thinking every child matters, yet fast-forward to this year and I was being told my child didn't matter.[32]

Laura found information, distributed by the IVRA, that veganism was protected under human rights law,[33] and set about launching a campaign to get vegan food on the school menu. She was ultimately supported by the school and the relevant local authority.

In 2021, Vegan Inclusive Education[34] conducted a survey[35] to examine the experiences of vegan children in primary and secondary schools throughout the UK. The survey attracted two hundred and fifty-two responses from pupils, with 85 percent reporting feeling discriminated against because of their vegan beliefs at school. The survey report revealed that:

- Fewer than 40 percent of respondents felt welcome as vegan pupil in their school.
- Less than 40 percent felt safe.
- Only 13 percent felt valued.
- 73 percent of respondents reported being teased about their vegan convictions or practices.
- 42 percent were bullied for their vegan beliefs at school. Twenty-five percent of the perpetrators were teachers or school staff. Of those teased or bullied, only 25 percent said their school had been swift and helpful in tackling the issue.
- The majority of vegan pupils (54 percent) reported that there were no vegan school meal options.
- Vegans experienced exclusion in cooking classes (63 percent), nutrition lessons (48 percent), on school trips (43 percent), in science classes (33 percent), and on topic work (25 percent).

The survey also includes comments from individual vegans: "[m]y son was bullied constantly and beaten up after school for being a vegan. His school did nothing to support vegan awareness and understanding of vegan culture. We had to find him a new school". And "I have had meat thrown at me, animal noises made at me". Survey participants reported a range of negative emotions: feeling misunderstood (53 percent), frustration (52 percent), sadness (51 percent), a heightened sense of difference (49 percent), anger (40 percent), anxiety (39 percent), feeling belittled (37 percent), embarrassment (36 percent), feeling socially isolated (36 percent), feeling undervalued (33 percent), having an impaired sense of belonging (31 percent), powerlessness (31 percent), humiliation (24 percent).

Programme Co-ordinator at Vegan Inclusive Education, Ruth Jenkins, explains that "[t]hese emotions distance students from the teachers and impair education".[36]

Vegan parents are frequently engaged in complaints with schools, following bullying and alleged attempts by school staff to encourage the vegan pupils to adopt the mainstream practices and values of non-vegans.[37] The issues, including repeated bullying, are often not effectively addressed by school staff despite numerous informal discussions on each occasion. It is not uncommon for these situations to escalate and, subsequently, jeopardize important relationships between the parents and the schools in question, even to the point of complete breakdown.

Vegan Issues in Secondary School

In 2017, *Metro* reported that a twelve-year-old vegan pupil at Richard Hale Secondary School in Hertfordshire, UK, took their own life after bullies threw meat at them.[38] It must be emphasized that there was no evidence that the child had intended to take their own life, and it is reported that the child's father believed that the death must have been accidental. In addition, the coroner was not convinced that the child had meant to kill themself and recorded an open verdict. Regarding the bullying, the child's mother informed the court that her child had been targeted regularly since arriving at the school because of being vegan. The child had become a heavy smoker to help with the bullying, had started self-harming, and had received counselling. The court heard that the child had had to eat outside because meat had been thrown at them in the school canteen. The child's mother had approached the school several times, but the bullying had not stopped. *Metro* reported that the coroner intended to write to the headteacher at the school to ask if policies are in place and up to date in respect of pupils who experience bullying and self-harm.

Case Study 18: Vegan Complaints about School's Raising of Animals for Slaughter

In 2018, a vegan parent complained that Priestlands Secondary School in Hampshire, UK, kept pigs on school ground to teach pupils how to rear pigs and fatten them up for slaughter. After being slaughtered, sausages made from the dead pigs' bodies were served in the school canteen as "Priestlands Porkers". It was argued that the school made "students and parents uncomfortable, by discriminating against their beliefs by condemning these pigs to death".[39]

Some of the issues the vegan parent wanted the school to address included the need to teach compassion. The parent was concerned that the pupils were not being given "an objective education with both sides of the story" (the truth about prejudice against some nonhuman animals and generally a vegan-inclusive perspective on raising other animals for slaughter). Campaigners set up an online petition to persuade the school not to send the piglets to slaughter, which attracted 58,190 supporters.[40]

In 2022, veganism in secondary education was examined in relation to educational psychology. Dr Hayley Lugassy completed a trailblazing PhD thesis on *Vegan Young People in England: an Exploratory Study on Their Identity, Relationships and Educational Experience,* which included a qualitative study to gain an understanding of the educational experiences of vegan young people aged eleven to eighteen in England.[41] Of interest to Lugassy is the interplay between vegan belief and its expression. They explore the legislative context for schools in relation to protected characteristics, principles of inclusive education and school belonging, theories of improving relationships between groups, theories of identity, adolescent identity development, and the role schools play in adolescent identity development. Lugassy highlights key themes relevant to vegan pupils' educational experience and their awareness of the need to carefully navigate the non-vegan school environment. Lugassy explains:

> My findings highlighted four key themes, Balancing Identity Disclosure and Raising Awareness; Intergroup Relationships and Interactions; The School System; and Protective Factors. These themes were found to be factors that foster and impede the social and emotional well-being of vegan young people.
>
> The young people shared feeling responsible for raising awareness of veganism to reduce animal cruelty and the environmental impact of the agricultural industry due to the perceived failure of the education system to educate young people on such issues. This perceived responsibility to raise awareness had to be carefully navigated alongside the negative perception of vegans amongst peers and staff. The vegan young people reported feeling wary of being open about their vegan identity because of this. Some of the vegan young people experienced bullying and social isolation as a direct result of them being open about their vegan beliefs.
>
> The long-term negative impact of bullying and social isolation is well documented, so veganism must be understood, respected, and accepted within the education system to ensure that children and young people are safe to be their authentic selves, as well as to reduce the burden vegan young people feel to educate others on complex issues such as climate change.[42]

How best to provide an education that encourages responsibility is one aim of a recent study into the way children think about moral issues relating to harming animals and eating meat. Authors Piazza, Simpson, and McGuire propose a development model for understanding that can help educators create effective educational environments that work with children's concern for nonhuman animals.[43]

Vegans in Further and Higher Education

Case Study 19: Vegans "Required" to Participate in Non-vegan Activities or Use Non-vegan Materials

In 2021, a college student was forced into a dispute with education provider South Gloucestershire and Stroud College when a module on Farm Husbandry, which involved working on a farm producing meat and dairy products and the possibility of visiting a slaughterhouse, was imposed as compulsory on a course the college had described as "great for people who love animals".[44] The module on the BTEC National Extended Diploma in Animal Management was listed as optional by the awarding body but was made mandatory by the college. The student's requests to opt for a different module were repeatedly denied; she was told she would not be given the opportunity to study an alternative module and that skipping the unit would result in an automatic fail. Alternatively, she was told to leave the college or enrolll in another course.[45] The application of relevant law supported the successful outcome in this case.

Vegans in further and higher education are sometimes "required" to use products derived from nonhuman animals in coursework and assessments. Vegan students taking courses in art and textiles, the sciences, aesthetics, beauty, and hairdressing courses have made requests for their needs to be met but are often met with instant refusals.

Trainee animal protection students have claimed that they have been discriminated against in their education on the basis of an assumption that because they are vegan, they will refuse to undertake some tasks.[46] In 2021, Donelle Gadenne observed a specific difficulty for vegan veterinary students in that they "typically enter veterinary medicine because they love animals and want to care for them. But aspects of their professional education dictate that they inflict pain on animals and sometimes kill them".[47]

The difficult issues faced by vegan veterinarians have long been observed. Gadenne refers to a 2007 publication by Professor Andrew Knight, commenting that veterinary education and training should cease using animals as training tools and utilize the now numerous humane teaching methods available.[48]

Gadenne further argues that training in plant-based nutrition for companion animals would be valuable,[49] and for a proactive approach to vegan inclusion in the veterinary profession:

> [w]here possible, veterinary practices should purchase vegan-friendly communal use products for their practices, such as hand creams and cleaning products, and provide plant-based milk for staff beverages. This change disadvantages no one since all veterinary professionals can (and may prefer to) use vegan-friendly

> products, and using vegan-friendly products would benefit [vegan veterinarians] and, of course, nonhuman animals.[50]

VEGANS IN EMPLOYMENT

The 2013 survey showed that some vegans in UK workplaces experienced unfair treatment regarding access to suitable food and personal protective equipment (PPE), and in terms of anti-vegan attitudes, jokes, and "banter". There was a range of complaints, some more serious than others, but all representing a lack of consideration for the needs of vegans in the workplace and a dismissive attitude toward veganism. Later surveys, conducted a few years into the dedicated campaign for vegan rights, provide evidence that the situation of vegans in employment remains an important issue to address. In 2019, Crosslands Solicitors surveyed one thousand vegans and one thousand employers and reported that "[p]rejudice against vegans is endemic . . . ". Crosslands found that 45 percent of employees felt discriminated against by their employers, and 31 percent felt harassed or unfairly treated. They also found that:

> The vast majority (94%) of bosses said it's wrong for vegans to push their beliefs onto others in the office. Nearly three-quarters (71%) said they should just focus on their work, while 13% said such behaviour can be distracting to other employees. Some vegans also said they had been specifically told not to discuss their beliefs with colleagues, or to tell customers.

Crosslands also reported that almost half of the one thousand employers surveyed said that they didn't do anything to accommodate vegans and didn't provide vegan food, but over three-quarters did cater for vegetarians' dietary beliefs requirements.[51]

Case Study 20: Termination of Vegan's Employment Contract

Twelve years ago, in 2011, an employment tribunal heard the case of vegan Joe Hashman, a well-known animal rights activist, who claimed that his employers had unlawfully terminated his employment contract when they became aware that he opposed fox hunting. Hashman claimed that his employers, Milton Park (Dorset) Ltd., discriminated against him on the grounds of his philosophical belief in the sanctity of life, which was related to his broader vegan moral outlook.

Mr. Hashman expressed their beliefs, which had affected them since their childhood, to the tribunal in a number of ways. They were actively concerned with preventing cruelty to other animals and explained that they felt that their philosophical belief was the largest and most prominent part of their identity and the guiding force in the way they lived their life. They explained that their belief affects every aspect of their life on a daily basis: they make conscious decisions about the food they eat, the clothes they wear, the work they are prepared to do, the places they are prepared to visit and how they spend their time and resources. They also expressed their belief that hunting is morally unacceptable and that it is wrong to take pleasure from killing other animals. Mr Hashman explained their overarching belief that "people should live their lives with mindful respect for animals and we all have a moral obligation to live in a way which is kind to each other, our environment, and our fellow creatures".[52]

Mr. Hashman was cross-examined about their beliefs for almost two hours. Counsel for the respondent questioned whether Mr Hasman genuinely held their professed beliefs and whether their statements about why they did, or did not do, certain things in the real world, were to be believed, and attempted to persuade the tribunal that Mr Hashman did not hold their professed beliefs, citing actions that were argued to be inconsistent with the beliefs in questions. For example, it was argued that in Mr Hashman's employment as a gardener, they might harm creatures living in the soil, especially worms, which might be cut in half when digging. Mr Hashman killed creatures that threatened food crops and was employed by people actively engaged in hunting who also owned a herd of "cattle" and who sold meat in their shop, and he wrote articles for publication in a pro-hunting magazine and was paid by the magazine for doing so.

Mr. Hashman explained that they lived as a vegan in a non-vegan world, which they referred to many times as the "real world", and that in the (non-vegan) real world, they had family responsibilities and had to work to earn a living, which invariably meant dealing with issues that presented moral dilemmas. For example, while they had worked as a gardener and had tended crops (and caused harm to worms and other creatures), they would not work in a chicken factory. In their real-world employment, Mr Hashman distinguished between vertebrates and other animals and exterminated creatures threatening cabbage crops in what they described as the most humane, least objectionable, and environmentally friendly way possible. They also explained that being paid to publish in a pro-hunting magazine offered them the opportunity to discuss their perspective with a wider audience. Mr Hashman knew that their beliefs were those of a minority and that change would come about through small steps because the moral issues that concerned them as a vegan were complex and difficult to solve.

The tribunal accepted Mr Hashman's explanations of their real-world dilemmas and issues and that they had cogent and coherent beliefs, despite activities that might be required in their employment, stating that "moral issues can involve difficult choices"[53] and "[s]ometimes one's moral decisions cannot be based on a simple set of black and white principles".[54]

Case Study 21: Provision of Personal Protective Equipment

In 2014, a vegan public sector employee made repeated requests for (available) vegan alternative PPE. The request was denied, and the employee submitted an arguably compelling formal grievance, which was eventually escalated to lawyers acting for the respective parties.[55] Unfortunately, the complainant decided not to progress the complaint to the employment tribunal and sought alternative employment. The reasons given were stress and anxiety relating to the legal process, and the length of time it was taking to progress the legal challenge.

In 2016, another vegan public sector employee complained that they had made repeated unsuccessful attempts, over the course of a few years, to obtain (available) vegan-friendly PPE, while their employer took action to accommodate the religious needs of a new colleague in a very timely manner, and at comparatively high cost. The vegan concerned escalated their complaint and was eventually accommodated.[56]

Case Study 22: Discrimination During Recruitment

In 2017, a London National Health Service (NHS) Trust advertised a vacancy for an occupational therapist in eating disorders and made it clear that vegans were not welcome to apply for the role. The advert stated that occupational therapists with vegan diets could not be considered, and, in further detail, the Trust elaborated, stating that veganism or other highly restrictive diets could not be accommodated.[57] On being advised of their legal duties by the IVRA, the Trust apologized and amended its advertisement.

Case Study 23: Vegans Accused of Extremism and Terrorism

Five vegans, four in professional public sector employment in different areas of the UK and one undertaking voluntary work in the public sector, reported that they felt unfairly treated on the grounds that their vegan activities either amounted to, or potentially amounted to, issues for anti-terrorism legislation. In one case, the vegan was formally investigated; in another, the vegan was warned not to speak about veganism; in a third, the vegan was told by a counter-terrorism training provider that they were "people to watch out for". The fourth was required to attend a meeting to discuss their veganism, and the fifth was informed that they would not be allowed to continue with their regular volunteering.[58]

Case Study 24: Vegan's Employment Contract Terminated

In 2020, the campaign for vegan rights was bolstered by the courage of a vegan in Britain who had the tenacity and capacity to endure the legal process and bring their case in front of an employment tribunal.

The vegan in this case, Jordi Casamitjana, claimed that their employer, the League Against Cruel Sports, had unfairly dismissed them because of their ethical veganism stance after they discovered, and shared with colleagues, details about the employer's investments in pension funds in companies that carried out animal testing and damaged the environment. Norwich Employment Tribunal held a preliminary hearing to determine whether ethical veganism could amount to a philosophical belief and a protected characteristic under the Equality Act 2010.

On the basis of the evidence presented, Judge Postle found it "easy to conclude that there is overwhelming evidence [before me] that ethical veganism is capable of being a philosophical belief and thus a protected characteristic under the Equality Act 2010".[59] The respondent in the case issued the following statement:

> As has been the subject of extensive media coverage, between 2018 and 2020 we were involved in Employment Tribunal litigation brought by our former employee Jordi Casamitjana. We are happy to make clear that Mr Casamitjana was a very valued employee of the League during the two periods he worked with us, showing a great deal of professionalism, expertise and commitment to the protection of animals.
>
> The only reason for the dismissal of Mr Casamitjana in 2018 was his communications to his colleagues in relation to our pension arrangements. Having revisited the issue we now accept that Mr Casamitjana did nothing wrong with such communications, which were motivated by his belief in ethical veganism.
>
> We are grateful to Mr Casamitjana for having raised the issue of pensions to us, which allowed us to change our default pension fund to an ethical one closer to our values.[60]

Between 2020 and 2023, at the time of writing, many vegans have reported a lack of support in employment for ethical pension options.

Case Study 25: Complaints about Vegan Provisions in Military Service

In 2021, *Plant Based News* reported that vegan soldiers in the armed forces have submitted complaints about the lack of vegan-friendly uniforms and limited vegan food.[61]

Case Study 26: Complaints from Vegans Working in the Animal Care Sector

In 2021, Donelle Gadenne reported that vegan veterinarians in the workplace had to navigate their way through vegan stigma, negative vegan stereotypes, and teasing from colleagues. Some vegans felt reluctant to mention their veganism to a potential employer in fear of judgment and discrimination, and some felt the need to manage and modify their behavior when around non-vegan colleagues so as not to be seen as "militant," "extreme," "pushy" or "preachy" vegans.[62]

Trainee vegan animal protection employees have complained that their training involved harming animals in a context that was contrary to their convictions. The application of the relevant provisions under the Equality Act 2010 ensured that the issues were resolved out of court.[63]

Case Study 27: Acknowledgment of Legal Protection for Vegans

During the recent COVID-19 pandemic, many vegan employees who were required to accept vaccination or lose their jobs were concerned that the vaccines were developed by using nonhuman animals.[64] Prior to rolling out the mandatory vaccination policy across the health and social care sector, in accordance with a legal requirement to give due regard to the impact of policies on people who have a "protected characteristic," vegans, for example, the UK government conducted an equality assessment.[65] The requirements of the equality duty are to give due regard to the need to:

- Eliminate discrimination, harassment, victimization, and any other conduct that is prohibited by or under the Equality Act 2010.
- Advance equality of opportunity between persons who share a relevant protected characteristic and persons who do not share it.
- Foster good relations between persons who share a relevant protected characteristic and persons who do not share it.

On the basis of research data collected, the UK government became aware that:

> A number of people may be opposed to vaccination in principle due to their beliefs, either religious or non-religious.

Although the protected characteristic to be examined under equality law is "religion or belief," and the assessment report did contain a section on *Religion or belief—people with different religions, beliefs, or no belief,* it effectively relegated the concerns of vegans with a broad-brush approach to non-religious beliefs and gave considerably more space to communicating with those practicing religious faiths. The report detailed the percentages of different faith groups working in the NHS and documented the types of vaccines approved by the Vatican or the British Islamic Medical Association. The assessment paid lip service only to the existence of "cultural or ethical" beliefs and failed to properly distinguish between the legal obligations to consider the impact of the policy on those with a protected characteristic on account of a qualifying philosophical belief, such as vegans, and those presenting beliefs about issues that were not protected characteristics, such as a belief in conspiracy theories. Consequently, this is how the equality assessment referred to "vegan":

> Some religious groups, such as Muslims, Jews and Hindus, or people whose *dietary practice is vegan* [emphasis added] or vegetarian could also refuse vaccination due to the reported presence of animal products, or by-products, or alcohol in COVID-19 vaccines . . . Employers will be encouraged (through guidance) to consider redeployment as an alternative to dismissal wherever a worker is unable/chooses not to get vaccinated. And as above we have considered exemptions for those who refuse the vaccine due to *religious beliefs* [emphasis added] and have opted not to provide this exemption. This type of exemption would be difficult to implement or prove and would likely significantly reduce the impact of the policy in achieving its aims of increasing levels of protection for both the workforce and patients. It may also cause tension between those who have been exempted and other staff who have been required to be vaccinated as a condition of deployment.

As can be seen, the legal duty to give due regard to the impact of the mandatory vaccine policy on individuals employed in the health care professions was, arguably, inadequately executed, notwithstanding that the outcome of the assessment was that no exemption would be available for any individual with protected religious or non-religious beliefs.

For the avoidance of doubt, the issue and points made are not that vegans are against vaccines; evidence clearly shows that they are not. Neither is the point to be made that vegans should have been given *special* attention. The point being made is that veganism and vegans were relegated and inadequately represented and referenced in the government's policymaking process. Circumstances such as these arguably perpetuate the primacy of consideration for individuals with religious beliefs and result in vegan employees feeling undervalued and overlooked.

In 2023, a preliminary tribunal heard the case of a vegan, Ms. T Owen (also discussed above in relation to access to services).[66] Ms. Owen brought proceedings against her employer, claiming unfair dismissal and religion or belief discrimination following the termination of her employment contract. Ms. Owen alleged that she was dismissed from their employment because they were vegan and refused the mandatory COVID-19 vaccination. The tribunal was unable to progress to adjudicate on this issue partly because it concluded that Ms. Owen did not evidence that they had genuinely held belief in ethical veganism, despite evidence provided and the complainant swearing an oath that they identified as an ethical vegan.[67]

Case Study 28: Unlawful Harassment in the Workplace

In 2022, Ms K Reilly brought a case concerning multiple issues, including allegations of harassment, some of which related to veganism as a protected characteristic.[68] The employment tribunal heard that the claimant was subjected to comments encouraging them to eat meat, handle meat products, and had meat products waved close to their face. The tribunal confirmed that the claimant's veganism met the test for protection, and that the unwanted conduct created an intimidating, hostile, degrading, humiliating, and offensive environment for Ms Reilly that constituted harassment under the Equality Act 2010.

CONCLUSION

Unfair treatment and discrimination against vegans remain largely invisible, partly for privacy and data protection reasons but also because vegans do not wish to be seen as "making a fuss" or "causing trouble". The consequence is that the true extent of the lived experience of vegans is unknown. Their feelings about having to discuss their concerns and experiences are much like anyone else's; they do not want to be involved in complaints, formal complaints, and certainly not escalated complaints, tribunals, or litigation. As can be seen from the discussion above, however, vegans experience prejudice and unfair treatment on a daily basis in a variety of different contexts, some of which are known to have caused them considerable stress, anxiety, and loss of employment—either as misconduct or as a result of raising formal grievances and negotiating a settlement out of court. The experiences described are mostly those in the public domain on account of privacy regulations but are a mere drop in the ocean. The issues presented, even those presented in older cases, remain relevant and offer important insights into why a campaign for the recognition of vegans in law and a concerted effort to defend and protect vegans are still necessary.

The next chapter explains the formation of the IVRA and the commencement and aims of the vegan rights campaign, established to support and defend vegans and advance veganism as a useful strategy in the animal protection movement.

NOTES

1. More can be found at PETA, "Animal-Derived Ingredients List," PETA, 2023, accessed November 22, 2023, https://www.peta.org/living/food/animal-ingredients-list/.

2. Some vegans rationalize the use of second-hand footwear and clothing on environmental grounds to avoid waste and not contribute to wasteful consumerism. On the other hand, some vegans have expressed an overriding urge not to obtain a benefit from an animal that has been killed for commodities.

3. Research into the issues began in 2013. A draft copy of a vegan equality survey, which was related to broader research, was carried out in 2013–2014 and was later uploaded by Lancaster University to its Research Portal. See Jeanette Rowley, "Veganism and Equality Research," Lancaster University, Research Directory, accessed July 20, 2023, https://www.research.lancs.ac.uk/portal/en/publications/veganism-and-equality-research(f7c7c455-d6b6-49a2-9766-863fc7a92213).html.

4. United Kingdom Equality Act 2010, s. 31, accessed July 15, 2023, https://www.legislation.gov.uk/ukpga/2010/15/notes/division/3/3/4.

5. Some details of this case are publicly available online. For example, see BBC News, "NatWest Worker Told Customer 'Vegans Should be Punched'," February 18, 2019, accessed July 8, 2023, https://www.bbc.co.uk/news/uk-england-bristol-47257996.

6. All cases in this category were unreported.

7. All cases in this category were unreported.

8. Daniel McNeil, "London Dungeon Announces They Will '"Ban" Vegans from Entering in January in Support of Beloved Character," *LondonWorld,* January 3, 2023, accessed July 8, 2023, https://www.londonworld.com/whats-on/london-dungeon-announces-they-will-ban-vegans-from-entering-in-january-in-support-of-beloved-character-3972614.

9. Polly Foreman, "London Dungeon Apologizes After 'Banning Vegans' for January," *Plant Based News*, January 9, 2023, accessed July 8, 2023, https://plantbasednews.org/culture/ethics/london-dungeon-apologizes-banning-vegans/.

10. Sian Traynor and Tim Hanlon, "Vegan Furious over Rude Note Written on Restaurant Menu after Meatless Enquiry," *The Mirror*, June 1, 2021, accessed July 8, 2023, https://www.mirror.co.uk/news/uk-news/vegan-furious-over-rude-note-24225814.

11. All cases in this category were unreported.

12. This can be an issue in mixed food production environments. For example, pieces of animal products have been found in "vegan" foods because the same manufacturing lines are used for both vegan and non-vegan foods. Residue and "pieces" can remain after the equipment has been "flushed." Some vegan foods are produced in vegan-only facilities.

13. All cases in this category were unreported.

14. All cases in this category were unreported.

15. Nicola Slawson, "Head Chef Resigns over 'Spiking' Vegan Meal Comments," *The Guardian*, January 3, 2018, accessed July 15, 2023, https://www.theguardian.com/lifeandstyle/2018/jan/03/head-chef-gets-death-threats-over-spiking-vegan-food-claim.

16. *Mr. M Ali v. Indian Cuisine Limited,* [2019] UK ET 2206359/2018.

17. *Ms. T Owen v. Willow Tower Opco 1 Ltd,* [2023] UK ET 2400073/2022.

18. The Vegan Society, "87% of UK Vegans Have Had at Least one Dose of Covid-19 vaccine," accessed April 22, 2024, https://www.vegansociety.com/news/news/87-uk-vegans-have-had-least-one-dose-covid-19-vaccine.

19. See, for example, PETA, "Animals and the COVID-19 Vaccine: PETA Answers Your Key Questions," 2021, accessed April 22, 2024, https://prime.peta.org/news/a-compassionate-guide-to-covid-19-vaccinations/. See also, guidance from The Vegan Society, "Vegan Society Response to Covid-19 Vaccine," 2020, accessed April 22, 2024, https://www.vegansociety.com/news/news/vegan-society-response-covid-19-vaccine, and The Vegan Society, "Medications," accessed April 22, 2024, https://www.vegansociety.com/resources/nutrition-and-health/medications.

20. All-Party Parliamentary Group on Vegetarianism and Veganism, "Respect for Religious and Philosophical Beliefs while Eating in Care," 2021, accessed July 22, 2023, https://vegappg.org.uk/wp-content/uploads/2021/11/VegAPPG-beliefs-respect-report-1.pdf. See also, https://vegappg.org.uk/inquiry/ and https://www.youtube.com/watch?v=1k0cBSMTOxk&feature=youtu.be.

21. All-Party Parliamentary Group on Vegetarianism and Veganism, "Respect for Religious and Philosophical Beliefs while Eating in Care," 2021, accessed July 22, 2023, https://vegappg.org.uk/wp-content/uploads/2021/11/VegAPPG-beliefs-respect-report-1.pdf, 5.

22. All-Party Parliamentary Group on Vegetarianism and Veganism, "Respect for Religious and Philosophical Beliefs while Eating in Care," 2021, accessed July 22, 2023, https://vegappg.org.uk/wp-content/uploads/2021/11/VegAPPG-beliefs-respect-report-1.pdf, 28.

23. All-Party Parliamentary Group on Vegetarianism and Veganism, "Respect for Religious and Philosophical Beliefs while Eating in Care," 2021, accessed July 22, 2023, https://vegappg.org.uk/wp-content/uploads/2021/11/VegAPPG-beliefs-respect-report-1.pdf, 19.

24. Stian Alexander, "Sneaky Lags Pretend to be Vegan in a Bid to Get Better Prison Dinners," *The Mirror*, November 5, 2022, accessed July 26, 2023, https://www.mirror.co.uk/news/uk-news/sneaky-lags-pretend-vegan-bid-28417598.

25. Independent Monitoring Boards, "Annual Report of the Independent Monitoring Board at HMP Warren Hill for Reporting Year June 1, 2021—May 31, 2022," October 2022, accessed July 26, 2023, https://cloud-platform-e218f50a4812967ba1215eaecede923f.s3.amazonaws.com/uploads/sites/13/2022/10/AMENDED-Warren-Hill-AR-21-22-final-for-circulation-without-track-changes.pdf.

26. The Vegan Society, "Prison Guards Impose an Oppressive Dietary Regime and Refuse to Allow Prisoners to Become Vegan, says Vegan Society Rights Advocate," November 10, 2022, accessed July 26, 2023, https://www.vegansociety.com/news/news/prison-guards-impose-oppressive-vegan-dietary-regime.

27. BBC News, "Vegan School Meal Options Promised After Mother's Campaign," November 5, 2019, accessed July 29, 2023, https://www.bbc.co.uk/news/uk-scotland-50249679.

28. Unreported.

29. Department of Health and Social Care, "The Nursery Milk Scheme," accessed July 17, 2023, https://www.nurserymilk.co.uk/.

30. Solihull Observer, "Solihull School's U-turn after Vegan Dad's Campaign to get Soya Milk on the Menu," July 2, 2021, accessed July 17, 2023, https://solihullobserver.co.uk/news/solihull-schools-u-turn-after-vegan-dads-campaign-to-get-soya-milk-on-the-menu/.

31. An example of the type of resources vegans have complained about would be BookTrust, "Milly Cow Gives Milk: Storytime and Craft with Julia Groves." *YouTube.* Video, July 30, 2021, accessed August 5, 2023, https://www.youtube.com/watch?v=9IuzNT4DALI. See also, resources for schools available at Agriculture and Horticulture Development Board (AHDB), https://ahdb.org.uk/education.

32. Charlotte Dobson, "Mum Wins Battle to get Vegan Free School Meals for her Daughter," *Manchester Evening News*, October 9, 2018, accessed August 6, 2023, https://www.manchestereveningnews.co.uk/news/greater-manchester-news/vegan-free-school-meals-bury-15254775.

33. Although the news report states that Laura researched vegan rights materials, it also states that she found that veganism is supported by "the Human Rights Act 2010." This is, in fact, an incorrect reference to legislation. The information that was distributed at that time was that veganism was protected under Article 9 of the ECHR, which informs protection for religion or belief under the Equality Act 2010. Nevertheless, this news example shows how vegans were becoming aware of their potential protection in law, which aligns with the mission of the IVRA.

34. Vegan-Inclusive Education, https://vieducation.co.uk/, accessed July 29, 2023.

35. Ruth Jenkins, "Is There an Aspect of Inclusion Your School is Missing?" *Primary First*, no. 1 (June 1, 2021): 38–43, https://issuu.com/synergyprint/docs/primary_first_issue_31/45.

36. Quoted in Vicky Simpson and Jared Piazza, "Vegan-Inclusive Education: An Interview with Ruth Jenkins," PHAIR Society, October 23, 2022, accessed October 23, 2023, https://phairsociety.org/2022/10/23/vegan-inclusive-education-an-interview-with-ruth-jenkins/.

37. All cases in this category were unreported.

38. Tanveer Mann, "Vegan, 12, Took His Own Life after Bullies Threw Meat at Him," *Metro*, September 29, 2017, accessed July 20, 2023, https://metro.co.uk/2017/09/29/boy-12-hanged-himself-after-bullies-threw-meat-at-him-because-he-was-vegan-6964518/.

39. BBC News, "Vegan Parent Complains about Lymington School's Pigs," January 23, 2018, accessed July 22, 2023, https://www.bbc.co.uk/news/uk-england-hampshire-42782437.

40. Ed Winters, "Stop Priestlands School from Sending Pigs to Slaughter!" Change.org, January 20, 2018, accessed July 22, 2023, https://www.change.org/p/priestlands-school-stop-priestlands-school-from-sending-pigs-to-slaughter.

41. Hayley Lugassy, "Vegan Young People in England: An Exploratory Study on their Identity, Relationships and Educational Experience," (PhD diss., University of East Anglia, 2022), https://ueaeprints.uea.ac.uk/id/eprint/89352/.

42. Hayley Lugassy, email message to author, July 24, 2023. PhD thesis and personal correspondence on file with author.

43. Jared Piazza, Victoria Simpson, and Luke McGuire, "Why Children Moralise Harm to Animals but Not Meat," *Trends in Cognitive Sciences* 27, no. 8 (2023): 685–688. https://doi.org/10.1016/j.tics.2023.05.004.

44. ITV News, "Bristol Vegan Student Forces College into U-Turn on Making her do Farming Module," April 14, 2021, accessed July 29–2023, https://www.itv.com/news/westcountry/2021-04-14/bristol-vegan-student-forces-college-into-u-turn-on-making-her-do-farming-module.

45. The Vegan Society, "Vegan Student Forced to 'Study Unit on Farming or Fail' Wins Case against College," April 12, 2021, accessed July 29, 2023, https://www.vegansociety.com/news/news/vegan-student-forced-%E2%80%98study-unit-farming-or-fail%E2%80%99-wins-case-against-college.

46. All cases in this category were unreported.

47. H.A. Herzog, T.L. Vore, and J.C. New, "Conversations with Veterinary Students: Attitudes, Ethics, and Animals," *Anthrozoös* 2, no. 3 (1989): 181–188. Quoted in Donelle Gadenne, "Veganism and the Veterinary Profession: An Incongruous Union? The Experiences of Vegan Veterinary Professionals Working in Small Animal Veterinary Practice in England," (PhD diss., Edge Hill University, 2021), 138, https://research.edgehill.ac.uk/ws/portalfiles/portal/48208175/Donelle_Gadenne_PhD_Thesis.pdf.

48. Andrew Knight, "The Effectiveness of Humane Teaching Methods in Veterinary Education," *Altex*, 24, no. 2 (2007): 91–109. Quoted in Donelle Gadenne, "Veganism and the Veterinary Profession: An Incongruous Union? The Experiences of Vegan Veterinary Professionals Working in Small Animal Veterinary Practice in England," (PhD diss., Edge Hill University, 2021), 253, https://research.edgehill.ac.uk/ws/portalfiles/portal/48208175/Donelle_Gadenne_PhD_Thesis.pdf.

49. Donelle Gadenne, "Veganism and the Veterinary Profession: An Incongruous Union? The Experiences of Vegan Veterinary Professionals Working in Small Animal Veterinary Practice in England," (PhD diss., Edge Hill University, 2021), 256, https://research.edgehill.ac.uk/ws/portalfiles/portal/48208175/Donelle_Gadenne_PhD_Thesis.pdf.

50. Donelle Gadenne, "Veganism and the Veterinary Profession: An Incongruous Union? The Experiences of Vegan Veterinary Professionals Working in Small Animal Veterinary Practice in England," (PhD, diss., Edge Hill University, 2021), 254, https://research.edgehill.ac.uk/ws/portalfiles/portal/48208175/Donelle_Gadenne_PhD_Thesis.pdf.

51. Crossland's Employment Solicitors, "Nearly Half of Vegans Feel Discriminated Against at Work," May 9, 2019, accessed August 8, 2023, https://www.crosslandsolicitors.com/site/hr-hub/nearly-half-of-vegans-feel-discriminated-against-at-work.

52. *Hashman v. Milton Park (Dorset) Ltd. (t/a Orchard Park),* [2011] UK ET 3105555/2009, paragraph 25.

53. *Hashman v. Milton Park (Dorset) Ltd. (t/a Orchard Park),* [2011] UK ET 3105555/2009, paragraph 56.

54. *Hashman v. Milton Park (Dorset) Ltd. (t/a Orchard Park),* [2011] UK ET 3105555/2009, paragraph 58.

55. All cases in this category were unreported.

56. All cases in this category were unreported.

57. The original post is no longer available online, but see The Vegan Society, "Vegans Welcome to Apply—it's the Law," June 13, 2017, accessed August 12, 2023, https://www.vegansociety.com/whats-new/news/vegans-welcome-apply-%E2%80%93-it%E2%80%99s-law.

58. All cases in this category were unreported but see Jeanette Rowley, "The Expert Series Spring 2021: Veganism, Counter Terrorism Strategy and Policing," The Vegan Society, 2021, accessed November 25, 2023, https://www.vegansociety.com/get-involved/research/research-news/expert-series-spring-2021-veganism-counter-terrorism-strategy-and-policing.

59. *Casamitjana Costa v. The League Against Cruel Sports*, [2020] UK ET 3331129/2018.

Controversially, the same judge, Robin Postle, had found a year earlier that vegetarianism is not a protected characteristic for the purposes of the Equality Act 2010 because, they proposed, unlike veganism, the complainant's belief lacked the required degree of cogency and was more likely opinion rather than a belief capable of meeting the legal test for protection in law. *Conisbee v. Crossley Farms Ltd*, [2019] UK ET 3335357/2018.

60. *Casamitjana,* (above) Consent Judgment 24–28 February and March 1, 2020.

61. Liam Gilliver, "Vegan Soldiers File Complaints against Armed Forces over Lack of Plant-Based Options," *Plant Based News,* May 13, 2021, accessed August 12, 2023, https://plantbasednews.org/culture/ethics/vegan-soldier-armed-forces-plant-based-options/.

62. Donelle Gadenne, "Veganism and the Veterinary Profession: An Incongruous Union? The Experiences of Vegan Veterinary Professionals Working in Small Animal Veterinary Practice in England," (PhD diss., Edge Hill University, 2021), 256, https://research.edgehill.ac.uk/ws/portalfiles/portal/48208175/Donelle_Gadenne_PhD_Thesis.pdf.

63. All cases in this category were unreported.

64. The Health and Social Care Act 2008 (Regulated Activities) (Amendment) (Coronavirus) Regulations 2021 came into force on November 11, 2021 and mandated the vaccination of care service employees unless medically exempt.

65. Department of Health and Social Care, "Making Vaccination a Condition of Deployment in Health and Wider Social Care Settings- Equality Impact Assessment," November 9, 2021, accessed August 12, 2023, https://assets.publishing.service.gov.uk/government/uploads/system/uploads/attachment_data/file/1032203/making-vaccination-a-condition-of-deployment-in-the-health-and-wider-social-care-sector-government-response.pdf.

66. *Ms T Owen v. Willow Tower Opco 1 Ltd,* [2023] UK ET 2400073/2022.

67. Also, because it ruled that Ms Owen didn't have the required continuity of service to bring a claim for unfair dismissal.

68. *Ms K Reilly v. RT Management Bridgeton Limited,* [2022] UK ET 4107984/2020.

Chapter 2

The Campaign for Legal Protection for Vegans and the International Vegan Rights Alliance

This chapter explains the creation and the aims of the IVRA and the history and development of the dedicated campaign for vegan rights. It documents the introduction of the idea for a campaign for rights for vegans and how an international network of lawyers, academics, and other influential supporters, who were working on and were interested in exploring the idea of using law to protect vegans and advance veganism, came together through Vegan Equality-Non-Discrimination (VEND) and the IVRA. The chapter also gives insights into the context and impetus for, and objectives of, these two novel groups and the motivating statistical records that revealed the growth of global interest in the idea of vegan rights. It documents the first funded international symposium and the creation of the Alliance's Declaration, as well as its conferences, themes under discussion, and collaborative projects.

THE BEGINNING

The beginning of the campaign for vegan rights is set in the context of the lived experience of vegan animal rights activists, the plethora of historical, philosophical, and animal rights literature, the diverse range of animal rights activism, and my personal commitment to campaigning, activism, and veganism. The context includes my personal experiences as someone who has been committed and motivated in my support of the animal protection movement, who has been involved in animal rights activism and has been around people involved in animal protection, who is a vegan parent, and who has also taken advantage of educational opportunities.

Drive and dedication can be found everywhere in the vegan animal rights movement, and personal experiences, opportunities, insights, and educational choices no doubt shape how individuals connect various dots in their thinking and personal reflection. However, novel ideas and activity in our combined efforts to dismantle and replace prejudicial social norms are built on what already exists. The campaign for vegan rights emerged in this context and built on existing philosophy, law, knowledge, and ideas about power and oppression.

The proposal to use vegan rights to defend the practice of vegans as a string to a bow in the animal rights movement drew on, highlighted, and brought together, in a new way, a range of existing information. The grounding idea, however, required a certain amount of explanation: veganism is an issue for legal justice, and using law to protect vegans is relevant to dismantling prejudice. Securing rights for vegans supports achieving rights for nonhuman animals, and the issue of legal rights for vegans is relevant to a critique of the exclusivity of the human rights project.

The rationale for the campaign was that there were existing legal grounds supporting rights for vegans which, if utilized, would help bring about changes in policy and practice. The envisaged changes would not merely ensure vegans would be protected from unfair treatment and discrimination, but they would also elevate the status of veganism because protection in law is, arguably, a benchmark of validity and standing in a democracy.

Legal protection can be seen as a top-down mechanism, offering support for the anti-oppressive measures sought by the vegan and animal rights community. It was envisaged that legal rights for vegans would promote, sustain, and advance veganism because the emerging social conditions would make it easier for others to adopt the vegan philosophy.

Tracing back personal influences or notable beginnings is a useful exercise. Mine include the following incidents. A conversation with a vegan friend detailing how their daughter was encouraged by teachers to drink cow's milk at infant school. Being ambushed and violently attacked on the road by male employees of a travelling circus. Being arrested for simply walking down a country lane alone while a fox hunt was in progress and being detained in a mobile prison parked for the day on land owned by the hunt master, whose family and staff served refreshments to the police officers on duty. Being prohibited from continuing with undergraduate study in science because of a personal refusal to perform an experiment on a mouse or to sit next to a peer performing the experiment and record their results.[1] Being excluded when "treats" were brought in for "all staff" by managers, none of which were ever suitable for vegans. And further, despite there being no hierarchy of protection for qualifying religions and beliefs in law, being ordered to move a bottle of alcohol (which had been left on my office desk as a gesture of thanks by the head of the department) in case it caused offense to a Muslim colleague in the office, while personally having to accept cow's milk visibly present in the office, the contents of the staff fridge, and the smell of colleagues' meat or fish lunches, often cooked in the office microwave. Other experiences have included being joked about and asked if I am a bird because I eat seeds, and being accused of child abuse by a so-called friend because I was raising my children vegan.

The point to be made is that, in the context of a vegan animal rights activist's real-world lived experiences, it is difficult to pinpoint the exact moment in time when the dots are joined in such a way that they inspire, motivate, or reveal a particular course of action as a matter of conscience and justice.

Notwithstanding the likely significance of being a long-term vegan, exposed to various circumstances, and having a range of insights about the treatment of vegans, it is probably fair to say that the demanding catalyst for life-changing animal rights activism, formative to establishing the campaign for vegan rights, was a document published in 2010 by the UK's Equality and Human Rights Commission ("the EHRC," "the Commission").

The EHRC has a statutory duty to monitor and oversee human rights and equality measures and, to accompany forthcoming equality legislation, the EHRC published guidance in the form of an *Employment Statutory Code of Practice: Draft for Consultation*.[2] The aim of the guidance was to help individuals and public and private organizations understand the meaning of provisions in equality legislation soon to come into force.

As the body tasked with overseeing human rights and equality measures in the UK, the Commission would have been aware of a range of important international and European legal obligations, guidance, and case law that determine the trajectory of standards for compliance in the UK. Importantly, the EHRC would have been aware that veganism was within the legal meaning of the human right to freedom of belief under Article 9 of the ECHR,[3] and that the forthcoming legislation also retained and developed the European Union Principle of Equality,[4] which required a broad application of the concept of "belief".[5] It came as no surprise, therefore, that to explain the legal meaning of "philosophical belief" the draft guidance for consultation gave examples involving veganism. It stated that "[a] belief need not include faith or worship of a God or Gods, but must affect how a person lives their life or perceives the world", and gave the following example:

> A person who is a vegan chooses not to use or consume animal products of any kind. That person eschews the exploitation of animals for food, clothing, accessories or any other purpose and does so out of an ethical commitment to animal welfare. This person is likely to hold a belief which is covered by the Act.[6]

In the section on *During Employment*, the Commission made the point that an employer must ensure that contractual terms, employment conditions, practices, policies, processes, or procedures do not directly or indirectly discriminate against employees with a "protected characteristic". The Commission noted that an area where discrimination might occur could be in relation to food. With the accommodation of the needs of vegans in mind, the Commission gave an example of how to give due consideration to the needs of vegans in the workplace:

> A big, multicultural firm has provided each kitchen area with a vegan space and a non-vegan space. Each space has a fridge and sink with cleaning cloths, microwave, separate utensils and crockery, all of which are colour coded either green for the vegan spaces or red for the non-vegan spaces. Staff members are strongly encouraged to use the spaces appropriately in order to respect the beliefs of their vegan colleagues.[7]

At the time the guidance was published, the *Mail Online* reported that "[a] spokesman from the commission explained that '[t]his is about someone for whom being vegan or vegetarian is central to who they are. This is not something 'thought up by the commission.'"[8]

The examples included in the guidance raised the profile of veganism. The guidance validated veganism as a recognized belief in law, pointed to the practical needs of vegans, and offered a formal point of reference for all vegans to use if and when necessary. Unfortunately, however, and very disappointingly, following the consultation process, the examples supporting vegans were removed from the guidance.

The removal of the examples from official guidance effectively hid the legitimacy of veganism in law, which was both a personal and professional concern.

FIRST STEPS

The deletion of the examples from the guidance published by the EHRC prompted initial research about the human rights and equality provisions that were relevant to the claims of vegans, and also motivated a Freedom of Information Request to the EHRC.[9] The details provided under the request did not adequately explain why the examples relating to veganism had been removed.

Observations from early research were intriguing. Although the correct term of reference for individuals with religious or non-religious life-directing principles was "religion or belief," many authoritative sources on the subject of international law and protection for "religion or belief" gave the impression, perhaps inadvertently, that the protection of religious beliefs was the only target of human rights standards and that only lip service needed to be paid to any protection granted by the courts for those with non-religious beliefs. Furthermore, while in 1993 the Commission of the ECtHR had considered a complaint from a vegan and found veganism to be within the legal meaning of the human right to freedom of thought, conscience, and religion under Article 9 of the ECHR,[10] this important case had not been utilized in any way to support vegans or advance veganism, and it was exceptionally rare to find it footnoted in legal research and textbooks. The importance of the case appeared to have been overlooked and was unknown in vegan and animal rights networks.[11] What was also intriguing was that an unsuccessful case involving ethical vegan Jerry Friedman in California had been heard under regulations protecting *religious* faith (emphasis added).[12] Both existing case law and the legal meaning of religion and belief needed further exploration.

The primary observation was that the internationally guaranteed right to freedom of thought, conscience, and religion, (which is often referred to as the right to "religion or belief"), was a fundamental human right that grounded the prohibition on interference and discrimination in all walks of life and was important for harmonized understandings of rights and equality provisions yet seemed to be interpreted differently in different jurisdictions. This observation indicated that the legal meanings of "religion" and "belief" required analysis to reveal common characteristics and principles for the application of law and for adequate and appropriate legal protection.[13] Such an analysis would be critical to establishing the scope of vegan rights and access to justice. For example, a common understanding could, arguably, be that the right to freedom of religion or belief can be explained in terms of the right to think and work out one's own moral and spiritual compass, to be free to express one's identity, and to practice the daily life-directing moral values and convictions intrinsic to the belief in question.[14]

This early examination of the legal meaning of religion and belief noted that it was well-acknowledged that the legal category "religion or belief" had raised issues of definition and understanding.[15] Religions, at least the traditionally recognized religions, appeared to have enjoyed recognized status in law, while the definition of "belief" and "philosophical belief" have, apparently, been relegated and proved to be more complex for the courts.[16]

In the context of the apparent confusion relating to protection for religion or belief, as recognized and illustrated in literature and case law, one would be excused for thinking it somewhat reasonable to use veganism as an example to explain non-religious "philosophical belief" for the purposes of complying with and applying relevant law. Veganism is an extremely useful example of a non-religious philosophical belief in law, it being a commitment to convictions and principles that require practical manifestation on a daily basis. Its inclusion in authoritative draft guidance in relation to the meaning of philosophical belief in equality law would, therefore, seem appropriate. In the words of the Human Rights Committee,[17] the protected category "religion and belief" is "broadly construed" and "[t]he same protection is enjoyed by holders of all beliefs of a non-religious nature".[18]

The early examination of a range of literature—including on protection for religion or belief, international treaties, and the materials of the Human Rights Committee—was formative to the campaign for vegan rights, but it also revealed that research grounding a campaign for vegan rights, and providing practical support for vegans involved in claims of unfair treatment or discrimination, needed to dig deep and wide. The research needed to encompass the negative experiences of vegans, the removal of the examples relating to veganism in the Draft Code of Practice, the apparent inadequate assessment of the issue in existing literature, the meaning of being equal in law for people with philosophical beliefs as opposed to religious beliefs, and published guidance supporting the protection of vegans. Together, these things not only represented the messy and incoherent environment for vegan rights, equality, and inclusion but also offered an opportunity to create clarity and create a new dimension to the campaign for animal rights.

The opportunity presented was not only to establish and utilize the existing legal framework relevant to the legal protection of vegans. The realization that a legal framework could explicitly grant protection for vegans, who stand with and speak for nonhuman animals, while at the same time withholding protective rights from the animals themselves, generated a significant degree of curiosity. It was clear that legal protection for vegans was also capable of grounding a critical perspective on the exclusivity of human rights. What was thought necessary was not merely establishing and promoting the legal framework within which rights for individual vegans could be established and accessed, but also introducing veganism as relevant to a critical analysis of (exclusive) human rights.

Subsequently, three concurrent actions flowed from these compelling ideas. The first was to secure appropriate specialist guidance for a research project. The second was to establish the social media account "Vegan Equality, Non-Discrimination" ("VEND") and to advocate for the rights for vegans. The third was to establish an international support group for collaborative exploration (the IVRA).

The objectives in relation to the research were threefold. The first was to explore the legal landscape and determine the strength of global protection for vegans in law. The second was to ground the campaign for vegan rights in more than individual human rights by showing, through an analysis of human rights, that protection for vegans relates to our collective concern with avoiding suffering. The third was to survey the vegan community about their daily lived experiences to provide evidence for appropriate attention and workstreams.

In relation to the grassroots groups VEND and IVRA, the aims were to promote solidarity, establish practical support for vegans around the world, and bring together a group of professionals and supporters—vegan academics, vegan lawyers, representatives from vegan organizations, etc.—to discuss the international legal provisions that could be used to protect vegans and advance veganism, and to work out and understand how international provisions were interpreted and given effect in the legislation and case law of different countries.

The overall commitment was to help change the social, political, and legal conditions in which veganism and vegans exist: to contribute to the required shift from entrenched prejudice toward other animals and vegans to entrenched compassion for others. This included advocating for protection for those who manifest compelling, life-directing convictions and compassion for other animals. The mission was to clarify and use law to defend vegans and help bring about changes in laws, policies, and practices around the world.

Formal supervision for the research began in the autumn of 2011, and plans for VEND and the IVRA were in progress and promoted publicly in small academic and activist circles. The research was more widely publicized in July 2012 to professionals at the Fifth International Equality, Diversity, and Inclusion Conference, in Toulouse, France, under the aptly named conference theme "Roar from the Edge",[19] and to the animal rights community at the Second International Animal Rights Conference, held in Luxembourg, through a presentation on veganism in law given on the main stage on Friday, September 14, 2012.[20]

THE CONVICTIONS OF VEGANS: A COMPELLING ANCHOR FOR VEGAN RIGHTS, EQUALITY, AND INCLUSION

Being immersed in the vegan, animal rights community for many decades already provided significant insights about prejudice against those who defended the moral status of nonhuman animals. It was not uncommon to hear about or be involved in discussions about the unfair treatment of vegans in schools, in the workplace, as consumers, or socially. The campaign for vegan rights was partly conceived in the context of this awareness of the lived experience of vegans. There was also, however, a need to explore and record the views of vegans to provide supporting evidence for anecdotal reports of unfair treatment and discrimination and obtain information about how aware vegans were of the legal principles that could be used to protect them.

As mentioned above, the idea to establish a campaign for vegan rights was presented to the animal rights community in 2012, at the Second International Animal Rights Conference, held in Luxembourg.[21] The idea was well-received, and a number of interested individuals were very keen to find out more and support the project. Support from animal rights activists in Luxembourg was reassuring, motivating, and inspiring, particularly because a presentation focusing on rights for vegans could easily give the impression that the idea for such a campaign was not and would not be grounded in respect for other animals, or be meaningful for animal protection in any other way. The interest and support received at the conference paved the way for the groundbreaking survey on vegan equality, launched in 2013.[22]

The survey was approved by the ethics department at Lancaster University in the UK and was set in the context of new British equality law. The aim was to find out how vegans felt about their experiences in everyday life in relation to the stated protection for individuals with convictions coming within the legal meaning of "philosophical belief". At this time, the idea of vegans claiming rights was largely unheard of; the idea and rationale for such a campaign were new.

One unsurprising observation from the survey was that most vegan respondents reported having to "put up" with negative comments about veganism, "jokes", and being singled out. Vegans also reported feeling that responding to comments about their veganism, even in a reasonable way, would create a worse atmosphere, which meant that they often avoided discussing their convictions or other elements of their beliefs and lifestyle. Respondents reported feeling unwelcome, like "outsider" and worse, covertly "required" to isolate their lifestyle, their knowledge, their insights about the treatment of other animals, and their own convictions from a holistic presentation of who they were. It was clear, though, that the vegan respondents were deeply committed to their vegan convictions despite the uncomfortable social situations they expected to endure and deal with on a daily basis.

At the time of the survey, in 2013, it was apparent that the legitimate status of vegans in law was not known in the vegan community.[23] The survey generated little interest and attracted only a small number of respondents. However, there were two critically significant motivating observations that were a catalyst for driving forward the global campaign for vegan rights.[24] The first was that the convictions of vegans for nonhuman animals were so fundamental to the identity of respondents and people who participated in discussions about the survey at vegan events that their legitimate status as individuals with legal status who could be protected from unfair treatment and discrimination did not register as significant to them when placed in the context of their understanding of the suffering endured by other animals. The idea of legal protection for them had not resonated as meaningful or important because their focus was on animal suffering; their concern for other animals was their priority, not the unfair treatment they endured themselves. This emphasized the importance of their convictions to their identity as vegans. The second observation was related to the first. Some respondents felt that their convictions about and concern for nonhuman animals were so entrenched and life-directing that the survey's reference to veganism as a "belief" concerned and offended them; the idea of being defined as holding what was perceived as *mere belief*, did not accurately reflect, or do justice to, the profound nature of their life-directing convictions.[25] This objection was absolutely understood. The objection to the use of "belief" in the survey refers to the "moral imperative" that the lives of nonhuman animals matter and that they must be protected from harm and suffering. The reference to "belief" in the survey and statements that vegans held a "belief" were found insulting to some. These observations emphasized an important point relevant to the international human right to freedom of belief: vegans communicated deeply compelling, character-forming, identity-defining, and life-directing moral convictions that they manifested on a daily basis in various areas of their lives, and they felt that these went far beyond the everyday definition and meaning of a "belief."

The survey confirmed the strong moral convictions of vegans, their (often daily) discomforts in social settings, and the fact that they did not benefit from established inclusion or equality policies and did not routinely refer to human rights or equality standards to deal with prejudice or unfair treatment. Rather, they routinely endured prejudice and manifestations of unfair treatment and discrimination. It was absolutely clear from the survey, however, that there were vegan people who were subject to what, on the face of it, looked like unlawful interference, discrimination, harassment, and victimization because they were vegan. International human rights law provides for, accommodates, and imposes very strict limitations on interference with such compelling convictions; everyone is entitled to benefit from the guaranteed human rights, and everyone is equal in law. It was clear from the survey, despite its small scale, that the vegan community would benefit from knowledge about legal principles and law, and that existing law could be put to good use to protect vegans and advance veganism.

There were clear grounds to continue with the mission to educate the vegan community about the relevance and usefulness of using their established legal rights as necessary, and to invoke the law in their defense when they requested support.

THE RESEARCH GROUNDING THE CAMPAIGN FOR VEGAN RIGHTS

There were three elements to the research underpinning the campaign for vegan rights. Comprehensive research would (a) reveal the views of vegans (outlined above), (b) identify and disseminate information about the legal provisions that were of use to vegans in their claims of unfair treatment and discrimination, and (c) provide a critical vegan theory on existing exclusive human rights.

Regarding the legal framework, it was necessary to conduct an examination of international materials on the human right to freedom of religion and belief and how this right was interpreted and given effect in regional human rights systems and domestic human rights and equality legislation. This research led to the discovery that veganism had been an issue for law in the United States, and that it had been raised as an issue for law in literature many years prior to the start of the dedicated campaign.[26]

An objective of the campaign for vegan rights was to have a positive impact on policies and practices that would have to be changed to include and accommodate vegan complainants. It was envisaged that this would result in better social and political conditions for the vegan community and help generate respect for, and normalize, veganism. As a result, practicing vegans would feel more supported, veganism would become more easily sustained, and people wishing to adopt veganism would benefit from policy changes and reduced obstacles in their daily practice, such as when at work or school. The strategy envisaged aimed to create new social and political contexts for veganism, which would then start to positively impact on the oppression of other animals and the prejudicial social and political conditions in which nonhuman animals and veganism currently exist.

To be effective when defending vegans, it would be necessary to examine the existing international human rights frameworks and the mechanisms in place for human rights standards to filter through as formative principles in regional and national law, regulations, and policies. It would be necessary to identify and point out gaps and failings on the part of those tasked with responsibility for implementing, maintaining, and enforcing rights and equality measures in all contexts. For example: on what grounds were vegan prisoners denied suitable work boots? How effective was prison policy in reflecting a vegan prisoner's human rights? What failings were there on the part of the public bodies concerned to entrench human rights effectively and appropriately in their everyday functions? What were the legal obligations and responsibilities of prison monitoring boards, and what failings were there in their everyday practice regarding the safeguarding and application of human rights standards? On what grounds might a vegan school pupil be "required" to handle non-vegan products in food technology classes, and how effective was school policy in ensuring that vegan pupils' rights were being safeguarded? What rights did vegans have if they wanted to invest in vegan pension funds? On what grounds did a school permit "authorized" absence, and could a parent refuse to allow the school to take their vegan child to a working farm? These types of issues frequently arise in the vegan animal rights community.

The research task would ultimately conclude that there were useful laws to protect vegans, but that filtering through human rights standards from the treaty level to domestic legislation and through to the everyday practices of, for example, schools, hospitals, prisons, the police, care homes, and employers was a complex process that revealed gaps and failings which subsequently denied vegans their right to live with compassion. The gaps would need to be pointed out and duties, obligations, responsibilities, interpretations, and meanings of policy would be argued over. Ultimately, in grievances, disputes would be litigated as breaches of legal duties and violations of rights.

A campaign for vegan rights that intended to include a dedicated service for defending vegan complaints did not exist, but research confirmed that there was a need for both. The use of the examples in the draft Code of Practice was not the frivolous and fanciful wishes of a specific member of the drafting team. They were legitimate examples of how the human right to freedom of belief should filter through into employment regulations.

Research confirmed that the human right to freedom of belief is considered to be so important to the human rights framework that it occupies a special place in the Human Rights Act 1998. Section 13 of the Act instructs courts and tribunals that when they are dealing with matters under the human right to freedom of thought, conscience, and religion, they "*must* have particular regard to the importance of that right" (emphasis added). This special mention of the right to freedom of thought, conscience, and religion is not without additional support. The European Court of Human Rights has the power to decide which applicants have suffered "significant disadvantage" and to disregard what it considered "trivial" cases for reasons of practical efficiency. Many thousands of cases are sent to the Court, and there has to be some mechanism to ensure it functions as effectively as possible. However, cases grounded by the right to freedom of belief, presented by applicants who claim that their dietary needs have been denied while in the care or control of state bodies, have not only been regarded as important but have been decided in favor of applicants.[27]

The right to freedom of thought, conscience, and religion was, therefore, noted as a powerful mechanism to support and defend vegans. It was found to be applicable in a wide range of contexts because it is a human rights standard that is laid down in the responsibilities and obligations of public authorities, in employment law, in law relating to education, and in European prison regulations. As it is relevant to the right to equality law, it also applies in a wide range of private sector contexts.

Members of the IVRA supported the research and the developing knowledge base and highlighted their own work and the issues for the protection of vegans in their own countries. Acquiring in-depth knowledge was fundamental to developing an understanding of the possibilities for the application of law in the effort to provide protection for vegans and veganism in different parts of the world. For example, we learned about the "gap" between the legal meaning of the international right to freedom of thought, conscience, and religion and protection for *weltanschauung* in Germany, which was unlikely to be sufficiently broad to accommodate the convictions of vegans. We learned about the important work being undertaken in Canada by Camille Labchuk, whose legal arguments for vegans to be included under "creed" have been highly influential at the Ontario Human Rights Commission and for developing policy. We learned that prisons in Austria were unlikely to accommodate the needs of vegans without a legal challenge, and that vegans were referred to as "strict vegetarians" in some cultures, including in Portugal, which mandated the provision of "strict vegetarian" food in public canteens.[28]

The first element of the research sought to identify support for vegan rights in human rights standards, jurisprudence, and other authoritative materials. In the UK, promising evidence was found in a 2009 case,[29] establishing the legal test for the protection of philosophical belief, and in a 2011 judgment[30] which acknowledged that the anti-hunting beliefs of an animal rights activist were related to their overarching vegan convictions.

It was imperative, though, to be able to adequately explain the rationale for the appeal to law to protect vegans, and to human rights as a way of contributing to animal rights. Typically, lay (and sometimes professional) perceptions about the purpose of human rights revolve around pressing issues, such as loss of life, limb, and liberty, and the idea that there exists a hierarchy of protection. It is acknowledged that there are a multitude of pressing issues to be addressed and that talking about human rights and equality provisions can often feel like treacherous ground to tread in an era of acknowledged privilege. However, it is important to remain focused on the status of and conditions for other animals. Pro-vegan discourses and activism support this overall focus by looking to breach the trivializing effect (and function) of the normative application of human rights and unquestioned rights discourse. Feminist-vegan advocate, activist, and independent scholar Carol Adams made an important point over three decades ago:

> Vegetarianism is trivialised, seen as a distraction from or incidental to the important aspects of history . . . relegated to the realm of the individual . . . seen

> from the lens of the individual . . . And in contrast to the pressing difficult topics of sexuality, politics, family, work, racism, sexual and domestic violence, vegetarianism is judged as irrelevant. [31]

A further reason for the need to adequately explain the rationale for the appeal to law to protect vegans and to human rights as a way of contributing to animal rights, was that for animal rights activists and vegan people, the appeal to human rights could be questionable at least, and, at worst, could be seen as a cynical attempt to prioritize people over other animals who are, after all, in dire need of our urgent attention.

Explaining the rationale for the appeal to law entailed a critique of the framework for protective rights *because* it offered a benefit to vegans whose primary claims are for other animals but simultaneously excludes nonhuman animals from its protective reach. Surely, if vegans were beneficiaries of protective rights, there must be a clear *a priori* and collective acknowledgment that nonhuman animals matter. If nonhuman animals matter and vegans are beneficiaries of human rights, then why are rights withheld from other animals themselves?

These thoughts formed the central question to deal with and fused with an established idea in human rights that modern human rights emerged following our collective response to the atrocities and suffering witnessed in world wars. The argument was that if human rights provisions could benefit vegans on the basis that their lived response to the suffering of other animals was cogent and serious, and our collective acknowledgment that the suffering of other animals matters to us could be defended under human rights law, we must also manifest our response to the suffering of nonhuman animals in protective rights for them too. Research efforts dealing with this issue ran alongside the activities of VEND and the IVRA and put forward a critical legal theory on exclusive, anthropocentric human rights.

The critical academic human rights research underpinning the campaign for vegan rights is published elsewhere.[32] It points out that modern human rights treaties, starting with the Universal Declaration of Human Rights, were a response to immense suffering witnessed by human beings during worldwide war. The research relied on an existing “suffering narrative” of human rights, a theory which is critical of individual claim rights and which recognizes, as central to the mission of human rights, the human duty to deal with harm and suffering experienced by others.

Existing critical human rights literature already mentioned the suffering of nonhuman animals and their invisibility in, and exclusion from, a rights enterprise that aimed to protect others from suffering. It also already mentioned, briefly, the central claims of animal rights activists as relevant to a suffering narrative of human rights.[33] It therefore seemed logical to explain the vegan presentation of the suffering of others as relevant to a rights enterprise whose target was the amelioration of suffering.

Of significant importance to the research was that because the mission of human rights—to ameliorate suffering—is conflated with the notion of human reason, the vegan human right to freedom of belief is guaranteed only insofar as everyone has an *individual* right to work out and be guided by their moral compass. This was acknowledged in the research as a limitation of the campaign for vegan rights. It recognizes that human rights protection is grounded in the *individual human right* to be guided by one's personal thoughts and conscience, and that because vegans can be protected under human rights law, it does not mean that the rights of vegans have priority or that veganism has or can take priority. It merely means that the individual vegan presentation of the suffering of others can feature in democracy at the level of law. Vegans can bring their convictions to law, and they can be respected on an individual basis in the adjudication of complaints raised.

In the research, however, the vegan presentation (or more accurately, representation) of "the other" and their suffering is argued to be the very nucleus of the envisaged rights enterprise. On this ground, the research developed a critique of human rights for conflating the mission to deal with suffering with traditional philosophy on the primacy of individual human reason when the recognition of our collective, apparently innate, response to suffering is clearly a primary driving force.

One of the central arguments in the subsequent dissertation was that the reasoning by which vegans can be protected under human rights—because they care about the suffering of other animals and live practically in alignment with their convictions—is observed to be a human characteristic evident across human communities. The idea that other animals have moral standing only in the reasoning of vegans is, therefore, false. Rather, an explanation of human dignity that is established on the grounds that humanity is endowed with reason intrinsically concerns the common conviction that the suffering of other animals matters. On this ground, the research presented veganism as the representation of a shared human concern to ameliorate suffering.

The argument of the thesis, therefore, was that human rights must reorient their foundation to reiterate, establish, and entrench suffering as the primary target of an *inclusive* (of other animals) rights agenda. The primary right to be protected is the right to be free from suffering because suffering is abhorrent to the human community, and humanity feels inescapably duty-bound to respond to suffering.

The critical human rights theory that was presented grounded the claim to vegan rights in the context of a confused system of exclusive anthropocentric human rights. It also highlighted the limitation of the centrality of the individual in human rights and, based on the fundamental human characteristic and desire, to respond positively to suffering, called for a reorientation of human rights away from human dignity and human reason and toward suffering as the primary target of protective rights.[34]

The points made were, therefore, that human rights reflect our common abhorrence for and response to suffering, that the international community agreed that all humanity was against causing suffering, and that vegan rights claims represented the suffering of others. A vegan suffering narrative of human rights, and the practice-based advocacy of VEND and the IVRA, formed a holistic approach to introducing veganism and vegan activism to human rights.

There was, however, one important point that was critical to emphasize at the outset of the rights approach to vegan advocacy and the campaign's supporting research. Although vegans themselves are as entitled as anyone else to benefit from guaranteed rights and equality, the foundational principle embedded in the bedrock of the vegan rights campaign was not "rights for vegans for themselves". Although it was acknowledged that individual vegans might possibly or probably obtain a tangible benefit from the use of legal measures in supported cases, it could not be emphasized enough that the target of defending a vegan's right to practice veganism in different contexts was primarily to validate veganism as the expression of living with compassion at the level of law in order to contribute to the mission to dismantle speciesist prejudice.

The campaign for vegan rights, as strategically devised, could be described as exploiting, or capitalizing on, human rights in an effort to contribute to animal rights by the back door, or through human representation. Regardless of how it was, is, or will be described, the target of the campaign was, and still is, to raise the moral standing of other animals who are denied a rights framework in a human system of justice. The foundational principle is that it is human beings who need to change our society, laws, policies, and practices to facilitate rights for other animals. It makes no sense to speak of animal rights if we do not also entrench and make living with compassion accessible as a human value.

THE CREATION OF VEND AND THE EARLY INTERNATIONAL VEGAN RIGHTS ALLIANCE

Vegan Equality Non-Discrimination was the name given to a public social media campaign to generate interest in the lack of vegan inclusion and equality, and the idea of rights for vegans. VEND made use of the 1993 case that confirmed veganism to be within the legal meaning of Article 9 of the ECHR and the EU principle of equal treatment entrenched in the European Directive

2000/78/EC. VEND was launched publicly in Luxembourg at the Second International Animal Rights Conference on Friday, September 14, 2012, following my delivery of a presentation on veganism and human rights provisions on the main stage of the conference. The idea of claiming rights for vegans as a contribution to the animal rights mission was well-received and generated a significant number of post-presentation expressions of interest, enquiries, and offers of support. The conference organizers kindly lent space for a further meeting between interested parties to discuss next steps for the vegan rights campaign, and gave permission for us to put advertising flyers around the venue.

The commitment and enthusiasm of our five-strong, small group were obvious, but we were met with a dose of potential reality, delivered by a member of the conference organizing team, who reminded us that "everybody has a new idea . . . but . . .".

The comment was profound, and it had personal resonance for me. As a committed vegan animal rights activist, I had a personal feeling of responsibility for introducing a new dimension to the animal rights movement, especially a campaign for vegan rights, even though its aim was to advance the animal rights cause. The sense of responsibility felt overwhelming and all-consuming. The newly introduced campaign was about human responsibility and had good intentions, but the possibility of being responsible for causing harmful divisions and controversy was ever-present.

The success of the VEND social media initiative in generating interest in the situations some vegans faced, which it achieved by maintaining and developing relevant discussion on vegan rights issues, was due to the early administrators and the availability of free social media. VEND attracted a wide range of interested parties and many topical discussions. VEND's optimism and inclusive presence were reflected in its logo, which was designed by a founding member.

The logo was a multi-colored circle with text across it and around the circumference. Ideas relevant to the design were inclusion, diversity, and positivity.

The multi-colored circle represented a unified and holistic approach to the campaign for vegan inclusion, equality, and rights. It was designed to be vibrant to reflect positivity and ensure global relevance. VEND's strapline was "Vegan Equality, Loud and Proud" and although no events were ever planned for VEND, social media engagement evidenced a great deal of support for the initiative.

Meanwhile, the IVRAwas also in formation and taking shape.

Creating and Promoting the International Vegan Rights Alliance

The strategic plan behind the formation of the IVRA was threefold. First, it would function as an organized global body which would be dedicated to developing legal recognition for veganism and the vegan rights cause. In this function, it would act as an international supportive peer group in which members would share research and key information, and would be committed to promoting legal knowledge and best practice standards for the avoidance of discrimination against vegans. It would become a unified voice committed to the legal status of vegans, publish consolidated positions on legal issues and become a strong platform for vegans around the world to feel supported.

Second, it was envisaged that the IVRA would become a focal point of professional legal activism for vegan rights and, through its work, establish and promote the legal principles on which vegans in different jurisdictions could be protected. Ultimately, it would challenge cases of unfair treatment and discrimination against vegans anywhere in the world. Through its newly created website, the IVRA would foster solidarity across the global vegan community, validate the experiences of vegans by acknowledging the unfairness of those experiences, and empower vegans by providing as much information and support as was possible.

The approach of the IVRA would promote the convictions of vegans as deserving of legal protection, but always in the context of the overriding concern with prejudice against nonhuman animals. Its overall purpose would be to entrench the convictions of vegans in law as a social and ethical legal issue, as a matter of justice.

The third aim of the IVRA was to contribute to academic animal rights discourse by introducing the rationale for, and research relating to, the protection of vegans under human rights and equality law, and by also introducing practice-based professional human rights activism to the campaign for animal rights. The intention was to bolster the interdisciplinary approach to animal rights with this new dimension of vegan rights theory and practice. It was envisaged that the holistic approach of the IVRA would encourage further discussion and new research.

To do this, members of the IVRA would collaborate on relevant workstreams and host conferences on vegan rights. The IVRA would thus function as the primary platform for discussing the issues faced by some vegans and act as a catalyst for more nuanced areas of research that could enhance, explain, and elaborate on protection for vegans, as well as encourage existing and new scholars to explore this subject area as a new dimension related to justice for nonhuman animals.

At the time of its formation, the IVRA had five members: a founding chair, a volunteer administrator, a volunteer website creator, and two representatives from different countries. Only two members had legal experience, and all had demanding employment and other life commitments. There was no expertise in the theory of social movements, and no specific, specialist expertise in project planning, organizational planning, governance, graphic design, or communications. Nevertheless, the commitment and desire to succeed were strong.

The first agreed action was to accept the offer of the creation of a website, which would act as a repository for information about legal principles and laws related to vegan rights and the academic research in progress, and which would hopefully function as a source of information that would lead to interested parties making contact. The website was launched in October 2012 and included a section where individuals from different countries could be listed as supporting the initiative.

The IVRA Manifesto

In its manifesto, the IVRA asserted that, under international law, vegans are entitled to a social order in which their vegan rights are respected and provided for. It promoted existing social and cultural rights as entirely relevant to supporting vegan dignity and the free development of the personality of vegans.

The manifesto of the early IVRA records its concerns. It existed to secure ambitious goals:

- The right for ethical veganism to be accepted legally and socially as an intelligent, workable, achievable, realistic system, capable of underpinning human social organization.
- The right to cruelty-free kitchen, bathroom, and personal products in all public authority establishments, in the workplace, and where the supply of these items is an intrinsic part of any service provision.
- The right to vegan food in all public authority establishments, the workplace, and service provision.
- The right to vegan education through the inclusion of vegan belief on educational curricula and unbiased teaching, including accurate information regarding the type, extent, and impact of the use of other animals in human society; the vegan diet as a method of reducing an individual's carbon footprint; the vegan diet as a method of maintaining world food security; and the relationship of animal cruelty to interlinked oppressions and human violence.
- The right to vegan medications and other necessary health intervention products, including vaccines.
- The right to suitable vegan infant formula.
- The right to a formal and legal definition of the word "vegan".
- The right to legally enforced, clear, and accurate labelling of foodstuffs and other consumables.
- The right to outcomes-based equality legislation which places direct duties on employers and providers of goods and services, such that a clear understanding of what is required is achieved.

- The right for ethical veganism to be respected as emotionally, intellectually, and spiritually meaningful in law as a legitimate belief system equal to other belief systems, such as various religions.
- The abolition of unrepresentative images and other visual representations of nonhuman animals used in commercial enterprises; for example: images and commercials that give a false impression of other animals as happy and enjoying their subjection, degradation, and oppression. These false representations of other animals create a degrading and offensive environment and are not in line with a government's responsibility to create the required social conditions for ethical veganism.
- Respect for the vegan worldview by the media is crucial. Enhanced media regulation will contribute to the positive social conditions required for ethical veganism.
- The right for vegans to be recognized in law as a legal minority, requiring protection from discrimination and unfair treatment.
- The right to fair, balanced, and accurate research into vegan nonhuman animal feed.

Within the first two years, IVRA had listed the support of members from nine countries.

The IVRA Logos

The first logo depicting and representing the Alliance was a simple image of a sunflower, colored green, with the scales of justice hanging from leaves on each side.[35] The adaption of the sunflower to include scales on each side was designed to represent vegan philosophy as a matter of and for legal justice.

Combining the scales of justice with the sunflower is intended to convey the message that justice necessarily requires fairness and balance for all living beings, and that a justice that serves the interests of vegans will also be a justice that points to the moral standing of other animals.

The use of this particular image of a sunflower was, however, later found to breach copyright owned by The Vegan Society and, although there was absolutely no animosity, the IVRA set about redesigning its logo, which presented an opportunity for a new, well-thought-out design.

The new design evolved in stages, and the final choice was an orange-colored globe with green-colored continents positioned in the "V" of "IVRA".[36] The "V" represented stalks with leaves at the top, on which unbalanced scales of justice were hung. This logo also carried the strapline "shifting the balance".

The use of the globe in this image signified the IVRA's ambitious worldwide mission. The plant stalks and leaves design of the "V" related to the idea of a seedling, which is common to grassroots initiatives, and in this instance represented emerging activism with potential for significant growth. It also related to the former image of the sunflower in that it referenced plant-based perspectives and living; that image was already associated with veganism. The unbalanced scales signified injustice. The strapline "shifting the balance" referred to the imbalance of legal protection and the status of nonhuman animals and the fact that addressing this imbalance was the mission of the professional legal activism of the IVRA.

The "shifting the balance" strapline also referred to uniting the protection of vegans and advancing veganism with the campaign for animal rights, and to IVRA's goal of shifting perceptions about veganism to ensure it was recognized as a philosophy of life that entailed sincerely and deeply held convictions; ones that were relevant to the human rights framework and equality law. It was envisaged that where there was resistance to the legal protection of vegans, the IVRA would challenge prejudice and discrimination, support equal rights for vegans, and advocate for the accommodation of their needs.

The overall intention of the logo's design was to give a clear message that the mission at hand was not only to positively impact on law for vegans, but also positively impact social values, policies, and practices and to look toward a future transformation of the way human society treats nonhuman animals.

Within a short period of time, enquiries were forthcoming and, over time, strong and effective connections and partnerships were formed. Presentations were given throughout the UK, Europe, and Australia. Through the IVRA website, the numerous presentations given around the world, and the collaborations formed, the IVRA was quickly established.

Early IVRA Initiatives

The IVRA encouraged "country representatives" to start discussions in their own countries about the issues vegans faced; to examine the relevant international legal principles and explore how these were given effect in their country's constitutions and equality laws; and to consider the potential for protection for vegans in their jurisdictions. In the UK, records showing the status of objectives and information updates provided to members between 2012 and 2013 included the following:

- The IVRA had received a response from the Equality and Human Rights Commission regarding the freedom of information request related to the removal of useful examples involving vegans in the Draft Code of Practice accompanying the Equality Act 2010.
- Commenting on the view published by the European Network of Legal Experts in the Field of Non-Discrimination, that veganism might be

considered a "single issue" belief and, therefore, not respected as a "belief" for the purposes of the principle of equality.

- Informing the UN that veganism is much more than a single-issue belief, highlighting its recent report that a plant-based diet has numerous benefits for the planet and that the UN was celebrating "Vegan Missy Higgins" on its website.
- Raising the issue at the highest level that vegan parents are unable to purchase infant formula and highlighting the intense distress caused to parents; urging that this should be dealt with as a matter of public health policy.
- Seeking information from the education minister about vegan-appropriate reading material in early-years education.
- Contacting human resource bodies and organizations to encourage support for vegans in the workplace, particularly with appropriate personal protective equipment, food, and kitchen facilities.
- Compiling data from members in different countries about incidents of unfair treatment and how various countries entrenched the principle of equality and the legal meaning of "belief" in law.
- Confirming arrangements with the (then) Swiss and Indian IVRA Representatives to meet and present a petition to the Special Rapporteur for Freedom of Religion and Belief at the offices of the United Nations in Geneva.

In 2013, the survey on vegan equality began. In 2014, basic information about the human rights principles grounding protection for vegans was compiled in a downloadable e-book. By 2016, the IVRA had handled numerous complaints from vegans, which were enormously helpful in understanding the wide range of issues vegans faced and which supported the development of vegan rights advocacy knowledge and practice.

To support the academic element of the campaign, a chapter introducing veganism to human rights was published in Palgrave Macmillan's Animal Ethics Series in 2016.[37] The draft survey report was already available online, and the German IVRA representative, Attorney Ralf Müller-Amenitsch, published *Vegan im Recht* (Vegan Rights). Discussions were held between Mr Müller-Amenitsch and Petr Kudelka, the IVRA's Austrian representative, to publish a version of *Vegan im Recht* in Austria. Ralf Müller-Amenitsch also helped co-host a funded symposium in Germany. On April 23, 2016, the IVRA held its first fully funded symposium on vegan rights in Berlin, Germany, in collaboration with Sebastian Zösch (later Sebastian Joy) and the German Vegetarian Union (VEBU), with representatives from twelve nations.

Presentations were given at the symposium by participants on the scope of legal protection for vegans in different countries, regional interpretations of the European Equality Directive, and on other issues, such as the provision of vegan food in public sector institutions in the context of human rights principles and obligations.

At the end of the symposium, the participants also discussed the possibility of adopting a Declaration. The draft points for inclusion related to the IVRA's published information and stated mission, and following consultation with the participants' recommendations and developments, the Declaration was finalized and adopted.

The draft Declaration begins by referring to The Vegan Society's definition of veganism and refers to reasons why people choose the vegan way of life. It then sets out a number of legal instruments that entrench and explain the human right to freedom of belief and lists other human rights applicable to the protection of vegans. On April 23, 2016, the participants representing the twelve nations at the first International Law Symposium on Vegan Rights formally adopted the Declaration and called for:

1) Guaranteed provision of vegan food in public institutions.
2) Uniform, mandatory labelling of vegan and vegetarian products, especially food.
3) Guaranteed provision of non-food vegan alternatives in public institutions, including (for illustrative purposes and without limitation of the general principle) educational assessments, uniforms, and medicines.
4) The development of broad policies and practices that support the growing vegan community.[38]

IVRA Statistics

Data from Google Analytics showed that during the first month after the launch of the IVRA's website, between October 12 and November 12, 2012, 145 people accessed the website in 239 sessions. By 2016, a sample report measuring statistics over five days, between August 26, 2016, and August 30, 2016, showed that on average 10,103 new visitors accessed the website in 10,138 sessions. By 2017, a sample of data provided by Google Analytics over four days, between July 17, 2017, and July 20, 2017, showed that on average 18,353 new visitors accessed the website in 18,433 sessions. More detailed analysis showed that the average number of unique daily visitors totaled around 4,500, and these new visitors were spending, on average, around six minutes on the website per visit.

Developments

The acceptance of the vegan rights campaign within the vegan community and the work, growth and success of the IVRA became of interest to a number of other organizations. In 2019, a decision was taken to gift the IVRA network and function to The Vegan Society, from where its important work continued. Chapter 5 provides details about the uptake and success of the work of the IVRA.

CONCLUSION

The creation of the International Vegan Rights Alliance and its research and practice-based functions have grounded and informed a holistic rights-based advocacy for the vegan community. Its popularity and growth represent its value to vegans and the appetite in the vegan community for professional activism that not only elevates the status of veganism and vegans but, importantly, links human rights and vegan justice with justice for other animals.

The next chapter presents evidence, gained from the research undertaken, that invoking human rights is legitimate to protect nonhuman animals directly and that the human rights of those who care about the suffering of nonhuman animals have academic and judicial support. It also explores the existing legal frameworks to show how vegans are legitimate beneficiaries of the human right to freedom of conscience and belief, and it shows the grounds on which they can be protected from unlawful interference and discrimination.

NOTES

1. The experiment was conducted by hanging a mouse by its tail to insert a thermometer into its bottom. It was repeated routinely by undergraduates every year.
2. On file with the author but now appears to be difficult to find online. A copy can be found at The Equality and Human Rights Commission, "Employment Statutory Code of Practice: Draft for Consultation," Employment Lawyers Association, accessed June 22, 2023, https://www.elaweb.org.uk/sites/default/files/docs/Draft%20Employment%20Code%20of%20Practice%201109798532.pdf.
3. *W. v. The United Kingdom*, No. 18187/91, Eur. Comm'n H.R. 1993.
4. Council of the European Union. "Council Directive 2000/78/EC: Establishing a General Framework for Equal Treatment in Employment and Occupation." *Official Journal* L 303 (2000).
5. See chapter 3.
6. Equality and Human Rights Commission, "Employment Statutory Code of Practice: Draft for Consultation," Employment Lawyers Association, accessed June 22, 2023, https://www.elaweb.org.uk/sites/default/files/docs/Draft%20Employment%20Code%20of%20Practice%201109798532.pdf, section 2.53.
7. Equality and Human Rights Commission, "Employment Statutory Code of Practice: Draft for Consultation," Employment Lawyers Association, accessed June 22, 2023, https://www.elaweb.org.uk/sites/default/files/docs/Draft%20Employment%20Code%20of%20Practice%201109798532.pdf, section 9.85.

8. Kirsty Walker, "Now Vegans are Covered by Harman's Equality Law," *Mirror Online,* March 8, 2010, accessed September 2, 2023, https://www.dailymail.co.uk/news/article-1256264/Harriet-Harmans-equality-law-cover-vegans-teetotallers-atheists.html.

9. The right to access information was granted in the UK by the Freedom of Information Act 2000.

10. *W. v. The United Kingdom*, No. 18187/91, Eur. Comm'n H.R. 1993.

11. One of the early activities at presentations on vegan rights was to award a free IVRA mug to anyone who knew that veganism had been protected under human rights law since 1993. The mugs frequently ended up going to the person who shouted out the closest year.

12. *Friedman v. Southern California Permanente Medical Group*, 102 Cal. App. 4th 39, 125 Cal. Rptr. 2d 663 (2002). See also, Mr Friedman discussing the case in Caryn Hartglass, "It's All About Food-Tamara Bedić, Jerold Friedman, Jordi Casamitjana: Vegan Discrimination Cases, Part I," Podcast, September 27, 2023, accessed November 21, 2023, https://podcasts.apple.com/us/podcast/its-all-about-food-tamara-bedi%C4%87-jerold-friedman-jordi/id387958221?i=1000629378227.

13. The use of the human right to freedom of belief for vegans does not suggest or imply that the experiences of vegans are comparable to those who are persecuted on account of their religious beliefs. The application of internationally agreed human rights law in all situations of loss of life, limb, and liberty, and a wide range of other dire situations remains critical. Under exploration are the concept and legal meaning of "religion or belief" and their social, political, and legal ramifications.

14. This right is not intended to protect religions or beliefs that violate common moral principles deemed important to humanity.

15. See chapter 3.

16. See discussion in chapter 3.

17. The Human Rights Committee oversees the implementation of the International Covenant on Civil and Political Rights. The Committee explains and clarifies the scope and meaning of the articles of the Covenant to provide authoritative guidance to contracting parties. Its authority derives from Article 40 of the Covenant. Information about the Committee can be found at https://www.ohchr.org/en/treaty-bodies/ccpr/introduction-committee.

18. See Human Rights Committee, "General Comment No. 22: The Right to Freedom of Thought, Conscience, and Religion (Article 18 of the International Covenant on Civil and Political Rights)," UN Doc. CCPR/C/21/Rev.1/Add.4, 1993. See chapter 3 for more information about the meaning of "religion and belief."

19. Barbara Myers, Irene Ryan, "Stream Five. Hear me Roar: Views from the Edge," 5th Equality, "Diversity and Inclusion International Conference," July 23–25, 2012, Toulouse Business School, Toulouse, France, https://www.edi-conference.org/streams.php?past_conf_id=26.

20. https://ar-conference.org/2012/details.php?id=39.

21. https://ar-conference.org/2012/details.php?id=39.

22. In 2015, a draft copy of the results of a survey carried out in 2013 was uploaded by Lancaster University to its website: https://www.research.lancs.ac.uk

/portal/en/publications/veganism-and-equality-research(f7c7c455-d6b6-49a2-9766-863fc7a92213)/export.html.

23. It should be noted that The Vegan Society had historically made several references to the possibility that veganism might be protected in law in some way, but a dedicated campaign had never been developed.

24. It was extremely uncomfortable to continue the mission, as explained later.

25. Survey respondents commented on this, as did other commentators, including those from established organizations.

26. In addition to *Friedman* above, see Sarah Soifer, "Vegan Discrimination: An Emerging and Difficult Dilemma," *Loyola of Los Angeles Law Review* 1709 (2003).

27. See, for example, *Jakobski v. Poland*, No. 18429/06, Eur. Ct. H.R. Fourth Section, Dec. 7, 2010, and *Vartic v. Romania* (No. 2), No. 14150/08, Eur. Ct. H.R. Third Section, Dec. 17, 2013.

28. In Italy, there has been an attempt to "reclaim" the word vegetarian to signify a vegan diet. See Carlo Prisco, "*The Right to Vegetarianism*," (Maryland: Hamilton Books, 2017). The law in Portugal mandating the provision of vegan food refers to "strict vegetarian" food. See Nuno Alvim, "The Protection of Vegans in Portugal: Law and Progress," in *Law and Veganism: International Perspectives on the Human Right to Freedom of Conscience*, ed. Jeanette Rowley and Carlo Prisco (London: Lexington Books, 2022), 107–120.

29. *Grainger plc and others v. Nicholson,* [2010] IRLR 4 EAT.

30. *Hashman v. Milton Park (Dorset) Ltd. (t/a Orchard Park),* [2011] UK ET 3105555/2009.

31. Carol J. Adams, *The Sexual Politics of Meat* (Cambridge: Polity Press, 1990), 154.

32. Jeanette Rowley, *Towards a Vegan Jurisprudence: The Need for a Reorientation of Human Rights* (PhD diss., 2017 and London: Lexington Books, 2020). For further references, see notes on "the social and political context for veganism" in the Introduction to this book.

33. For example, see Costas Douzinas, *The End of Human Rights: Critical Legal Thought at the Turn of the Century*, (Oxford: Hart Publishing, 2000).

34. Human dignity can be redrawwn to intrinsically include compassion for other animals.

35. Images may still be found online, such as the one at "Pinterest": https://www.pinterest.co.uk/pin/328551735295081541/.

36. Ownership rights to IVRA artwork were transferred to The Vegan Society by the IVRA in 2019. The logo referred to can be viewed on various IVRA materials including conference banners, one of which is published on the Vegconomist website. See Vegconomist, "Lawyers Gather at Conference to Discuss Vegan Rights," 31 May, 2019, accessed February 17, 2024, https://vegconomist.com/society/lawyers-gather-at-conference-to-discuss-vegan-rights/.

37. Jeanette Rowley, "Human Rights are Animal Rights: The Implications of Ethical Veganism for Human Rights," in *Critical Perspective on Veganism,* eds. Jodey Castricano and Rasmus Rahbeck Simonsen (Switzerland: Springer, 2016), 67–93.

38. A copy of the IVRA Declaration can be seen on the website of Vegan Australia, https://d3n8a8pro7vhmx.cloudfront.net/veganaustralia/pages/10064/attachments/original/1579571581/Concluding-Declaration-of-the-1st-International-Law-Symposium-on-Vegan-Rights.pdf?157957158, accessed September 26, 2023. The twelve nations represented in the Declaration were England, Scotland, Canada, Germany, Austria, Estonia, Finland, Luxembourg, Greece, Romania, India, and the Netherlands. The Declaration was supported more widely by national representatives who were unable to be present, including those from the United States of America, Australia, and South Africa. Vegan groups and associations represented include IVRA, VEBU, The Vegan Society, Animal Justice, Go Vegan Scotland, Luxembourg Vegan Society, and Estonian Vegan Society.

Chapter 3

Research Validating and Supporting Rights for Vegans

Given that the mission of the campaign for vegan rights and the function of the IVRA center on the suffering of nonhuman animals and deal with entrenched oppression and prejudice, some readers might reasonably ask: why should we validate the claims of yet another group of people making human rights and equality claims when no amount of alleged unfair treatment or discrimination against them can compare to the suffering endured by other animals? This question can be answered briefly in a single statement: it doesn't make sense to campaign for animal rights without also dealing with the manifestations of prejudice and building a social, political, and legal infrastructure on which animal rights have a chance of becoming a reality.[1]

The failure of human society to respect the moral standing of other animals and their rights, and the need for stronger representation in our system of justice, both require changes in *human* practices. It makes no sense to speak of animal rights if we do not also pay attention to both the overt and covert manifestations of exploitation and prejudice, address them, and start building the kind of human society we want and need to create. Basically, if we want rights for nonhuman animals, then we must also set about *creating* a society that shows respect for the lives, moral standing, and rights of other animals in the way it functions.

On this view, paying attention to how *we live* means we need to expose every covert manifestation of animal exploitation and prejudice, including how these manifestations are perpetuated by, thus far, unquestioned policies and practices that we come across in our everyday lives. This is critical because it is these policies and practices at the everyday level that contribute in no small way to regulating our outlook on the world. For example, we may be raised in a vegan family but once we start compulsory education, we might struggle to obtain vegan food and nutritious drinks because the defaults at the policy level involve state-sponsored exploitation and consumption of other animals. In education, we will likely encounter false narratives about farmed animals and be deceived into believing we are not participating in causing suffering. We will often be expected to participate in visits to working farms to "pet" lambs without being told the truth about their short lives or the reality for their mothers, and we may be inconvenienced and financially burdened if we do not participate in the school milk scheme. As an aside, the legal definition of milk is "mammary secretions obtained from one or more milkings . . .,"[2] and although there are exceptions to the rules, such as for "coconut milk," plant milks are not officially recognized as milk[3] and are, therefore, exempt from subsidies provided under the school milk scheme.

There are many forms of activity that directly and indirectly contribute to the campaign for animal rights. Some involve direct action, and some are focused on critically assessing welfare laws and bringing legal actions for violations of legal provisions. Some campaigns are diet-related and focus on human health, some point to climate and environmental sustainability measures, some revolve around wider issues of oppression and prejudice, some will be high-profile, and others will be going on in the background at various levels. Arguably, all are useful in their own way, helping bring about the changes we need to see, particularly as many strands of interconnection can be found in analysis and different issues speak to different groups of supporters. The benefit of these multiple strands of advocacy is that they provide a rich and evolving social, political, and legal landscape in which the moral standing of nonhuman animals is represented and the suffering we subject them to is highlighted.

What can also help is using our human and equality rights, as vegans, to challenge institutional disregard for the conditions we have created for other animals. By claiming our rights to equality and inclusion, we can directly impact the policies and practices that perpetuate unaddressed prejudice and exploitation and interfere with or prevent us from practicing our compassionate convictions. For example, by challenging a school policy which states that only cow's milk or water can be consumed on school premises, we can achieve inclusion and normalize the consumption of healthy alternatives to cow's milk in school. By challenging an educational or employment training policy that requires harm to be inflicted on nonhuman animals, we can introduce new, morally responsible training methods.

It is acknowledged that this type of animal rights activism will sometimes result in tangible benefits for a human complainant: vegans will benefit from appealing to their legal rights, and measures will be implemented that provide for *their* needs. But without the introduction of policies and practices that accommodate vegans and, through this, the entrenchment of respect and compassion for other animals, how can we introduce rights for nonhuman animals? Surely, their rights depend on the duty we have both to stop harming them and to entrench a principle of doing no harm as a value in our social, political, and legal frameworks.

The process of transformation from prejudice to compassion can benefit from a demand for the formal recognition and validation of veganism as a "philosophy and way of living which seeks to exclude—as far as is possible and practicable—all forms of exploitation of, and cruelty to, animals for food, clothing or any other purpose," and a rights-based approach to creating the social conditions in which people who live according to this philosophy are supported, and in which others can more easily adopt and manifest the vegan philosophy.

By claiming and defending our right to live according to the vegan philosophy, policies are amended. This, then, "promotes the development and use of animal-free alternatives for the benefit of animals, humans and the environment". Nonhuman animals do not benefit from a rights enterprise, but humans do, and there are powerful mechanisms for change that already exist but that have, thus far, not done much heavy lifting in the campaign for animal rights.

On the view presented—that a vegan rights approach to animal rights is valid and offers a novel and useful way to support the animal rights campaign—the question "why should we protect and defend vegans?" is turned on its head to "why shouldn't we?" The questions, then, become the following: What existing support can be found? What are the principles and legal provisions we can use? Where can we find these principles and provisions?

This chapter presents some of the research undertaken to support a vegan rights narrative. It explains why a vegan rights-based approach to animal rights is valid by presenting three elements of how a vegan rights narrative supports the campaign for animal rights.

First, it points to supportive academic and judicial opinion about how individuals with ethical convictions about the treatment of nonhuman animals can effect change via the human right to freedom of conscience.[4] Second, it explains relevant principles and provisions of human rights law. Third, it explains how the human right to freedom of belief features in European equality law.

By exploring these three relevant elements of the vegan rights narrative, this chapter hopes to persuade the reader that vegan rights have an important role in the campaign for animal rights, that the idea is already evident in judicial reasoning, and that vegans are legitimate beneficiaries of existing international human rights and equality provisions that can be put to good use.

ACADEMIC AND JUDICIAL SUPPORT FOR APPEALING TO HUMAN RIGHTS TO SUPPORT ANIMAL RIGHTS

In 2014, Michael Hass's introductory textbook on human rights acknowledged that concern for animal rights might seem irrelevant in a book about human rights but that, in fact, "animal rights" refers to human conduct. Hass understands that animal rights is relevant to human rights because the human rights mission is about protecting the weak, the powerless, and those vulnerable to abuse: a point made in historical critical literature on human rights.[5] Hass, therefore, makes the critical point, relied on in the vegan rights narrative, that animal rights is relevant to human rights because it is about human responsibility.[6]

In 2020, Tom Sparks commented that human rights are acknowledged as a vital tool to achieve change for individuals, but said that "[t]o seek . . . to harness the potential of human rights institutions and discourse to advance animal welfare and animal rights may appear farfetched: one could be forgiven for a certain scepticism concerning the availability of space for animal concerns in this deliberately human-centred area of law and policy".[7] Sparks is not explicitly concerned with capitalizing on the (vegan) human right to freedom of conscience to bring about policy changes that support dismantling prejudice toward other animals, how vegan rights impact on cases involving nonhuman animals, or what the protection of vegans in human rights might say about the orientation of the rights enterprise,[8] but is specifically interested in how the European Court of Human Rights ("ECtHR," "the Court") deals with matters concerning Convention rights in relation to animal protection. Sparks points to "indications of certain modest advances which offer opportunities for animal welfare and rights concerns to be considered within the framework of human rights",[9] and recognizes the "zone of confluence, in which human and animal wellbeing and rights coincide insofar as it can be demonstrated that protecting the one benefits the other".[10] In view of this, Sparks promotes an existing principle of the vegan rights campaign:

> Articulating those confluences within the language of the ECHR [European Convention on Human Rights] and other human rights frameworks has the potential to catalyse the development of animal welfare as a sub-genre of the international human rights story, as well as to provide norms, ideas and impetuses which will cross into other jurisdictions and disciplines, and scholars should now take up this task.

The idea of the intersection of animal rights and protection for people with compassionate convictions under human rights law has, thus, gained traction.

One important human right at the intersection of animal and human rights that is relevant to the discussion is the human right to freedom of conscience.[11]

The direct significance of the right to freedom of belief for the protection of vegan convictions was explicitly recognized at the European Court of Human Rights in 1993.[12] Additional evidence shows that the human right to freedom of conscience has value for animal rights and that there is judicial recognition for the idea that the human right to freedom of conscience actively supports our moral responsibility to other animals *within* the human rights framework. The right to freedom of conscience can be seen to play an important role in cases involving ethical convictions about nonhuman animals, and the relevance of the applicability and function of this right has also been robustly defended by partly dissenting judges when the Court has decided that there is no need to examine the right to freedom of conscience itself and has ruled in favor of applicants on other grounds. The point is that the right to freedom of conscience/belief is important and available to those with ethical convictions about nonhuman animals, and when the importance of the right is relegated in favor of other rights, there are judges who will insist that the application of the right itself should not be overlooked, as the examples below illustrate.

THE IMPORTANCE OF THE RIGHT TO FREEDOM OF CONSCIENCE IN CASES CONCERNING ANIMAL PROTECTION

In the 1999 case of *Chassagnou and Others v. France*,[13] the Court accepted that the ethical convictions of the applicants were relevant to an assessment of whether it was proportional to require landowners with ethical convictions against hunting to be burdened by a compulsory transfer system which required them to transfer hunting rights to a hunting association. The Court ruled in favor of the applicants, but only insofar as their ethical convictions were relevant to other rights under the ECHR ("the Convention," "ECHR"), namely the right to freedom of association (Article 11) and property rights under Article 1 of Protocol 1. The applicants had invoked the right to freedom of thought, conscience, and religion (Article 9 of the Convention), arguing that:

> the right guaranteed by Article 9 could not be reduced to the right to shut oneself away inside one's own house or on one's own property without being able to express and give an outward material form to one's moral stance. The fact, therefore, that they were obliged to tolerate hunting on their land, although they themselves were opposed to hunting, constituted in their opinion an infringement of their freedom of thought.

The Court recognized that the convictions of the applicants fell within the scope of the right to freedom of thought, stating that:

> [t]he applicants are opposed to hunting on ethical grounds and the Court considers that their "convictions" in this respect attain a certain level of cogency, cohesion and importance and are therefore worthy of respect in a democratic society.

And:

> although opposed to hunting on ethical grounds, they [the applicants] are obliged to tolerate the presence of armed men and gun dogs on their land every year. This restriction on the free exercise of the right of use undoubtedly constitutes an interference with the applicants' enjoyment of their rights as the owners of property.

The Court concluded that:

> Compelling small landowners to transfer hunting rights over their land so that others can make use of them in a way which is totally incompatible with their beliefs imposes a disproportionate burden which is not justified under the second paragraph of Article 1 of Protocol No. 1. There has therefore been a violation of that provision.

The Court also ruled that compelling someone to be a member of an organization that is fundamentally contrary to their own convictions and obliging them under its rules is not fair and infringes Article 11. With regard to Article 9, the Court stated that:

> the Court considers that in the light of the conclusions it has reached with regard to Article 1 of Protocol No. 1 and Article 11 . . . it is not necessary to conduct a separate examination of the case from the standpoint of Article 9.

As can be seen in this case, the Court ruled in favor of the applicants on account of their qualifying ethical convictions under the right to freedom of conscience, even though it decided that it did not need to examine the case under Article 9 directly. The case shows the value of the human right to freedom of conscience in cases concerning animal exploitation because the applicants' Article 9 rights were fundamental to property rights and the right to freedom of association under Article 11. However, despite this, the importance of the right to freedom of thought, conscience, and religion in its own right in this case was raised in the *Separate Opinion Of Judge Fischbach Concerning Article 14,* who made the following important points:[14]

- The case necessitates a separate examination from the standpoint of Article 9.
- Respect for freedom of thought and conscience goes to the very heart of the case.
- Article 9 beliefs are closely bound up with the personality of each individual and determine the decisions they take about the type of life they wish to lead.
- It is undeniable that the question of preservation of our environment, and of wild animals in particular, is now a much-debated one in our societies.
- The applicants had an absolute right to freedom of belief.
- There are rules to be followed regarding lawful interference with manifesting genuine beliefs. The question to be examined is to what extent is it legitimate under Article 9 of the Convention to oblige individuals to take part in an activity incompatible with their beliefs?
- The applicants were obliged to take part in an activity that serves essentially private interests and were required to assist the practice of a "sport" in which only a small proportion of the population takes part, doing so in total contradiction with their most deeply held beliefs.
- I therefore conclude that there has been a violation of Article 9.

Similarly, in the later case of *Herrmann v. Germany* (2012),[15] which also concerned the involuntary membership of a hunting organization of a landowner opposed to hunting, the Court again ruled in favor of the applicant under Article 1 of Protocol 1 (property rights).

In this case, the applicant, Mr Günter Herrmann, submitted that compulsory membership in the hunting association had deprived them of the possibility of acting in accordance with their moral beliefs, and that a requirement to sacrifice their freedom of conscience was not justified under Article 9 of the Convention. The Court found in Mr Herrmann's favor regarding property rights, stating that the obligation to tolerate hunting on their property "imposes a disproportionate burden on landowners who, like the applicant in the present case, are opposed to hunting for ethical reasons." Despite this, however, it held by a majority of sixteen votes to one that it was not necessary to examine separately the complaint under Article 9 of the Convention. This motivated an extensive, partly concurring, and partly dissenting opinion by Judge Pinto of Albuquerque,[16] who pointed out at length the importance of Article 9 in cases where applicants have qualifying ethical convictions for other animals.

Judge Pinto first makes the point that the case is about a conscientious objection to hunting, and then reflects on "mankind's true moral test" in recognition of a pressing interface between human rights and our responsibilities to nonhuman animals necessarily being adjudicated at the European Court of Human Rights. Judge Pinto is acutely aware that our concern for nonhuman animals requires us to consider our obligations to other animals within the context of a human rights framework. Judge Pinto considers the ways nonhuman animals are protected by the Convention as human property, and as part of a healthy, balanced, and sustainable environment. The judge also mentions that the human right to freedom of expression accommodates clear public interest in various matters concerning animal welfare and that there is no Convention right to hunt or right to take part in person in ritual slaughter.

Judge Pinto then explains that nonhuman animals are no longer considered objects but are recognized as individual living beings capable of experiencing fear, suffering, and pain: a value enshrined in Conventions, at the United Nations, and in various legislation. Animal sentience is recognized in the Treaty of Amsterdam, which imposes duties throughout the European Union, obliging member states to pay full regard to the welfare of other animals.

On the issue of human rights, Judge Pinto remarks that human rights are not trivialized by issues concerning nonhuman animals. Rather, "they are enriched with the sense of mankind's full responsibility for the destiny of other species, natural ecosystems and, more broadly, the environment."

Judge Pinto also cites a range of historical literature to point out that a "respectable philosophical tradition advocates a change in the way humans deal with animals, based on the premise of the shared nature of all human and non-human animals," and notes that there are many other people who would agree with Mr Herrmann's ethical convictions. Moreover, the judge notes that the right to object to hunting on conscientious grounds is within the scope of protection of Article 9 because it is a belief that is cogent and has cohesion and importance, and it is, thus, worthy of respect in a democratic society.

Ultimately, Judge Pinto wants the right to freedom of conscience to perform its paramount role in cases where legal rules impact moral convictions for other animals. In this case, the judge asserts that:

> the applicant faced a conflict of conscience between a legal rule and a higher ethical value. It is time to release him from this conflict by affirming that his claim is right and the impugned legal rule is wrong. In sum, I find that Article 9 has been breached by the respondent State, on account of both the compulsory membership of a hunting association, referred to above, and the obligation on the applicant to tolerate hunting by third parties on his land.

The discussion above shows that the appeal to human rights in the interest of animal rights is supported by evidence that the right to freedom of thought, conscience, and religion can function to protect those with convictions about nonhuman animals in situations where a requirement made of them causes a conflict of conscience. Such an appeal is regarded as enriching human rights on account of the "dignity of all creatures."[17] The discussion also shows that the academic domain of human rights has acknowledged and recognized the intertwined nature of human and animal rights as an issue concerning human responsibility for what happens to other animals: a responsibility concerning and involving human rights stakeholders who are given tools in law to advance the development of a higher status for nonhuman animals.

The fact that this human right protects vegans and, moreover, has judicial support in cases concerning convictions for nonhuman animals are reasons for using it to protect vegans to advance animal rights. The evidence being the impact on legislation, policy, or practices: the ruling in *Chassagnou and Others v. France* brought about changes in member states' legislation.[18]

The next section examines in detail the human right to freedom of conscience and its scope and application in order to explain how those who adopt and live according to the vegan philosophy are legitimate beneficiaries of human rights, and why their claims for inclusion and protection are valid and reasonable.

THE HUMAN RIGHT TO FREEDOM OF THOUGHT, CONSCIENCE, AND RELIGION

The modern human right to freedom of thought, conscience, and religion has evolved over hundreds of years from a concern for religious freedom. The starting point, for the purpose of the present discussion, is the Universal Declaration of Human Rights ("UDHR," "the Declaration"). The provisions of the UDHR are grounded in the acknowledgment of and respect for the inherent dignity and equality of all people and were drafted by representatives from around the world. The Declaration was proclaimed by the United Nations General Assembly in Paris in December 1948. The UDHR does not have legal force itself but has global significance, having inspired multiple human rights treaties that give effect to and develop its provisions and mission. In particular, the formative principles of the inherent dignity of all people features in treaties, constitutions, and case law around the world.

Article 18 of the Declaration explains the right to freedom of thought, conscience, and religion. It states that:

> Everyone has the right to freedom of thought, conscience and religion; this right includes freedom to change his religion or belief, and freedom, either alone or in community with others and in public or private, to manifest his religion or belief in teaching, practice, worship and observance.

There is no rigid definition of the human right to freedom of thought, conscience, and religion as proclaimed by the Declaration,[19] but it does not only concern the right to freedom of religious beliefs. It also applies to beliefs which may be regarded as a system of philosophy rather than a formal religion.[20]

In addition to Article 18, a number of other articles are relevant for the purposes of the present discussion on the validity of veganism in human rights. Under Article 1, all human beings are born free and equal in dignity and rights. Article 2 provides that "[e]veryone is entitled to all the rights and freedoms set forth in this Declaration, without distinction of any kind, such as race, colour, sex, language, religion, political or other opinion, national or social origin, property, birth or other status." Article 7 confirms that everyone is "equal before the law and are entitled without any discrimination to equal protection of the law. All are entitled to equal protection against any discrimination in violation of this Declaration and against any incitement to such discrimination." Article 19 provides that "[e]veryone has the right to freedom of opinion and expression; this right includes freedom to hold opinions without interference and to seek, receive and impart information and ideas through any media and regardless of frontiers," and Article 26 explains the right to education, with Article 26(2) indicating that the function of education includes strengthening respect for human rights and promoting understanding:

> Education shall be directed to the full development of the human personality and to the strengthening of respect for human rights and fundamental freedoms. It shall promote understanding, tolerance and friendship.

The rights proclaimed by the UDHR are subject to strict limitations on interference. Article 29(2) explains that lawful interference must be grounded in a law that is necessary for a legitimate reason:

> In the exercise of his rights and freedoms, everyone shall be subject only to such limitations as are determined by law solely for the purpose of securing due recognition and respect for the rights and freedoms of others and of meeting the just requirements of morality, public order and the general welfare in a democratic society.

As can be seen, from the outset, the international community committed to entrenching a universal value for an individual's right to determine one's own value system, whether this be grounded by religious or non-religious, philosophical beliefs, and convictions. The right was declared to be available to everyone, without distinction, free from discrimination; everyone would be free to express their opinions, and education, in its function to develop the human personality, would respect their values. In addition, the human rights declared by the international community could only be limited by a law that was required for a good reason in the interests of democracy.

The United Nations carried out further work on the rights contained in the Declaration and gave them legal effect in the much later International Covenant on Civil and Political Rights (ICCPR).[21] Article 18 of the ICCPR reiterates the right to freedom of thought, conscience, and religion and goes further, prohibiting coercion so that people are able to adopt a belief of choice and, importantly, signifying the relationship of the right to freedom of conscience to the rights of parents and guardians of children in state education:

1. Everyone shall have the right to freedom of thought, conscience, and religion. This right shall include freedom to have or to adopt a religion or belief of his choice, and freedom, either individually or in community with others and in public or private, to manifest his religion or belief in worship, observance, practice, and teaching.
2. No one shall be subject to coercion which would impair his freedom to have or to adopt a religion or belief of his choice.
3. Freedom to manifest one's religion or beliefs may be subject only to such limitations as are prescribed by law and are necessary to protect public safety, order, health, or morals or the fundamental rights and freedoms of others.
4. The States Parties to the present Covenant undertake to have respect for the liberty of parents and, when applicable, legal guardians to ensure the religious and moral education of their children in conformity with their own convictions.

The individual freedom to work out and live according to one's own philosophical or religious value system was, therefore, recognized as potentially being negatively impacted by entrenched views and practices that effectively prevent the adoption of a different set of religious or moral values or beliefs. The important element of a guaranteed right to freedom of conscience is self-direction, which depends on having a choice to decide for oneself. This was recognized by the United Nations, which then included an intrinsic prohibition on coercion to ensure everyone has a free choice. In addition, the United Nations recognized that a state education system could potentially breach the right to freedom of conscience and the right to free choice if it teaches and reinforces biased views that are contrary to those of people who wish to raise their children according to a particular and different value system. The right to freedom of conscience, therefore, is promoted as a value that must be entrenched as intrinsic to the provision of state education.

In addition, State Parties to the Covenant agreed to recognize and promote the rights it contains and to ensure they are made available to everyone, including by taking steps to legislate, if necessary to give effect to the rights in the ICCPR, and to ensure effective remedies in response to infringements. Thus, State Parties to the Covenant have both positive and negative duties.[22]

The Human Rights Committee has provided authoritative guidance on interpreting Article 18[23] and has emphasized the paramount importance of this right by iterating that the prohibition on interference must be strictly interpreted and reiterating the limitation on unlawful interference: "this provision cannot be derogated from, even in time of public emergency."[24] This strict prohibition on interference is justified on the grounds that:

> the concept of morals derives from many social, philosophical and religious traditions; consequently, limitations on the freedom to manifest a religion or belief for the purpose of protecting morals must be based on principles not deriving exclusively from a single tradition.[25]

It has also confirmed a number of points (some quoted below, and some paraphrased):[26]

- "[t]he right to freedom of thought, conscience and religion (which includes the freedom to hold beliefs) in Article 18(1) is far-reaching and profound; it encompasses freedom of thoughts on all matters, personal conviction . . . ."
- "Article 18 protects theistic, non-theistic and atheistic beliefs, as well as the right not to profess any religion or belief."
- "The terms belief and religion are to be broadly construed."
- "Article 18 is not limited in its application to traditional religions or to religions and beliefs with institutional characteristics or practices analogous to those of traditional religions."
- "The Committee therefore views with concern any tendency to discriminate against any religion or belief for any reasons, including the fact that they are newly established . . . "
- Article 18 "does not permit any limitations whatsoever on the freedom of thought and conscience or on the freedom to have or adopt a religion or belief of one's choice."
- The observance and practice of a belief include dietary norms.
- The freedom to "have or to adopt" a belief necessarily entails the freedom to choose a belief . . . .
- Article 18(2) bars coercions that would impair the right to have or adopt a belief, to recant a belief, or to convert.
- Policies or practices having the same effect are similarly inconsistent with the right to freedom of thought, conscience, and religion.
- "The same protection is enjoyed by holders of all beliefs of a non-religious nature."

- Education about ethics is acceptable if it is given in a neutral and objective way.
- The liberty of parents or legal guardians to ensure that their children receive a moral education in conformity with their own convictions, under 18(4), is related to the guarantees of the freedom to teach a religion or belief stated in Article 18(1).
- Education regarding religions and beliefs is inconsistent with the right to freedom of thought, conscience, and religion unless provision is made for non-discriminatory exemptions or alternatives that would accommodate the wishes of parents and guardians.
- No manifestation of beliefs may amount to propaganda for hatred that constitutes incitement to discrimination.
- "Persons already subject to certain legitimate constraints, such as prisoners, continue to enjoy their rights to manifest their religion or belief to the fullest extent . . . "
- "The freedom from coercion to have or to adopt a religion or belief and the liberty of the parents and guardians to ensure religious and moral education cannot be restricted."
- "In interpreting the scope of permissible limitation clauses, States parties should proceed from the need to protect the rights guaranteed under the Covenant, including the right to equality and non-discrimination."

As these salient points show, the human right to freedom of thought, conscience, and religion recognizes that human beings have, and need to live according to, life-directing values and convictions. Its purpose is to ensure that people are free to believe in religious *or* non-religious convictions and that they benefit from the required social, political, and legal conditions to be able to manifest their values and convictions practically in their daily lives.

In 1981, the United Nations adopted an additional Declaration, focused specifically on the human right to freedom of belief. The Declaration on the Elimination of all Forms of Intolerance on and of Discrimination Based on Religion or Belief[27] has no legal force, its purpose being to confirm the agreed moral standards. It makes a number of points relevant to the case for defending and protecting vegans in their struggle to manifest the vegan philosophy in their daily lives.

The target of the Declaration is dealing with discrimination on the grounds of religion or non-religious belief. The Declaration first reiterates international respect and support for the observance of human rights, equality, and the principle of non-discrimination, and, importantly, recognizes that holding a belief is one *of the fundamental elements in a person's conception of life,* that freedom of belief should be fully respected and guaranteed, and that freedom of belief should contribute to (inter alia) social justice. The Declaration then sets out a number of agreed measures for eliminating discrimination based on belief, starting with Article 1, which restates the absolute right to believe, the qualified right to practice (which, as noted above, is subject to a law that is required for a good reason), and the prohibition on coercion that impairs the freedom to have a belief of choice. Article 2 provides, firstly, that "[n]o one shall be subject to discrimination by any State, institution, group of persons, or person on the grounds of religion or belief," before going on to explain the meaning of "intolerance" and "discrimination." Article 2(2) states:

> For the purposes of the present Declaration, the expression "intolerance and discrimination based on religion or belief" means any distinction, exclusion, restriction or preference based on religion or belief and having as its purpose or as its effect nullification or impairment of the recognition, enjoyment or exercise of human rights and fundamental freedoms on an equal basis.

Article 4 then explains the measures States must take to eliminate discrimination:

1. All States shall take effective measures to prevent and eliminate discrimination on the grounds of religion or belief in the recognition, exercise, and enjoyment of human rights and fundamental freedoms in all fields of civil, economic, political, social, and cultural life.
2. All States shall make all efforts to enact or rescind legislation where necessary to prohibit any such discrimination . . . .

Article 5 pays particular and comprehensive attention to the rights of parents and guardians in the education of their children. Article 5(1) focuses on the rights of parents and guardians to family arrangements regarding the moral education of the children in their care. Article 5(2) focuses on the right of the child to education. It states that:

> Every child shall enjoy the right to have access to education in the matter of religion or belief in accordance with the wishes of his parents or, as the case may be, legal guardians, and shall not be compelled to receive teaching on religion or belief against the wishes of his parents or legal guardians, the best interests of the child being the guiding principle.

Article 5(3) requires (inter alia) that the child shall be protected from discrimination on the grounds of their belief, and Article 5(4) accommodates the expressed wishes of children who are not under the care of their parents or guardians in relation to religion and belief. Article 5(5) looks to protect children, requiring that:

> [p]ractices of a religion or belief in which a child is brought up must not be injurious to his physical or mental health or to his full development, taking into account Article 1, paragraph 3, of the present Declaration, (which states the strict limits on interference).

Article 6 gives some examples of what might be included in the manifestation of a belief, and Article 7 requires the rights and freedoms expressed in the Declaration to be made available in national legislation.

In Europe, the ECHR, which was being drafted around the time of the UDHR, guarantees the right to freedom of religion and belief in Article 9. Article 9 is structured differently from Article 18 of the ICCPR (Article 18 was developed over time). It does not include an explicit prohibition on coercion, nor does it include, as an element of the right to freedom of thought, conscience, and religion, education rights. These are, however, dealt with in other ways: the prohibition on coercion has been dealt with in legal cases at the European Court of Human Rights as implicitly included in the text of Article 9, and education is dealt with under a separate protocol.

Part one of Article 9 reiterates the absolute individual right to believe, and part two confirms that interference with the practice of beliefs is strictly limited to the specified conditions:

1. Everyone has the right to freedom of thought, conscience, and religion; this right includes freedom to change one's religion or belief and freedom, either alone or in community with others and in public or private, to manifest his religion or belief, in worship, teaching, practice and observance.
2. Freedom to manifest one's religion or beliefs shall be subject only to such limitations as are prescribed by law and are necessary in a democratic society in the interests of public safety, for the protection of public order, health or morals, or for the protection of the rights and freedoms of others.

Regarding the right to education, Article 2 of Protocol 1 of the ECHR provides that:

> No person shall be denied the right to education. In the exercise of any functions which it assumes in relation to education and to teaching, the State shall respect the right of parents to ensure such education and teaching in conformity with their own religious and philosophical convictions.

Guidance on the Protocol from the European Court of Human Rights confirms that the right to education and respect for the religious and philosophical convictions of parents are related to the human right to freedom of thought, conscience, and religion,[28] as provided in Article 18(4) of the ICCPR.[29] The European Court of Human Rights has also stated that the meaning of "education" under the Protocol extends to the "whole process" of education, including school policies and practices that are not directly related to the teaching and learning curriculum. The Court has clarified that the education of children concerns adults transmitting their beliefs, culture, and other values to the young, and that rights under the Protocol are not limited to activities related to teaching or instructing pupils. Rather, the Protocol is applicable to "each and every function undertaken in the sphere of education."[30]

The Court has also emphasized an existing principle that respect for the moral convictions of parents implies that the content of a curriculum should be delivered in an *objective, critical and pluralistic* manner. In particular, the Court has confirmed that "[t]he State is forbidden to pursue an aim of indoctrination that might be considered as not respecting parents' religious and philosophical convictions. That is the limit that must not be exceeded."[31,32]

Under the ECHR, Member States have a positive duty to "secure to everyone within their jurisdiction" Article 9 rights,[33] "without distinction on any ground . . . "[34]

THE PROTECTION OF PHILOSOPHICAL BELIEFS

The right to freedom of thought, conscience, and religion is given legal effect in different parts of the world in different ways, and some countries have historically taken a more restrictive approach than others, despite authoritative guidance on the breadth of scope of protection.[35] The scope of protection under the right to freedom of belief is broad and, as confirmed above, there is no hierarchy between a protected religious and a protected non-religious belief; although it is reported that, historically, traditional religions were regarded to fall within the scope of protection of Article 9 with more ease than non-mainstream religions and beliefs, and a burden of proof was imposed on adherents of non-traditional religions or beliefs to prove the existence of their belief systems.[36]

Though historical records confirm that the term "religion" was difficult to define, let alone the concept of a non-religious philosophical belief,[37] developments over time have resulted in a deeper understanding of the normative inclusive scope of the right to freedom of thought, conscience, and religion, and the recognition that "[r]eligions and beliefs reflect an abundance of diverse teachings," including many different doctrines, norms of conduct, dietary practices, and other conduct.[38]

For a philosophical belief to qualify for protection at the European Court of Human Rights, a legal test, which the Court has developed over time, requires the belief to be genuinely held and the professed beliefs to attain a certain level of cogency, seriousness, coherence, and importance.

In the development of this legal test, being "convinced" by, and committed in theory and practice to, the professed convictions are factors that have featured in the discussion about what constitutes the legal meaning of philosophical belief. In the 1978 case of *Arrowsmith v. the United Kingdom,*[39] a case concerning whether pacifism was within the scope of the legal meaning of the right to freedom of religion and belief, the UK government explained its view that:

> the word "belief" connotes and requires the holding and expression of spiritual or philosophical convictions, which, while not necessarily organised in the same sense of a religion, nevertheless have an identifiable formal content.

The opinion of the Commission of the Court (as it was then prior to restructuring) in this case was that:

> Pacifism as a philosophy, and in particular, [as defined by the UK Government] falls within the ambit of the right to freedom of thought and conscience. The attitude of pacifism, may therefore be seen as a belief ("conviction") protected by Article 9(1).

In 1981, the Court considered the case of an applicant who complained that being obliged to be buried in a cemetery with Christian symbols denied the right to manifest their own beliefs by having their ashes scattered in their garden after their death. In this case, the Court indicated that an assessment of an application for unlawful interference with the manifestation of a belief will include whether the belief in questions expresses "some coherent view" on "fundamental problems,"[40] clearly signalling that legal protection under the right to freedom of belief concerns and is likely to be reserved for matters that are more than strong personal motivations or personal desires.

The following year, in 1982, the Court examined the legal meaning of "convictions" in the case (discussed above) brought by parents of school pupils who objected to the use of corporal punishment at their respective children's schools.[41] The case of *Campbell and Cosans v. the United Kingdom* considered whether there had been a violation of the right to education, and specifically, whether the use of corporal punishment failed to respect the rights of the parents to education and teaching in conformity with their philosophical convictions, as guaranteed by the second sentence of Article 2 of Protocol 1. The Court first reiterated the wording of Article 2, before considering the legal meaning of "philosophical convictions":

> No person shall be denied the right to education. In the exercise of any functions which it assumes in relation to education and to teaching, the State shall respect

> the right of parents to ensure such education and teaching in conformity with their own religious and philosophical convictions.

The Court stated that the ordinary meaning of the word "convictions" is akin to the term "beliefs" appearing in Article 9 of the Convention (which guarantees freedom of thought, conscience, and religion), and also stated that it denotes "views that attain a certain level of cogency, seriousness, cohesion, and importance." The Court deemed the parents' "philosophical convictions" on corporal punishment in education worthy of respect in a democratic society, not incompatible with human dignity, and involving a weighty and substantial aspect of human life and behavior, namely the integrity of the person.

These cases, examined at the European Court of Human Rights, illustrate that the legal meaning of "belief" for the purposes of the Article 9 Convention right to freedom of thought, conscience, and religion includes cohesive, non-religious philosophical convictions where they represent clear, logical, and reasoned thought (cogency) on serious and important issues. The cases clearly indicate the Court's intention to comply with the broad scope of meaning attached to the right to freedom of conscience, as required by the ICCPR, and explained in guidance provided by the Human Rights Committee in General Comment 22 (above).

Thus, as can be seen from the discussion above, the principles of equality and inclusion ground agreed international law and formal legal guidance, underpinning the right to freedom of religion or belief. The case law of the European Court of Human Rights shows how the principle of inclusion is applied and confirms that those who adopt and live according to genuinely held qualifying non-religious convictions are legitimate beneficiaries of the human right to freedom of belief and can be protected from unlawful interference. Accommodating non-religious beliefs and convictions under the right to freedom of religion and belief is, therefore, legitimate and reasonable, as is protecting adherents of said beliefs and convictions from unlawful interference.

In 1993, the Commission of the Court (as it was then, prior to restructuring), considered the case of a vegan prisoner who complained that a requirement to work in the prison print shop infringed their Article 9 rights because, they alleged, they would be required to work with ink dyes that had been tested on nonhuman animals. Although, in this case, the Commission decided that the prison had not acted unlawfully, it nevertheless found that "the Vegan convictions with regard to animal products fall within the scope of Article 9 para. 1 (Art. 9–1) of the Convention."[42] Since then, the Court has published guidance, stating that the protection for veganism concerns an individual's "opposition to the manipulation of products of animal origin or tested on animals."[43]

The protection of human rights and fundamental freedoms is also an important value in the European Union (EU), which has confirmed its commitment to the principle of respect for non-religious philosophical beliefs in its treaties.[44] Guidelines on the promotion and protection of freedom of religion or belief, published by the European Union, explain that "[t]he EU does not consider the merits of the different religions or beliefs, or the lack thereof, but ensures that the right to believe or not to believe is upheld." They explain that the right to freedom of thought, conscience, and religion is a universal right that applies to all persons equally and "needs to be protected everywhere and for everyone regardless of who they are, where they live, and what they believe or do not believe in." The guidance reaffirms the importance of relevant provisions in the UDHR, the ICCPR, and guidance provided by the Human Rights Committee in General Comment 22. It also reasserts the positive obligation on Member States to ensure that adequate and effective domestic legislation is in place to guarantee the right to freedom of thought, conscience, and religion.[45]

The Charter of Fundamental Rights of the European Union[46] reaffirms the importance and commitment to international human rights obligations common to Member States, including observation of the ECHR and the case law of the European Court of Human Rights.[47] In fact, respect for human rights and freedoms is necessary for membership of the EU.[48] The right to freedom of thought, conscience, and religion is set out in Article 10 of the Charter:

1. Everyone has the right to freedom of thought, conscience, and religion. This right includes freedom to change religion or belief and freedom, either alone or in community with others and in public or in private, to manifest religion or belief in worship, teaching, practice, and observance.
2. The right to conscientious objection is recognized, in accordance with the national laws governing the exercise of this right.

The Charter also sets out a "principle of non-discrimination" in Article 21, which provides that:

1. Any discrimination based on any ground such as sex, race, color, ethnic or social origin, genetic features, language, religion or belief, political or any other opinion, membership of a national minority, property, birth, disability, age or sexual orientation shall be prohibited.

The EU "principle of equal treatment" was entrenched in the Union with the Council's adoption of Directive 2000/78/EC which established a general framework for equal treatment in employment and occupation.[49] Its purpose was to combat discrimination in employment and occupation on various grounds, including religion or belief.[50] The Directive doesn't define a "belief" for the purposes of the Directive or its implementation, but it sets out the provisions under which equality would be achieved.

Equal treatment would be achieved by prohibiting direct and indirect discrimination, harassment, and, where anti-discrimination measures were relied on by individuals seeking redress, victimization. Direct discrimination was defined in the Directive as treating a person less favorably than another on the grounds of a protected characteristic. Indirect discrimination could be subsequent to an apparently neutral provision, criterion, or practice that puts [protected] persons at a particular disadvantage compared with other persons, subject to that provision, criterion, or practice being objectively justified by a legitimate aim and the means of achieving that aim being appropriate and necessary. Harassment was explained as unwanted conduct that takes place with the purpose or effect of violating the dignity of a person and of creating an intimidating, hostile, degrading, humiliating, or offensive environment. Victimization was described as any adverse treatment of an employee in response to an attempt to enforce the principle of equality. The implementation of this Directive had enormous value in reinforcing legal protection for vegans in the UK.

LEGAL PROTECTION FOR VEGANS IN THE UK: A CASE STUDY

The UK is a signatory to both the ICCPR and the ECHR. The ECHR is incorporated into domestic law by the Human Rights Act 1998. In 2005, in *R (Williamson) v. Secretary of State for Education and Employment*,[51] a case in which the meaning of philosophical convictions and the scope of Article 9 of the ECHR were discussed in relation to the corporal punishment of children and relevant provisions of the Human Rights Act 1998, Lord Walker commented that "[p]acifism, vegetarianism and total abstinence from alcohol are uncontroversial examples of beliefs which would fall within Article 9 . . . ."[52]

On the implementation of Directive 2000/78/EC, discrimination against those with qualifying religions and beliefs became unlawful. The Directive was given legal force in 2003 by the Employment Equality (Religion or Belief) Regulation, which defined "religion or belief" as any religion, religious belief, or similar philosophical belief.[53] The meaning of "similar" philosophical belief was uncertain and promoted various comments in the House of Lords during the motion to approve the Regulation, including in relation to the ICCPR and Article 9 of the ECHR. Lord Brennan suggested that:

> The word "similar" in these regulations is used in relation to the quality of the belief, not its nature. The phrase "similar philosophical belief" addresses the state of mind in which someone holds *that* belief to the same thinking quality as a religious belief. It is not used to assimilate it in any way with a religion.[54]

Lord Lester of Herne Hill QC sought reassurance that "the intention is to protect atheists, agnostics, rationalists, secularists, humanists and all the others who make up the ungodly and irreligious . . .,"[55] to which the Government Minster moving the motion, Lord Sainsbury of Turville, replied:

> It is clearly the intention that where people have strongly held views, which include humanism, or atheism or agnosticism, they would be covered under the phrase "or similar philosophical belief."[56]

The reference to "similar" philosophical belief was not maintained in the later Equality Act 2006. Instead, the legislation referred to "belief" as meaning any religious or philosophical belief. The reasoning for the removal of the word "similar" is given by Baroness Scotland, who referred to legal reasoning from the case law of the European Court of Human Rights, discussed above:

> we have removed the word "similar". . . from the definition of "belief." It now reads, "any religious or philosophical belief," rather than, as in the regulations, "any religious or similar philosophical belief." I assure the noble Baroness and the noble Lord, Lord Lester, that there is no sinister motive in that. The intention behind the wording . . . is identical to that in the employment regulations. However, in drafting . . . it was felt that the word "similar" added nothing and was, therefore, redundant. This is because the term "philosophical belief" will take its meaning from the context in which it appears; that is, as part of the legislation relating to discrimination on the grounds of religion or belief. Given that context, philosophical beliefs must therefore always be of a similar nature to religious beliefs. It will be for the courts to decide what constitutes a belief . . . but case law suggests that any philosophical belief must attain a certain level of cogency, seriousness, cohesion and importance, must be worthy of respect in a democratic society and must not be incompatible with human dignity.[57]

In a 2007 Employment Appeal Tribunal, it was confirmed again that the test for determining whether "views" can properly be considered to fall into the category of a philosophical belief must refer to the legal reasoning of the European Court of Human Rights in its assessment of *Campbell and Cosans v. the United Kingdom*, which laid down the precedent that philosophical convictions should have sufficient cogency, seriousness, cohesion, and importance and be worthy of respect in a democratic society.[58]

In 2009, the Baroness's statement played a role in a seminal case which again discussed the legal meaning of "philosophical" belief. In *Grainger plc and others v. Nicholson*,[59]it was confirmed that a belief must be of a similar cogency or status to a religious belief, that the jurisprudence of the European Court of Human Rights is directly material, and any limitations on the concept and scope of a philosophical belief can be derived from that.

In this case, Mr Nicholson complained that their employment was terminated because they had a strongly held philosophical belief about climate change and the environment. Mr Nicholson believed that we must urgently cut carbon emissions to avoid catastrophic climate change. The philosophical belief was presented to the employment appeal tribunal as being "that mankind is heading toward catastrophic climate change and therefore we are all under a moral duty to lead our lives in a manner which mitigates or avoids this catastrophe for the benefit of future generations, and to persuade others to do the same." Mr Nicholson explained how their beliefs directed their daily life in practice:

> It is not merely an opinion but a philosophical belief which affects how I live my life including my choice of home, how I travel, what I buy, what I eat and drink, what I do with my waste and my hopes and my fears. For example, I no longer travel by airplane, I have eco-renovated my home, I try to buy local produce, I have reduced my consumption of meat, I compost my food waste, I encourage others to reduce their carbon emissions and I fear very much for the future of the human race, given the failure to reduce carbon emissions on a global scale.

With reference to Baroness Scotland's statement on the meaning of "philosophical belief" for the purpose the principle of equality, the honorable Mr Justice Burton acknowledged three main issues for consideration in the case:

1. How far, if at all, the belief said to qualify for protection under the Regulations is required to be similar to a religious belief?
2. What limits (if any) should be placed upon the words "philosophical belief"? (the employer in this case arguing that)
(a) it must be a "settled" belief, part of a system of beliefs; and/or
(b) it must be a philosophical belief and not a political belief, one based upon political opinions, such as, for example, fascism; and/or
(c) it must not be a scientific belief based upon conclusions drawn from science and resulting from research or the gathering of information.
3. Whether the authorities in relation to the European Convention on Human Rights ("ECHR"), Article 9 and Article 2 of Protocol 1 in particular, are of relevance, or indeed persuasive or conclusive in this field . . . [particularly] the judgment of the European Court of Human Rights

> in *Campbell and Cosans v. United Kingdom* . . . a case in which the complainants successfully alleged that the system of corporal punishment in Scottish state schools offended their *philosophical convictions* under Article 2 of Protocol 1 of the ECHR.

With reference to relevant authorities, including the jurisprudence of the European Court of Human Rights, the tribunal referenced in the report "Summary" that "[t]he belief must be of a similar cogency or status to a religious belief" and established the criteria under which a philosophical belief can be determined:

(i) The belief must be genuinely held.
(ii) It must be a belief and not an opinion or viewpoint based on the present state of information available.
(iii) It must be a belief as to a weighty and substantial aspect of human life and behavior.
(iv) It must attain a certain level of cogency, seriousness, cohesion, and importance.
(v) It must be worthy of respect in a democratic society, be not incompatible with human dignity, and not conflict with the fundamental rights of others.

On these criteria, a genuinely held belief in man-made [*sic*] climate change was found to be capable of being a philosophical belief for the purpose of the 2003 Religion and Belief Regulations and used as an example of a qualifying philosophical belief by the Equality and Human Rights Commission.[60]

In 2011, an employment tribunal considered the case of Joe Hashman again under the 2003 Regulations.[61] As explained in chapter 1, Mr Hashman complained that their employer had unlawfully terminated their employment contract on account of their philosophical belief in the sanctity of life, which manifested in anti-hunt activism. The tribunal referred to the binding precedent introduced by *Grainger*, and tested Mr Hashman's beliefs against the criteria.

The tribunal confirmed that the authorities to be considered included Article 9 of the ECHR and the jurisprudence of the European Court of Human Rights. The tribunal also recognized that the 2003 Regulations derive from Article 9 of the Convention and that philosophical beliefs are to be determined by the criteria emerging from an assessment of relevant authorities and jurisprudence, but that the threshold requirements must not "be set at a level which will deprive minority beliefs of the protection they are intended to have under the Convention."[62]

The tribunal acknowledged that Mr Hashman's belief comprises vegan convictions, environmentalism and animal rights activism, and found that the sanctity of life is truly part of their philosophical belief, both within the ordinary meaning of such words and within the meaning of the 2003 Regulation.

In 2010, the UK government introduced the Equality Act 2010. In this Act, "belief" means "any religious or philosophical belief and a reference to belief includes a reference to a lack of belief." The explanatory notes accompanying the Act state that the definition of the protected characteristic "religion or belief" is broad, in line with the freedom of thought, conscience and religion, guaranteed by Article 9 of the ECHR. Also, the criteria for determining what is a "philosophical belief" are that it must:

- be genuinely held;
- be a belief and not an opinion or viewpoint based on the present state of information available;
- be a belief as to a weighty and substantial aspect of human life and behavior;
- attain a certain level of cogency, seriousness, cohesion, and importance;
- be worthy of respect in a democratic society, compatible with human dignity, and not conflict with the fundamental rights of others.

In 2020, an employment tribunal ruled that a belief in ethical veganism could be protected under the Equality Act 2010. Judge Postle stated: "I am therefore satisfied and find it easy to conclude that there is overwhelming evidence before me that ethical veganism is capable of being a philosophical belief and thus a protected characteristic under the Equality Act 2010."[63]

In this case, the importance of Article 9 of the Convention and the human rights process are clear. The relevance of the 1993 case at the European Court of Human Rights concerning the vegan prisoner was cited as an authority. The judge reiterated the relevance of the ECHR and the significance of the human right to freedom of thought, conscience, and religion, as granted under Article 9. Judge Postle noted that:

- The relevant provisions of the Equality Act 2010 consciously mirror Article 9 of the European Convention on Human Rights.
- The freedom to hold and manifest belief is to be enjoyed without discrimination as defined by Article 14 of the European Convention on Human Rights.
- Freedom of thought, conscience, and religion as one of the foundations of a democratic society within the meaning of the Convention . . . is one of the most vital elements that goes to make up the identity of believers and their conception of life.

- Pursuant to Section 3 of the Human Rights Act 1998, domestic legislation must be read insofar as possible to give effect to Convention rights.
- It would be both bizarre and, by reason of Section 3 of the Human Rights Act 1998, unlawful if a belief were recognized under the Conventions but not under the Equality Act 2010.
- Article 9 is not confined to the freedom to hold a belief, but includes the right to express and practice one's belief.

The discussion above shows that vegans can be protected under the human right to freedom of belief and protected from discrimination by equality legislation deriving from the guarantee of that right. It also shows that there is academic and judicial support for the practice of protecting individuals with moral convictions about other animals, specifically to make the human right to freedom of belief work harder and better for other animals, to help bring about change by elevating their status in our system of justice. Moreover, the discussion surely leaves the reader in no doubt that the claims of vegans in their appeal to law are not fanciful but are valid and legitimate calls for their genuine convictions about other animals to be taken seriously and accommodated in a legal system that respects their human rights and in a democracy that already recognizes that nonhuman animals are vulnerable to human power and abuse.

The question posed, therefore, concerning why we should protect vegans, or why we should care about the rights of vegans when it is the suffering of other animals that is our concern, turns on its head: why we should not, given that nonhuman animals do not currently benefit from rights and depend on us to stand with them and to speak with them in whatever way we can.

In 2014, former Special Rapporteur for freedom of religion and belief, Heiner Bielefeldt, acknowledged that religion or belief discrimination in the workplace is an underexplored issue, but did report that in relation to reasonable accommodation in the workplace:

> appropriate infrastructure already exists or is in the process of development. Accommodating religious or belief-related diversity in the workplace has become a standard practice in many public institutions and private companies. One example is respect for specific dietary needs originating from religious prescripts or other conscience-based reasons.[64]

In 2016, Mr Bielefeldt reported that the international community had made "enormous strides in recent decades" regarding the right to freedom of belief, including a prohibition on discrimination.[65] Mr Bielefeldt also spoke of "concealed forms of discrimination," where an environment of apparent neutrality that doesn't intend to target a specific community can conceal discrimination with regard to (inter alia) dietary practices. The Special Rapporteur states that:

> Overcoming the various forms of discrimination in the field of religion or belief, including indirect and structural discrimination, is a complex task that requires moving beyond mere formal equality towards substantive equality, including by adopting measures of reasonable accommodation.

CONCLUSION

This chapter has explained that the idea of vegans claiming their rights in law is valid and has academic and judicial support in terms of registering concern for nonhuman animals. It has also shown the legitimacy of the rights claims of vegans under the relevant legal frameworks.

The rationale presented for the legal protection of vegans is to help deal with entrenched prejudice toward, and exploitation of, nonhuman animals. The argument is that the resort to law not only helps deal with direct, indirect, and structural discrimination in the effort to live with compassion for nonhuman animals, but it creates changes in everyday policy and practice that register respect for other animals. For example, as a result of the legal argument for plant-based milk alternatives to be included in government-funded health programmes, to avoid discrimination against vegans, the Scottish Government amended its legislation and now provides funding for plant-based alternatives to cow's milk.[66] Legal arguments for the inclusion of plant-based food in public institutions have led to the majority of local authorities in the UK reporting that they now provide for vegans: a significant change that has taken place in a few years of a rights-based approach to vegan advocacy.[67]

There is no doubt that claiming vegan rights to introduce policy and practices that support animal rights is animal rights activism "by the back door," but it is a string to a bow, a key to a, thus far, locked door to opportunities, a way of raising the profile of human compassion for nonhuman animals in our daily lives, a way of being accommodated, defended, and respected in law. If we have the opportunity to do this work, the question is why wouldn't we take it and try to make the most of it?

On the view presented, defending our right to live as vegans positively contributes to the campaign for animal rights by creating the social conditions in which veganism is sustainable and people can adopt veganism more easily. This change, however, is not achieved without a struggle, and it necessarily depends on a dedicated commitment to developing legal arguments for defending vegans' rights in all contexts, as well as assessing the social, political, and legal contexts in which the vegan expression of compassion exists.

The next chapter explains how some of the research and legal provisions used in the campaign for vegan rights apply to the issues faced by vegans described in chapter 1.

NOTES

1. See works by David Nibert as examples of observations of mechanisms of speciesist prejudice.

2. See Council Regulation (EEC) No. 1898/87 of July 2, 1987, on the Protection of Designations Used in Marketing of Milk and Milk Products, *Official Journal* L 182 (July 3, 1987), 36–38.

3. This issue has been discussed within the IVRA since its inception and at its conferences. Over recent years, the problem of legal restrictions on the labelling of vegan food items has become more widely commented on and generated academic articles. For resources from within the vegan community, see, for example, the European Vegetarian Union and its position paper, available at https://www.euroveg.eu/school-milk/ and Jeanette Rowley, "Dairy's Identity Crisis: Digesting the Socio-politico-legal Landscape," The Vegan Society, April 13, 2023, accessed January 28, 2024, https://www.vegansociety.com/get-involved/research/research-news/dairy-identity-crisis-digesting-socio-politico-legal-landscape.

4. For simplicity, this chapter does not develop a discussion on the issue of protection for freedom of conscience and freedom of belief but relies on freedom of conscience grounding freedom of belief with regard to the protection of vegans.

5. Critical human rights scholars Upendra Baxi and Costas Douzinas make this point.

6. Michael Hass, *International Human Rights: A Comprehensive Introduction*, 2nd ed. (Oxon: Routledge, 2014), 503–514.

7. Tom Sparks, "Protection of Animals Through Human Rights: The Case-Law of the European Court of Human Rights," in *Studies in Global Animal Law*, ed. Anne Peters, Beiträge zum ausländischen öffentlichen Recht und Völkerrecht 290, Berlin, Heidelberg: Springer, 2020, https://doi.org/10.1007/978-3-662-60756-5, 153.

8. For a detailed examination, see Jeanette Rowley, *Towards a Vegan jurisprudence, The Need for a Reorientation of Human Rights* (PhD diss., 2017, London: Lexington Books, 2020).

9. Tom Sparks, "Protection of Animals Through Human Rights: The Case-Law of the European Court of Human Rights," in *Studies in Global Animal Law,* ed. Anne Peters, Beiträge zum ausländischen öffentlichen Recht und Völkerrecht 290, Springer, Berlin, Heidelberg: Springer, 2020, https://doi.org/10.1007/978-3-662-60756-5, 153.

10. Tom Sparks, "Protection of Animals Through Human Rights: The Case-Law of the European Court of Human Rights," in *Studies in Global Animal Law,* ed. Anne Peters, Beiträge zum ausländischen öffentlichen Recht und Völkerrecht 290 (Berlin, Heidelberg: Springer, 2020), https://doi.org/10.1007/978-3-662-60756-5, 13.

11. This right is explored in detail later in this chapter.

12. *W. v. The United Kingdom*, No. 18187/91, Eur. Comm'n H.R. 1993.

13. *Chassagnou and Others v. France*, Grand Chamber Judgment, April 29, 1999, App. Nos. 25088/94, 28331/95, and 28443/95.

14. Separate Opinion of Judge Fischbach Concerning Article 9, ECHR in *Chassagnou and Others v. France,* 46.

15. *Herrmann v. Germany*, No. 9300/07, Eur. Ct. H.R. Grand Chamber, June 26, 2012.

16. Partly Concurring and Partly Dissenting Opinion of Judge Pinto de Albuquerque in *Herrmann v. Germany*, 38–42.

17. Partly Concurring and Partly Dissenting Opinion of Judge Pinto de Albuquerque in *Herrmann v. Germany*, 38–42.

18. See para. 36, *Herrmann v. Germany.*

19. Although it is generally acknowledged as complex.

20. Phillip Halpern, "Preliminary Report of the Proposed Study on Discrimination in the Matter of Religious Rights and Practices," UN Doc., E/CN.4/Sub.2/162 (1954), accessed, December 11, 2023, https://digitallibrary.un.org/record/783698.

21. United Nations, "International Covenant on Civil and Political Rights," G.A. Res. 2200 A, 21 UN GAOR, Supp. (No 16) 53, UN Doc. A/6316 (1966).

22. Michael Hass explains this as an affirmative obligation for governments to provide the infrastructure to guarantee accountability for violations, and a negative obligation for governments to refrain from interfering with the exercise of rights.

23. Human Rights Committee, General Comment No. 22: The Right to Freedom of Thought, Conscience, and Religion (Article 18 of the International Covenant on Civil and Political Rights), UN Doc. CCPR/C/21/Rev.1/Add.4, 1993.

24. HRC General Comment 22, para. 1.

25. HRC General Comment 22, para. 8.

26. HRC General Comment 22, paras. 1–8.

27. GA Res. 36/55, November 25, 1981. UN Doc. A/36/51.

28. Council of Europe, European Court of Human Rights, "Guide to Article 2 of Protocol No. 1: Right to Education," Updated August 31, 2022, accessed July 15, 2023. https://www.echr.coe.int/documents/604084/839313/Guide_Art_2_Protocol_1_ENG.pdf.

29. United Nations, International Covenant on Civil and Political Rights, GA Res. 2200 A, 21 UN GAOR, Supp. (No 16) 53 UN. Doc. A/6316 (1966), accessed July 15, 2023, https://www.un.org/en/development/desa/population/migration/generalassembly/docs/globalcompact/A_RES_2200A(XXI)_civil.pdf.

30. *Campbell and Cosans v. United Kingdom*, No. 48 Eur. Ct. H.R. (Ser. A) (1982), 33.

31. *Campbell and Cosans v. the United Kingdom*, 35.

32. For a more detailed discussion of veganism and the right to education, see Jeanette Rowley and Edie Bowles, "Veganism, Law and Education in the United Kingdom," in *Law and Veganism: International Perspectives on the Human Right to Freedom of Conscience*, eds. Jeanette Rowley and Carlo Prisco (London: Lexington Books, 2022).

33. Article 1, "The High contracting Parties shall secure to everyone within their jurisdiction the rights and freedoms defined in Section 1 of this convention."

34. Article 14, "The enjoyment of the rights and freedoms set forth in this Convention shall be secured without discrimination on any ground such as sex, race, colour, language, religion, political or other opinion, national or social origin, association with a national minority, property, birth or other status."

35. It is well-documented in UN reports that drafting the human right to freedom of religion and belief presented difficulties for members representing Islamic nations.

36. Paul M. Taylor, *Freedom of Religion: UN and European Human Rights Law and Practice* (Cambridge: Cambridge University Press, 2005), 208.

37. See for example, the historical rejection of secularism and philosophical beliefs in *Wisconsin v. Yoder*, 406 U.S. 203, 215–216 (1972), https://tile.loc.gov/storage-services/service/ll/usrep/usrep406/usrep406205/usrep406205.pdf. See also, the recognition that a system of ideas and practices associated with a "religion" might evolve according to social conditions: Wilson and Deane JJ, in *Church of the New Faith v. Commissioner for Pay-roll Tax (Vict.),* 154 CLR, 120, 173 (1983).

38. United Nations, General Assembly, "Interim Report of the Special Rapporteur on Freedom of Religion or Belief," A/71/269 (August 2, 2016), para. 11.

39. *Arrowsmith v. United Kingdom*, App. No. 7050/75, Eur. Ct. H.R. [1980].

40. *X. v. Germany*, No. 8741/79, Eur. Ct. H.R. Mar. 1981.

41. *Campbell and Cosans v. United Kingdom*, No. 48 Eur. Ct. H.R. (Ser. A) (1982).

42. *W. v. The United Kingdom*, No. 18187/91, Eur. Comm'n H.R. 1993. The applicant's veganism was held to be within the scope of Article 9(1), but the Commission decided that unlawful interference with the vegan's practice had not taken place because there was a law required for a good reason, that being that the prison rules requiring prisoners to work in the print facility were in place to maintain order in the prison.

43. Council of Europe, European Court of Human Rights, "Guide on Article 9 of the European Convention on Human Rights: Freedom of Thought, Conscience and Religion," updated August 31, 2022, accessed August 22, 2023. https://www.echr.coe.int/documents/d/echr/guide_art_9_eng.

44. See, for example, the Maastricht Treaty and the Treaty of Amsterdam. A statement of respect for non-religious and philosophical organizations can be found in Declaration 11, annexed to the Treaty of Amsterdam.

45. Council of the European Union, "EU Guidelines on the Promotion and Protection of Freedom of Religion or Belief," June 24, 2013, accessed August 27, 2023. https://www.eeas.europa.eu/sites/default/files/137585.pdf.

46. *Official Journal* C 364/01 (December 18, 2000).

47. See "Preamble," para. 5.

48. Article 2 of the consolidated version of the Treaty on European Union states that:

The Union is founded on the values of respect for human dignity, freedom, democracy, equality, the rule of law, and respect for human rights, including the rights of persons belonging to minorities. These values are common to the Member States in a society in which pluralism, non-discrimination, tolerance, justice, solidarity, and equality between women and men prevail. Article 49 includes "Any European State which respects the values referred to in Article 2 and is committed to promoting them may apply to become a member of the Union. "Consolidated Version of the Treaty on European Union." *Official Journal* C326/1 (2012).

49. Council Directive 2000/78/EC: Establishing a General Framework for Equal Treatment in Employment and Occupation, *Official Journal, L* 303 (2000). (Passed under article 13 of the Treaty of Amsterdam).

50. The grounds were listed as religion or belief, disability, age, and sexual orientation.

51. [2005] UKHL 15, 2 A.C. 246.

52. Para. 55.

53. The Directive did not mention a requirement that a belief must be "similar" to a religious belief.

54. "Employment Equality (Religion Or Belief) Regulations 2003" *Hansard* HL Deb., vol. 649, col. 789 (June 17, 2003).

55. Ibid. col. 790.

56. Ibid, col. 793.

57. "Equality Bill," *Hansard*, vol. 673, col. 1109, July 13, 2005.

58. *McClintock v. Department of Constitutional Affairs*, [2008] IRLR 29.

59. *Grainger plc and others v. Nicholson*, [2010] IRLR 4.

60. See, Equality and Human Rights Commission, "Religion or Belief Discrimination," accessed November 2, 2023, https://www.equalityhumanrights.com/equality/equality-act-2010/your-rights-under-equality-act-2010/religion-or-belief-discrimination?return-url=https%3A%2F%2Fwww.equalityhumanrights.com%2Fsearch%3Fkeys%3Dclimate.

61. *Hashman v. Milton Park (Dorset) Ltd. (t/a Orchard Park),* [2011] UK ET 3105555/2009.

62. *Williamson* [2005] para. 23.

63. *Casamitjana v. The League Against Cruel Sports*, [2020] UK ET 3331129/2018.

64. United Nations, General Assembly, "Interim Report of the Special Rapporteur on Freedom of Religion or Belief," A/69/261 (August 5, 2014),

65. United Nations, General Assembly, "Interim Report of the Special Rapporteur on Freedom of Religion or Belief," A/69/261 (August 5, 2014), 19–20.

66. Scottish government, "The Milk and Healthy Snack Scheme (Scotland) Regulations 2021," https://www.legislation.gov.uk/ssi/2021/82/schedule/1. Guidance can be found at: Scottish Government, "Scottish Milk and Healthy Snack Scheme: Statutory Guidance," https://www.gov.scot/publications/scottish-milk-healthy-snack

-scheme-statutory-guidance-local-authorities-participating-registered-day-care-settings/, accessed September 1, 2023.

67. In 2019, complaints from vegans about the lack of vegan food across the public sector were significantly higher than they are now in 2024. The campaigns of various organizations and health messaging are acknowledged as impactful alongside formal complaints made by vegans and the confirmation that veganism is a protected characteristic for the purposes of equality law. In the last four years, the nature of complaints has shifted significantly from there being no vegan food to the poor quality of vegan food provided. For insights, see The Vegan Society, "Catering for Everyone," accessed November 28, 2023, https://www.vegansociety.com/get-involved/campaigns/catering-everyone.

Chapter 4

How Research, Law, and Guidance Apply to the Issues Faced by Vegans

Preceding chapters have provided insights into some of the experiences faced by vegans, the rationale for their protection, the professional legal activism directed toward supporting and protecting them, and some of the important legal research supporting the global campaign for vegan rights.

This chapter refocuses on the complaints of vegans in Britain by returning to some of the issues reported by vegans in chapter 1 to illustrate the practical value and application of some of the research conducted during the campaign for vegan rights.

Cases I supported prior to the 2020 tribunal confirmation that veganism is a protected characteristic under the Equality Act 2010 relied on observations of law and relevant legal guidance. Particularly important was the fact that veganism was confirmed in 1993 to be within the scope of protection of the ECHR,[1] which meant that vegans in public sector contexts were entitled to invoke human rights protection when in relationships with government bodies.[2] Prior to 2020, there was no explicit precedent that vegans could rely on confirming their protection under equality law or in private sector contexts,[3] but on the strength of the evidence obtained through research, it was clearly logical and correct to argue that the protected characteristic of religion or belief included veganism and that vegans should, therefore, benefit from the prohibition on discrimination under the Equality Act 2010.

The evidence relied on included (inter alia) the case of *Campbell and Cosans v. the United Kingdom,* which had identified that philosophical convictions were akin to a "belief" for the purposes of legal protection. This authority had been recognized in *Williamson*,[4] and the tribunal in the case of *Hashman*[5] had acknowledged that Mr Hashman's beliefs about fox hunting were related to their commitment to the vegan philosophy.

The case of *Grainger* had established the legal test for assessing whether a "belief" could be protected under the Equality Act 2010, and it was discovered in the research for the campaign for vegan rights that the legal test was derived from the jurisprudence of the European Court of Human Rights.

On the evidence provided, cases I supported prior to the tribunal confirmation in 2020 that vegans were legitimate beneficiaries of the Equality Act 2010 were well-informed and well-grounded, and it was only a matter of time before a vegan case would be heard by a tribunal.

This chapter starts with a general overview of the relevant provisions of the Equality Act 2010. It then sets out sections specifically related to the prohibition on discrimination in the provision of services, education, and employment under separate headings.

THE EQUALITY ACT 2010

The Equality Act 2010 prohibits discrimination against individuals with protected characteristics, one of which is religion or belief, which readers will by now understand includes the beliefs and convictions of vegans. The Equality Act protects vegans in employment, education, and in wider society as consumers of goods, facilities, and services.[6]

Under the Equality Act, direct and indirect discrimination are prohibited, along with harassment and victimization. In addition, there are provisions relating to education and specific obligations relevant to the public sector. All these categories are relevant to the protection of vegans, and the main general principles will be explained in turn.[7]

The Meaning of Religion or Belief under the Equality Act 2010

The definition of religion or belief is aligned with the freedom of thought, conscience, and religion, guaranteed by Article 9 of the ECHR. The criteria for determining a non-religious "belief" are as set out in the *Grainger* test (see chapter 3). The belief must be genuinely held, be a belief and not an opinion, concern a weighty and substantial aspect of human life and behavior, attain a certain level of cogency, seriousness, cohesion, and importance and be worthy of respect in a democratic society. It must be compatible with human dignity and not conflict with the fundamental rights of others. Section 10 of the Equality Act 2010 explains the meaning of religion or belief:

(1) Religion means any religion, and a reference to religion includes a reference to a lack of religion.

(2) Belief means any religious or philosophical belief, and a reference to belief includes a reference to a lack of belief.
(3) In relation to the protected characteristic of religion or belief—
(a) A reference to a person who has a particular protected characteristic is a reference to a person of a particular religion or belief;
(b) A reference to persons who share a protected characteristic is a reference to persons who are of the same religion or belief.

Direct Discrimination

Direct discrimination happens when the reason for a person being treated less favorably than another is a protected characteristic. Section 13(1) of the EA 2010 provides that:

(1) A person (A) discriminates against another (B) if, because of a protected characteristic, A treats B less favorably than A treats or would treat others.

Indirect Discrimination

Indirect discrimination happens when a policy or practice which is applicable to everybody particularly disadvantages an individual with a protected characteristic unless the policy can be objectively justified. To be justified, the policy must be shown to have a legitimate aim, and any disadvantage caused must be shown to be proportional to meeting the aim of the policy. Indirect discrimination can also happen if a policy or practice is a deterrent to someone with a protected characteristic and results in them experiencing a disadvantage. Section 19 of the EA 2010 provides that:

(1) A person (A) discriminates against another (B) if A applies to B a provision, criterion, or practice which is discriminatory in relation to a relevant protected characteristic of B's.
(2) For the purposes of subsection (1), a provision, criterion, or practice is discriminatory in relation to a relevant protected characteristic of B's if—
(a) A applies, or would apply, it to persons with whom B does not share the characteristic,
(b) it puts, or would put, persons with whom B shares the characteristic at a particular disadvantage when compared with persons with whom B does not share it,
(c) it puts, or would put, B at that disadvantage, and
(d) A cannot show it to be a proportionate means of achieving a legitimate aim.

Harassment

Harassment is any unwanted conduct related to a protected characteristic when it has the purpose or effect of creating an intimidating, hostile, degrading, humiliating, or offensive environment, or when it violates the individual's dignity. Section 26 of the EA 2010 provides that:

(1) A person (A) harasses another (B) if—
(a) A engages in unwanted conduct related to a relevant protected characteristic, and
  (b) the conduct has the purpose or effect of—
  (i) violating B's dignity, or
(ii) creating an intimidating, hostile, degrading, humiliating, or offensive environment for B.

Victimization

Victimization happens when an individual treats a person badly because they have done what is referred to as a "protected act." A protected act for the purposes of victimization is raising an issue related to equality protections under the EA 2010 or alleging breaches of equality provisions. Victimization can also take place when an individual treats another person badly because they suspect that person has done or intend to do a protected act. Section 27 of the EA 2010 provides that:

(1) A person (A) victimizes another person (B) if A subjects B to a detriment because—
  (a) B does a protected act, or
  (b) A believes that B has done, or may do, a protected act.
(2) Each of the following is a protected act—
  (a) bringing proceedings under this Act;
(b) giving evidence or information in connection with proceedings under this Act;
(c) doing any other thing for the purposes of or in connection with this Act;
(d) making an allegation (whether or not express) that A or another person has contravened this Act.

Public Sector Equality Duty (in force 2011)

The Public Sector Equality Duty (PSED) applies to specified public bodies.[8] They must give due regard to the three elements of the duty when exercising their functions. Useful provisions under section 149 of the EA 2010 provide that:

> (1) A public authority must, in the exercise of its functions, have due regard to the need to—
> (a) eliminate discrimination, harassment, victimization, and any other conduct that is prohibited by or under this Act;
> (b) advance equality of opportunity between persons who share a relevant protected characteristic and persons who do not share it;
> (c) foster good relations between persons who share a relevant protected characteristic and persons who do not share it.
> (2) A person who is not a public authority but who exercises public functions must, in the exercise of those functions, have due regard to the matters mentioned in subsection (1).
> (3) Having due regard to the need to advance equality of opportunity between persons who share a relevant protected characteristic and persons who do not share it involves having due regard, in particular, to the need to—
> (a) remove or minimize disadvantages suffered by persons who share a relevant protected characteristic that are connected to that characteristic;
> (b) take steps to meet the needs of persons who share a relevant protected characteristic that are different from the needs of persons who do not share it;
> (c) encourage persons who share a relevant protected characteristic to participate in public life or in any other activity in which participation by such persons is disproportionately low.
> (5) Having due regard to the need to foster good relations between persons who share a relevant protected characteristic and persons who do not share it involves having due regard, in particular, to the need to—
> (a) tackle prejudice, and
> (b) promote understanding.
> (6) Compliance with the duties in this section may involve treating some persons more favorably than others; but that is not to be taken as permitting conduct that would otherwise be prohibited by or under this Act.

Having set out the general principles of law and guidance grounding the campaign for vegan rights, we can now revisit and discuss how they feature in some of the issues experienced by vegans.

At the outset, it is important to state that only a court can interpret legislation and decide if discrimination has taken place based on all the facts.

The discussion of the issues faced by some vegans follows the structure of and refers to the issues recorded in chapter 1, beginning with the issues faced by vegans as consumers of goods, facilities, and services.

VEGANS AS CONSUMERS OF GOODS, FACILITIES AND SERVICES

Section 29 of the Equality Act 2010 explains the meaning of provision of services:

(1) A person (a "service-provider") concerned with the provision of a service to the public or a section of the public (for payment or not) must not discriminate against a person requiring the service by not providing the person with the service.
(2) A service-provider (A) must not, in providing the service, discriminate against a person (B)—
    (a) as to the terms on which A provides the service to B;
    (b) by terminating the provision of the service to B;
    (c) by subjecting B to any other detriment.

Interpretation

31(7) A reference to a service provider not providing a person with a service includes a reference to—

(a) the service provider not providing the person with a service of the quality that the service provider usually provides to the public (or the section of it that includes the person), or
(b) the service provider not providing the person with the service in the manner in which, or on the terms on which, the service provider usually provides the service to the public (or the section of it that includes the person).

Vegan Consumer of Financial Services

Case Study 1: NatWest Bank Customer Service

The first case discussed in this category in chapter 1 arose in 2019, and involved a vegan customer who was verbally abused by a customer service assistant at NatWest Bank when applying for a loan. A bank provides services, and the Equality and Human Rights Commission provides guidance for banks, reminding them that they must not unlawfully discriminate because of a protected characteristic when giving or refusing people access to financial services, such as loans.[9]

Aside from basic customer service expectations and issues, in terms of the legislation, the bank's customer service operative had arguably treated the vegan less favorably because of their veganism by saying that "all vegans should be punched in the face." The bank operative was providing the service in a hostile and less courteous manner and caused the customer a significant amount of distress.[10] On the face of it, this was, therefore, a case of direct discrimination under the EA 2010. The vegan customer was treated less favorably than others because they were vegan. There is no justification for direct discrimination and on the strength of the evidence for the protection of vegans in law, the NatWest customer was entitled to make a claim for compensation.

The Equality and Human Rights Commission publishes guidance on how to work out the value of a discrimination claim for injury to feelings.[11] At the time, the value of compensation for a one-off incident would be within the lower band and would attract an award in the region of £900–£8,600. It is important to note that the aim of compensation is to compensate a claimant for genuinely injured feelings, not to punish the service provider.[12]

While compensation, if awarded, offers an individual vegan a tangible benefit, the purpose of the campaign for vegan rights is to advance a culture of respect for veganism, encourage a shift in policies and practices that support vegans, and make veganism more accessible and sustainable. In this case, the most beneficial outcome of the campaign for vegan rights was that the case received a significant amount of publicity, which raised veganism as an issue for anti-discrimination law. Further, and importantly, although NatWest did not admit that discrimination had taken place, it nevertheless committed to improving its customer service and equality, diversity, and inclusion (EDI) training across its entire staff.[13] This embedded veganism in the EDI agenda for thousands of NatWest employees and generated requests for information and in-house presentations, including from other high street banks, on accommodating the needs of vegans.

Vegan Consumers of Holidays and Trips

Case Study 2: Vegans Excluded from Booking an Excursion

The case of John, William, and Joseph, who wanted to join a tour of the Second World War sites in Normandy, was also dealt with prior to the confirmation that vegans were protected under the EA 2010. This case also involved prejudice against vegans and, on the face of it, was a case of direct discrimination. It is evident from the facts that they were treated less favorably than other people because they were vegan. While the tour operator did ask about dietary requirements, it was not prepared to accommodate the dietary needs of vegans and, worse, was not even prepared to accept bookings from vegans on the grounds of its prejudicial perception that its other guests would not want vegans on the trip. The tour operator, therefore, discriminated against the three vegans. It refused to provide them with its services, defended its practice of directly discriminating against them, and effectively implemented and enforced a practice of excluding vegans, all of which, on the face of it, breached the legal duties of service providers.

Although, for the three friends, the discrimination they experienced was an incident that caused injury to feelings, and they did submit a complaint and request advocacy, they did not wish to escalate the matter or claim compensation.

Following lengthy advocacy discussions on behalf of the three friends, which included disseminating relevant information and sharing links to helpful online sources of information, John, William, and Joseph were eventually reassured that the tour operator now understood equality provisions and its legal duties as a service provider. The operator accepted that their prejudice against vegans was unjustified and unfair, and manifested in potentially unlawful practices that, on the face of it, breached equality law obligations. After being provided with information and being signposted to further reading, the tour operator committed to improving its inclusion and dietary needs practices, offered the three vegans a discount to join the tour, and provided a written apology to all three vegan customers.

In terms of the mission of the campaign for vegan rights, this case elevated the philosophy of veganism and changed business practice.

Case Study 3: Failure to Provide Vegan Food

Irene's and Dave's experience was after the confirmation that vegans are protected under the Equality Act 2010. However, there was no evidence of discrimination against them as vegans. Although the tour operator in this case explicitly stated that all dietary needs would be accommodated, clearly intending to be inclusive and non-discriminatory in terms of legal obligations, it relied on service providers abroad and had not considered the possibility of not being able to meet its contractual duties. In this case, the problem was not discrimination against the vegans by the tour operator, but typical social norms and cultural and material issues in the "real world" and the subsequent availability or supply of vegan food and meals in shops, restaurants, and hotels. The outcome in this case was more relevant to consumer law than anti-discrimination law, and Irene and Dave received a substantial refund on the grounds that they had not received what they expected and for a lack of care in the provision of the service.

It would be unrealistic to argue that this case advanced veganism or protected vegans. In fact, it would not be surprising if the tour operator amended its terms and conditions to expressly limit its responsibility for the provision of specific food abroad. However, these kinds of cases certainly produce good results; as a consequence, tour operators do everything they can to accommodate dietary needs, even if they need to expressly limit liability. Cases such as these remind tour operators that they must examine their operations and devote time and effort to meeting the needs of customers. These cases also offer insights into the lived experience of vegans, harmonization, and different interpretations and application of equality law in various countries, and they inform research relevant to the principle of inclusion.

Of relevance in this regard, for example, is the German interpretation of the legal meaning of "belief" for the application of the European Union's Equality Directive.[14] The International Vegan Rights Alliance' member for Germany, Attorney Ralf Müller-Amenitsch, explains that the German word *weltanschauung* can be interpreted as "conviction," and although the EU Equality Directive requires a broad approach to the meaning of "belief," the German concept of "weltanschauung" was unlikely, at that time, to include the convictions of vegans.[15]

Similarly, Marie Laffineur-Pauchet explains that there are difficulties advancing veganism and protecting vegans in France in the context that the "gastronomic meal of the French," which contains courses of animal products, including meat, fish, and cheese, is included in the United Nations Educational, Scientific and Cultural Organization's (UNESCO's) list of Intangible Cultural Heritage of Humanity.[16] The UNESCO Intergovernmental Committee was informed that the gastronomic meal of the French plays an active social role and is part of the French identity. The Committee noted that "[i]ndividuals called "gastronomes" who possess deep knowledge of the tradition and preserve its memory watch over the living practice of the rites, thus contributing to their oral and/or written transmission, in particular to younger generations."[17]

Although the specific issue presented by the vegan complainant did not produce what might be regarded as an immediate useful social, political, or legal outcome relevant to the campaign for vegan rights or animal rights, insights into the context for the potential for legal protection for vegans in different countries are relevant and required for a thorough understanding of the socio-politico-legal context for the protection of vegans around the world. Presentations given on the lived experience of vegans and the harmonization of equality law by network representatives have enriched the campaign's knowledge base and have been discussed during conferences.

Vegan Consumers of Entertainment

Case Study 4: Vegans Publicly Targeted in a Joke about Being Denied Access to an Entertainment Venue

The case concerning The London Dungeon banning all vegans from entry during January and branding Veganuary as "VeBANuary", was particularly alarming given that it was 2023, thirteen years on from the Equality Act 2010 coming into force and three years after the Norwich employment tribunal confirmed in its ruling that veganism is a protected characteristic for the purposes of the Equality Act 2010. It was a marketing gimmick rolled out during Veganuary, the month now associated with celebrating veganism and inviting non-vegans to consciously consider the vegan philosophy and adopt veganism.

A London Dungeon spokesperson responded to complaints from the vegan community, saying that it was not implementing a genuine ban on vegans and apologizing for causing upset.

The questions to be answered in this case concerned not only what legal duties applied, whether The London Dungeon (its owners are Merlin Entertainments) acted lawfully and whether vegans were discriminated against, but also concerned whether the Dungeon acted responsibly and whether it was reasonable for vegans to feel offended by the "joke."

Given that veganism is protected under human rights law and is a protected characteristic for the purposes of the Equality Act 2010, the question of whether it was reasonable for vegans to feel offended by the "joke" can be answered by replacing vegans with other groups of people with protected characteristics and who are protected by law. It is important to keep in mind that the prohibition on discrimination against all people with protected characteristics applies equally and that there is no hierarchy of protection.[18]

Firstly, we can consider replacing vegans with another subset of the protected characteristic "religion or belief." As we noted above, "[r]eligion means any religion and a reference to religion includes a reference to a lack of religion." And "[b]elief means any religious or philosophical belief and a reference to belief includes a reference to a lack of belief."

On these grounds, we can replace vegans with Christians and consider the reasonableness of a marketing campaign denying Christians entry to the Dungeon during a recognized period of celebration that The London Dungeon effectively trivializes and dismisses by rebranding the occasion negatively. It would not be surprising to learn that Christians and the general public felt offended or that they regarded the campaign to be ill-thought-out and in very bad taste.

We can also take a step further and consider the marketing strategy in relation to other protected characteristics. There are nine protected characteristics which include race, gender reassignment, disability, and sexual orientation. Each of these protected characteristics protects individuals and communities that have historically struggled to benefit from protective rights and the principles of equality, diversity, and inclusion. It is fair to say that if The London Dungeon had used any of these protected groups in its marketing campaign, there would be justifiable widespread outrage and condemnation. It is also unlikely that the Dungeon would have targeted any of these groups. This speaks to entrenched prejudice.

When we consider the Dungeon's intentions in the context of other protected characteristics, we might realize more easily the potential for causing offense and public outrage. We can easily see why it is unfair, unlawful even, to mock and joke about other protected groups. However, because prejudice toward other animals is commonplace, entrenched in our language, our education system, consumerism, and in the very structure and organization of our society, the Dungeon failed to appreciate that mocking veganism and vegans is wrong. These are the very reasons, though, why the protected characteristics exist: because people with protected characteristics are vulnerable to unfair treatment and discrimination and are protected so that wider society learns to respect and accommodate them equally.

To answer the question of whether it was reasonable for the vegan community to be upset by the Dungeon's use of veganism in its marketing gimmick, we should refrain from relegating veganism and structuring the protected groups of individuals in a hierarchy based either on where we subjectively position them in terms of individual need, or on the extent of discrimination or intolerance experienced by different groups. For the purpose of this exercise, we must remain focused on the rationale for the right to equality and the spirit and intention of the prohibition on discrimination.

The Declaration of Principles on Equality, published by The Equal Rights Trust ("The Trust"), reiterates the inherent dignity of the human person[19] and recognizes that the right to equality "reaffirms the inter-relatedness of equality and dignity articulated in Article 1 of the Universal Declaration of Human Rights."[20] The Declaration states that:

> The right to equality is the right of all human beings to be equal in dignity, to be treated with respect and consideration and to participate on an equal basis with others in any area of economic, social, political, cultural or civil life. All human beings are equal before the law and have the right to equal protection and benefit of the law.

Human dignity has been said to include individuals or groups feeling "self-respect and self-worth." It is "concerned with physical and psychological integrity and empowerment." The dignity of a person can be "harmed by unfair treatment premised upon personal traits" and "when individuals and groups are marginalized, ignored, or devalued . . . ."[21]

As pointed out above, under the Equality Act 2010, harassment, which is applicable to the protected characteristic of religion or belief, is unwanted conduct that has the *purpose or effect of violating dignity* (emphasis added) or creating an intimidating, hostile, degrading, humiliating, or offensive environment.

Harassment, under the EA 2010, is, essentially, only available in an employment context, but in other contexts, it can translate to direct discrimination.

In the campaign for vegan rights, what is critical in this case, and important to emphasize, is that compassion for nonhuman animals is presented as intrinsic to human dignity. Based on the facts and guidance presented, The London Dungeon did not act responsibly. It violated the dignity of vegans and discriminated against them by treating them less favorably than other consumers and providing its service to them on less favorable terms. Members of the vegan community felt extremely offended by the Dungeon's proposed marketing strategy *because* it violated their dignity as people with convictions that focus on our collective duty and responsibilities to nonhuman animals.

An additional issue in this case was that The London Dungeon holds the Learning Outside the Classroom Quality Badge (LOtC), awarded by the Council for Learning Outside the Classroom (CLOtC). The LOtC Quality Badge is a national award for educational provision, recognized by the Department of Education. The CLOtC states that "[t]he LOtC Quality Badge provides you with a framework to ensure you are the best you can be."[22] The "quality indicators" required for this award include compliance with the Equality Act 2010 and encouraging socially responsible attitudes and behaviors: important considerations to ensure young pupils feel valued, included, and respected.

As a result of the backlash from the vegan community, The London Dungeon cancelled its marketing plans quickly. However, through its conduct, it had brought itself—along with its parent company, Merlin, and the CLOtC—into disrepute. All were held accountable for disrespecting the vegan community and implementing poor equality standards. The situation was an opportunity to disseminate information about veganism and the equality principles and laws they all claimed to uphold.

Vegan Consumers of Food

The issues presented in this section of chapter 1 included seven typical examples of complaints received from vegans about their experiences as consumers of food.

Case Study 5: Poor Quality of Service in Restaurant

In the first case regarding issues relating to the provision of vegan food, a vegan consumer dining in an Edinburgh restaurant accidentally came across an offensive note written by a member of staff who had clarified all the vegan options. The note read, "The vegan sh**e has been circled." The customer was reported to have been in disbelief and felt insulted, shocked, angry, and upset by the attitude of staff.

Food service providers breach their legal duties when they do not provide their normal quality of service to someone with, or because they have, a protected characteristic. As already stated, only a court can decide whether discrimination took place, but on the available facts, the vegan customer was treated less favorably because of their veganism through a less courteous manner, which also left them feeling shocked, upset, and insulted. An additional question is whether the restaurant created an intimidating, hostile, degrading, humiliating, and offensive environment, capable of constituting harassment under the Equality Act. In a case such as this, the subjective feeling of the aggrieved party would be relevant to a legal assessment of the case, along with a consideration of whether it was reasonable for the aggrieved party to feel the way they did.

Case Study 6: Vegans Denied Service

In the second case, concerning the provision of vegan food in a restaurant in the Southwest of the UK, it will be recalled that the restaurant actually advertised that all dietary requirements could be accommodated. In this case, it was established that the restaurant provided for a wide range of other dietary needs, some at short notice, that there were suitable vegan menu items, and that other meals could be adapted with very little effort.

The discussions revealed that the refusal to provide vegan food was not well-grounded, was unreasonable, and was, potentially, a case of direct discrimination. It was accepted that the restaurant felt unable to allow the vegan customers to supply their own vegan food on health and safety grounds, but it was pointed out that unless the restaurant could provide a good reason for refusing to serve the vegans, it was potentially in breach of its duties as a service provider subject to the Equality Act 2010.

The vegans involved did not wish to escalate the matter and were happy with an apology and a revised menu that indicated which items were already suitable or could be adapted for vegan customers.

Case Study 7: Vegan Given Non-vegan Food

The next case discussed in this section of chapter one concerned a vegan customer who was given the wrong pastry by a server at a well-known takeaway shop. The vegan in this case was distraught because, in their words, they had in their mouth "the flesh of an animal and they had not eaten meat for over thirty years." Vegans, as well as vegan rights advocates, will know that this experience would have been traumatizing for the vegan. However, the distress caused was the result of a mistake, and there was no evidence of discrimination.

In complaints of this nature, the vegan does not typically consider what outcome they want. They are distressed and emotional. They might want to see changes to policy and/or practice. Occasionally, they want evidence of changes made, and sometimes they want an apology. In cases such as this, vegans often can't think of a single useful outcome that comes close to addressing how they feel. Discrimination claimants can sometimes benefit from a scale of financial awards that are grounded in "injury to feelings," but when vegans suffer the psychological impact of a food service mistake such as this, they often report that remedies easily available to them under consumer law are "a joke."[23]

Under consumer law, it is a statutory requirement that goods provided must match their description. A service provider must also provide their service with reasonable care and skill.[24] If a vegan does not receive what they expected and paid for, they are generally entitled to a refund or replacement.

Vegans in this kind of situation have reported a range of responses from food service providers, from being ignored to being treated courteously and being offered a refund and free replacement and, in different contexts, sometimes being offered a voucher for a free meal at a different time. Dealing with a food service complaint in this latter way can be regarded as reasonable and professional and will, undoubtedly, go some way to reassuring the customer that the mistake has been acknowledged and that the food service provider is keen to rectify the mistake and compensate the customer.

Often, however, vegans report that a refund and a free replacement do not do justice to the psychological harm caused. In theory, a vegan could attempt to bring a case for psychological damage, but there are currently no legal precedents that can be relied on and no evidence from case law that such a claim would have a reasonable chance of success. Cases invoking food safety law primarily involve physical harm, such as serious cases of food poisoning and allergic reactions. Food safety law is relevant, however, in cases of malicious cross-contamination of vegan food.

Case Study 8: Vegans Suspect Malicious Food Spiking

The next case referred to in chapter one involved online ordering and home delivery of vegan pizzas. When the pizzas arrived, they were confirmed to be vegan, but large pieces of chicken were strewn around inside the boxes. The vegans in receipt of the pizzas accused the food provider of discrimination and of maliciously contaminating the vegan food. The vegans had no evidence for either allegation, but nevertheless submitted a formal complaint by using the complaints mechanism available on the Food Standards Agency's website.[25]

Allegations of intentional food spiking of vegan food are not uncommon, and although in most situations it can be difficult to prove, there is cause for concern, as evidenced by the next two cases, also discussed in chapter 1.

Case Study 9: Suspected Malicious Food Spiking Reported in News

The first of the two case studies on the subject of intentional spiking involved a chef who had cooked for and served vegans and had then posted on social media "[p]ious, judgemental vegan (who I spent all day cooking for) has gone to bed, still believing she's a vegan," and was reported to have also posted "[s]piked a vegan a few hours ago." The chef later denied that they had intentionally and maliciously contaminated the vegan's food.[26]

Case Study 10: Evidence of Routine Adulteration of Vegan Food

The second of these two cases, *Mr M. Ali v. Indian Cuisine Limited,* explained how an employment tribunal heard details about the routine adulteration of vegan food at a restaurant.

Vegans who are not served with the food they asked for and are concerned that their food has been knowingly adulterated can make a formal complaint to the local authority's food safety enforcement team for examination in the context of food safety and trading standards law. Under food safety law in Britain, it is unlawful to sell "to the purchaser's prejudice" any food which is not of the nature or substance requested. It is also unlawful to falsely describe or present food in a way that is likely to mislead consumers as to its nature or substance or quality.[27]

Food service providers are subject to a vast array of regulations and standards that are in place to prevent the causing of harm to consumers. These include rules about hygiene and how food is to be stored, prepared, and cooked, accurate food labelling and avoiding contamination and potential cross-contamination. These rules apply to the provision of vegan food.[28]

The Food Standards Agency recognizes the dietary needs of vegans and states:

> Veganism is a lifestyle choice consumers make based on a range of factors, including ethical, environmental, and nutritional. Food labelled as vegan should not be made from or with the aid of animals or animal products.[29]

Research to support vegans with their food-related complaints has established that Trading Standards operate according to a number of existing general principles for best practice in storing, preparing, and cooking vegan food. They include:

- Storing vegan food separately from non-vegan food.
- Clearly labelling vegan products and ingredients.
- Using separate preparation areas for vegan food, if at all possible.
- Using separate kitchen equipment and utensils to prepare and cook vegan food.

- Cleaning equipment and shared spaces thoroughly.
- Using separate appliances, such as fryers and grills, to cook vegan food.
- Providing staff training regularly.
- Providing gloves for staff working in mixed food environments.
- Ensuring staff and consumers have access to accurate information in response to questions from vegan customers, preferably in printed form.

Information gathered on the rules around the provision of food has been useful for vegans making formal complaints about poor food standards and service and has informed impactful catering campaigns.

Vegan Litigant: The Threshold for Evidence of Ethical Veganism

Case Study 11: Vegan Accessing Tribunal Services

The next case discussed in chapter one concerns a vegan accessing tribunal services with an allegation of discrimination in employment.[30] The issue for our purposes was not the basis of the claim itself (a requirement to be vaccinated), but the tribunal's ruling that the claimant had not provided sufficient evidence that they were an ethical vegan.

The claimant had declared that they objected to the consumption of animal products on ethical grounds and identified as an ethical vegan. Their daily practice included not wearing leather; they took their own vegan food to work and they wore gloves if required to handle non-vegan items during their employment. They followed a strict vegan diet and didn't use products that were tested on animals or products that contained ingredients derived from animals.

The tribunal had been invited to accept that the claimant had a genuine belief in ethical veganism, having given a sworn statement and evidence. However, despite accepting that the claimant followed a vegan diet and avoided using some products that were not vegan, the tribunal did not conclude that they genuinely held a belief in ethical veganism because, in its view, the claimant had not provided sufficient evidence of practice. The tribunal judge stated that: "[i]t is not enough, in my judgment, for her to say she is an ethical vegan. She needs to demonstrate that she genuinely holds that belief."

The human right to freedom of belief protects personal beliefs and acts which are "generally recognised" as "intimately linked to the belief."[31] A question, in this case, concerns whether the tribunal went too far in its demand for further evidence of practice.

Vegan convictions "with regard to animal products"[32] or "opposition to the manipulation of products of animal origin or tested on animals,"[33] are generally recognized to manifest in the adoption of the vegan diet and avoidance of participation in the exploitation of nonhuman animals as far as is possible and practicable. The claimant in this case gave evidence of their ethical vegan beliefs and how they manifested on a daily basis.

A tribunal must necessarily examine whether a claimant genuinely holds the belief in question, but guidance explains that the examination of a claimant's professed beliefs is a limited enquiry: individuals cannot always be expected to express themselves with cogency or precision, and the conditions for recognition or threshold requirements should not be set at a level which would deprive minority beliefs of the protection they are intended to have under the Convention. Lord Nicholls has stated that "it is not for the court to embark on an inquiry into the asserted belief and judge its 'validity' by some objective standard" such as the extent to which the claimant's belief conforms to or differs from the views of others.[34] These principles are observed in tribunal reports.[35]

In this case, however, the tribunal was highly critical of the vegan's presentation of evidence because it was not a comprehensive body of information similar to that in *Casamitjana.* The tribunal even went as far as remarking that the claimant's employment was inconsistent with the extent of the belief, as described in *Casamitjana,* because it required the claimant to sometimes wear gloves at work.[36] It is imperative that the threshold for the legal protection of vegans is not set so high that they feel prevented from taking up employment. As employment Judge Guyer stated in *Hashman:*

> I do not consider I should reject his claims to holding a set of cogent and coherent beliefs, because he remained working where he was, rather than opting to bring to an end one of his means of livelihood. Sometimes one's moral decisions cannot be based on a simple set of black and white principles.[37]

A complainant who is not happy with a first instance employment tribunal decision can lodge an appeal, but what is also needed for continued policy developments supporting vegans is an approach to ethical vegans by judges that acknowledges nuanced practice and does not set the bar too high. This is important in order to achieve compliance with the spirit and intention of the human right to freedom of belief and to facilitate its proper function.[38]

Vegans Accessing HealthCare Services

Case Study 12: Vegan Forced to Handle and Cook Animal Products

The next section in chapter one explained the wide-ranging issues grounding vegan complaints in healthcare contexts.

In addition to the prohibition on discrimination under the EA 2010, the healthcare sector is subject to the Public Sector Equality Duty. The PSED requires public bodies to go further than avoiding discrimination. They must also have an approach to decision-making that eliminates discrimination, advances equality of opportunity, and fosters good relationships. In relation to vegans specifically, this means that those with decision-making powers must be mindful of the following:

- Eliminating direct and indirect discrimination, harassment, and victimization against vegans.
- Advancing equality of opportunity between vegans and non-vegans.
- Fostering good relations between vegans and non-vegans.

The cases presented in the report *Respect for Religious and Philosophical Beliefs while Eating in Care* in 2021 show a failure on the part of the care providers to adhere to legal duties, and the healthcare sector as a whole needs to understand its legal obligations to vegans and do better, including in the way it responds to complaints from vegans about falling short of legal obligations. The campaign for vegan rights and a rights approach to effective advocacy have ensured that individual vulnerable vegans in healthcare have been able to submit informed formal complaints, and the use of the provisions of the EA 2010, along with an explanation of the PSED, have resulted in individual vegans obtaining adequate information from their doctors, and in the provision of vegan food and vegan alternative medications (that were available and affordable).

In addition to frequent claims of unfair treatment and discrimination against vegans, pressing issues in health and social care concern the treatment and care of older vegans, the treatment of vegans in clinical care settings (including the treatment of vegans with disordered eating), and the treatment of vegans with compromised capacity.

The chair of the IVRA provided formative information to support Vegetarian for Life's work in this area.[39] A legal assessment of, specifically, David's case (see case study 12 in chapter 1) includes consideration of the legal duty on state bodies not to unlawfully interfere with David's beliefs. In this case, the requirement to handle and cook non-vegan food constituted interference that denied David their right to live according to their convictions. The legitimate aim in this case was, clearly, to be able to cook a meal, but a requirement to handle and cook non-vegan products was, arguably, not a proportional way to achieve the legitimate aim. There was, arguably, a clear violation of David's Article 9 right to freedom of belief, and a breach of the PSED to eliminate discrimination and create equality of opportunity. In addition, there are potential breaches of law relating to a requirement to the best interests of those with reduced capacity.[40]

Vegans in Detention

Case Study 13: Protecting the Rights of Vegan Prisoners

The next issue in chapter 1 explained how registered vegans were monitored at a UK prison. The application of law applicable to this issue included violation of Article 9 rights under human rights law, equality law, the PSED and law relevant to the Independent Monitoring Board who had failed to problematize the issue in its published report, and merely stated that "[r]equests for special diets, especially vegan diets, are carefully monitored, and prisoners who are found to be eating non-vegan food are removed from the list."

As a result of communicating law and legal duties, the policy at Warren Hill was cancelled with immediate effect, and the statutory duties and responsibilities of the IMB to recognize that prisoners are particularly vulnerable and its duty to prevent their ill-treatment were raised at the national level.

VEGANS IN EDUCATION

The provisions of the EA 2010 relating to education state that bodies responsible for individual schools must not discriminate against pupils. However, the stated prohibitions do not apply to anything done in relation to the content of the school curriculum. This is to ensure that equality law does not prevent schools from teaching a broad syllabus that is designed to expose pupils to a wide range of ideas. However, the way the curriculum is taught must not subject pupils to discrimination. Section 85(2)(a) provides that:

The responsible body of such a school must not discriminate against a pupil—

- (a) in the way it provides education for the pupil;
- (b) in the way it affords the pupil access to a benefit, facility, or service;
- (c) by not providing education for the pupil;
- (d) by not affording the pupil access to a benefit, facility, or service;
- (e) by excluding the pupil from the school;
- (f) by subjecting the pupil to any other detriment.

In addition, we will recall that the ICCPR and the ECHR guarantee the right to education and respect for the rights of parents to education that aligns with their moral convictions. In the UK, the right to education is guaranteed by a legal provision entrenched in the ECHR. Article 2 of Protocol 1 states:

> No person shall be denied the right to education. In the exercise of any functions which it assumes in relation to education and to teaching, the State shall respect

> the right of parents to ensure such education and teaching in conformity with their own religious and philosophical convictions.[41]

Vegan Issues in Nursery

As seen in chapter three, case law has established that education is not limited to teaching pupils but is to be interpreted as the "whole process" of educating and includes policies and practices unrelated to the curriculum. On this basis, the lack of alternatives to cow's milk for vegan pupils at nursery school is arguably an issue for the right to education, equality law, and the PSED. Vegan pupils don't have the benefit of free milk, which is, arguably, a detriment and discriminatory. The vegan rights approach to supporting vegan parents and pupils includes a legal challenge to the Nursery Milk Scheme.

Case Study 14: Vegan Complaints about the Lack of Vegan Milk in Nursery

The Nursery Milk Scheme is governed by The Welfare Food Regulations 1996, which define "milk" as whole or semi-skimmed liquid cow's milk.[42] Information referring to the type of milk provided under the Scheme is included on the current Nursery Milk Scheme website. It states:

> You may be reimbursed for any pasteurised cows' milk, including whole and semi-skimmed, under the Nursery Milk Scheme. The milk can be organic.
>
> The Nursery Milk Scheme does not include fully-skimmed milk, goat's milk, soya milk, lactose free milk, fluoridated milk or unpasteurised milk, milk with added flavours, colours, vitamins or other additives.
>
> You can claim for any powdered infant formula for babies up to 12 months, that is based on cows' milk, satisfies the nutritional requirements of babies and is suitable from birth.
>
> You may **not** claim for follow-on milk, ready-to-feed milk, anti-reflux, goat's milk and plant milk.[43]

Statutory guidance requires Early Years Foundation Stage (EYFS) settings to obtain information about children's special dietary requirements before they attend the setting and record and act on the information provided about children's dietary needs. Some of the stated aims of the EYFS are to ensure quality and consistency for all children, create good partnerships between settings and parents or carers, and provide equality of opportunity and anti-discriminatory practice, ensuring that every child is included and supported.[44]

In guidance on "meeting cultural needs," The Children's Food Trust for Public Health England states that "[s]ettings must ensure that they make appropriate provision for parental preferences including cultural and religious food sensitivities," and "[i]t is important that requests for special diets are handled sensitively and appropriately, and this can be included as part of a policy, describing how these are managed, and the procedure that is followed."[45] In the guidance, step five of "[s]even steps to planning healthy meals, snack and drinks" requires providers to "[m]ake sure you cater for the cultural and dietary needs of all the children in your care. . . . " In addition, recommended menu plans at the time of this specific complaint included soya alternatives, explicitly in support of vegan children.[46]

A vegan rights approach to the exclusion of plant-based alternatives to cow's milk, under the government-run Nursery Scheme, began in 2019, with a request to the overseeing body, the Department for Health and Social Care, to change the governing legislation and the publication from the Rights Network of a "legal opinion."[47]

A consultation process ensued in England, which to date has included an Equalities Analysis,[48] a call for evidence on research and studies relating to bioavailability of micronutrient fortificants from plant-based drinks, and information from manufacturers of plant-based milk alternatives on processing and manufacturing methods.[49] A report from the Working Group with recommendations on plant-based drink consumption is due to be published in 2024.[50] This report will determine whether a legal challenge can progress.

The vegan rights approach was, however, instrumental in bringing about changes to Scottish legislation, which does now include funding for early years providers to supply non-dairy alternatives to cow's milk on ethical grounds.[51] This is a perfect example of what the IVRA set out to achieve.

Vegan Issues in Primary School

Case Study 15: School's Cow's Milk or Water-Only Policy

Case study 15 involved Mr Roberts and their four-year-old child, who had moved from nursery, where their needs had been accommodated, to reception, where they were no longer able to drink their plant-based milk with their peers at milk time and were told they would have to drink water instead. The school's policy clearly caused the child a particular disadvantage and detriment. The child was denied the opportunity to benefit from the free provision of a nutritious drink and prevented from taking their own drink into school.

This dispute lasted around nine months and, ultimately, a robust and comprehensive rights approach was applied that included principles and provisions from both human rights and equality law, as well as guidance on nutrition. Following a presentation of the legal arguments, the outcome of this case was much more than Mr Roberts had hoped for. The governing body[52] not only recognized and accommodated the child's need to have soya milk in school as an alternative to cow's milk, but also recommended that the school's water-only policy must be reviewed with a view to including a dairy-free alternative to the milk provided under the "Cool Milk" scheme. It also committed to critically examining whether the "Cool Milk" cow's milk marketing narrative was appropriate to be included within school policy and related literature, and committed to funding the child's soya milk.[53]

After nine long months, Mr Roberts was, understandably, relieved and happy with the outcome, but also reeling from circumstances and a lengthy process the family should never have had to endure. As a result of one parent's courage, tenacity, and determination that their child should benefit from inclusion in education, the school milk provision policy was overhauled. All pupils would now be able to opt for a plant-based alternative to cow's milk. This is exactly the kind of policy overhaul envisaged by the IVRA.

Case Study 16: Vegan Complaints about Educational Resources

The next issue discussed in chapter one concerns complaints from parents about the lack of vegan-appropriate educational materials and the promotion of biased educational materials that conflict with vegan values and convictions. A vegan rights approach to this issue applies the Public Sector Equality Duty, which obliges schools to go further than merely avoiding discrimination against vegans. All public bodies, including schools, must have due regard to the need to remove disadvantages, create equality of opportunity, and promote good relationships between vegans and non-vegans in the interests of tackling prejudice and promoting understanding.

The use of the PSED in a request from parents for vegan-friendly learning resources, combined with information about vegan rights and legal duties in education, has resulted in at least one school providing a number of vegan-friendly books in the school library.[54] The PSED, arguably, has the potential to ground further changes that will support vegans in education and contribute to the mission of the vegan rights campaign to make visible the exploitation of nonhuman animals.

A further element of a vegan rights approach to vegan issues in education relies on the requirement that educational curricula should be delivered in a *critical, objective, and plural* way to ensure respect for philosophical convictions. This is specifically and particularly relevant to an educational culture in which "Every Child Matters," as noted by vegan teacher training provider, Laura Chepner.[55]

Case Study 17: Issues for Vegan Inclusion in Education

A vegan rights approach to the provision of vegan food in schools is included in The Vegan Society's "Catering for Everyone" campaign.[56] In relation to the principle that from the outset, everyone in education matters, it is important to register the negative experiences of vegans in primary, secondary, and higher education, which include bullying, biased education, and non-inclusive educational requirements. What is clear is that avoiding discrimination in education and accommodating the needs of vegans *requires* honesty and a transparent approach to the exploitation of nonhuman animals.

Case Study 18: Vegan Complaints about School's Raising Animals for Slaughter

In the case of Priestlands Secondary School in Hampshire, the IVRA published an open letter to the school, outlining foundational legal duties.[57] The school eventually returned the pigs to their former "owner" and committed to a consultation and discussion about whether to raise piglets for slaughter in the future. The school is reported to have stated that it respects the vegan philosophy but is proud to serve the whole community.[58]

While a claim of discrimination in relation to the content of the curriculum is not available, serving the whole community requires that the curriculum be taught in a balanced manner. One of the most important changes required in this regard is the explicit inclusion of veganism in school equality, diversity, and inclusion policies and training policies—especially in relation to the requirement to teach a balanced curriculum, the legal duties toward veganism as a protected philosophical belief, and the explanation of the applicability of the PSED to veganism as a protected characteristic.[59]

From the outset, the IVRA recommended a rights approach to vegan advocacy in education.[60] This guidance is supported by the research of Jenkins, Lugassy, Piazza, Simpson, and McGuire, and those historically working in the field of critical animal pedagogy, such as Dinker and Pederson,[61] and now grounds the education work of The Vegan Society.[62] Its first rights-based vegan inclusion in education conference was held in 2022,[63] and supportive educator materials and training for continuing professional development (CPD) are now available.[64]

Case Study 19: Vegans "Required" to Participate in Non-vegan Activities or Use Non-vegan Materials

The duty not to discriminate applies across the education sector, and responsible bodies can be governing bodies, proprietors, or management boards. Private training providers are not subject to the education provisions of the

EA 2010 (unless they have public functions) but are subject to provisions for service providers.

A student was unable to claim discrimination in respect of the content of their college curriculum, but was able to argue that the way the curriculum was being delivered subjected them to discrimination because a requirement to participate in activities on a working farm violated their right to freedom of belief as a vegan. In this type of case, the aim of a training programme must be taken into account, but if there is another way to meet the overall learning objectives that does not cause unreasonable hardship, then it is, arguably, not proportional to require the student to endure the disadvantage. In this case, the overall learning outcomes could be met by permitting the student to take a different module. The college was also subject to the PSED, which required it to have due regard to the needs of students with protected characteristics. These considerations are also relevant to students seeking accommodation of their needs in different contexts and assessments.

VEGANS IN EMPLOYMENT

Part Five of the Equality Act 2010 makes it unlawful for an employer to discriminate against, harass, or victimize employees or job applicants because of a protected characteristic. For the purpose of our discussion, this means that an employer cannot discriminate against, harass, or victimize a vegan employee or a vegan job applicant. The prohibitions apply across a broad range of areas related to employment, such as in the selection of applicants, the terms of employment, opportunities for development (such as through training, selection for promotion, access to other employment benefits), or any other area where detriment could be caused.

Section 39 EA 2010 lays down the following:

(1) An employer (A) must not discriminate against a person (B)—
(a) in the arrangements A makes for deciding to whom to offer employment;
(b) as to the terms on which A offers B employment;
(c) by not offering B employment.
(2) An employer (A) must not discriminate against an employee of A's (B)—
(a) as to B's terms of employment;
(b) in the way A affords B access, or by not affording B access, to opportunities for promotion, transfer, or training or for receiving any other benefit, facility, or service;
(c) by dismissing B;
(d) by subjecting B to any other detriment.
(3) An employer (A) must not victimize a person (B)—

(a) in the arrangements A makes for deciding to whom to offer employment;
(b) as to the terms on which A offers B employment;
(c) by not offering B employment.
(4) An employer (A) must not victimize an employee of A's (B)—
(a) as to B's terms of employment;
(b) in the way A affords B access, or by not affording B access, to opportunities for promotion, transfer, or training or for any other benefit, facility, or service;
(c) by dismissing B;
(d) by subjecting B to any other detriment.

Section 40 sets out the prohibition on harassment:

(1) An employer (A) must not, in relation to employment by A, harass a person (B)—
(a) who is an employee of A's;
(b) who has applied to A for employment.

Information and advice on employment-related issues can be obtained from services such as the Advisory, Conciliation and Arbitration Service (ACAS)[65] and Citizens Advice,[66] but there are also significant opportunities for vegan organizations to support employers with information and guidance on veganism and measures they can take to ensure their vegan employees feel valued and included.[67]

Case Study 20: Termination of Vegan's Employment Contract

The first employment case discussed in chapter one was the 2011 case of Mr Hashman. The relevant historical legislation and application of the law have already been outlined. It will be sufficient, therefore, to briefly mention again that the relevant European Union anti-discrimination law, which itself recalls and reiterates respect for fundamental rights, informs British equality law, and that both recognize "belief" as being on a par with religion. The tribunal in this case recognized relevant jurisprudence, and that the 2003 Regulations derive from Article 9 of the European Court of Human Rights.

Although Counsel for the Respondent tried to persuade the tribunal that Mr Hashman's beliefs were not cogent, coherent, or genuinely held, and that they were opinions bound up with politics, the tribunal accepted that Mr Hashman's beliefs met the legal test laid down in *Grainger.* Namely, that Mr Hashman's beliefs were genuinely held, derived from their philosophical commitment to the sanctity of life and animal welfare, they affect every area of their life and are cogent, serious, coherent, and important. Their beliefs did not conflict with the fundamental rights of others as there is no fundamental human right to engage in blood sports. The tribunal found that Mr Hashman had protected philosophical belief.

Case Study 21: Provision of Personal Protective Equipment

The next two cases in chapter one discuss the accommodation of needs in employment. In both cases, the vegans involved had made repeated requests for vegan-friendly personal protective equipment and, in both cases, the requests were ignored. If either of these cases had been heard by a tribunal, there would, first, need to be a ruling as to whether their philosophical beliefs met the legal test. Assuming that the applicants evidenced that they met the legal test for philosophical belief successfully, a tribunal would then need to consider all the facts before applying the relevant legislation.

In the first case, the standard issue personal and protective equipment (PPE)[68] was, arguably, a provision, practice, or criterion that caused the vegan applicant a particular disadvantage. The employer would have had to show that it had an "objective justification" for the practice. It would have to show this by explaining the legitimate aim to be met and that if any discrimination was evident, it was proportional to meeting the legitimate aim.

It was argued in this case that the vegan met the test set out in *Grainger* and that the employer indirectly discriminated against the vegan employee by requiring them to use the standard issue, non-vegan PPE. Evidence was provided that accommodating the needs of the vegan employee required little effort and would not cause the employer unreasonable hardship. While it was accepted that the employer had a legitimate aim in its requirement that employees use PPE, it was not accepted that discrimination caused was proportional to meeting its aims and it could not, therefore, claim it had an objective justification for the requirement. The vegan in this case did not progress their case, but it is known that the employer did change policy and practice to support those who requested vegan-friendly PPE.

In the second case, the repeated requests from a vegan employee for (available) vegan PPE were dismissed, avoided, and ignored for at least two years. When the employer spent a considerable sum of money to accommodate the needs of a new colleague with religious beliefs, the vegan employee felt devalued and unfairly treated. In this case, it was argued that the vegan employee met the *Grainger* test and that the employer directly discriminated against them because they treated them less favorably than they treated others. The vegan in this case did not need to apply to a tribunal and obtained full vegan-friendly PPE.

In addition, in both of the above cases, the Public Sector Equality Duty was invoked because both were public sector employers and were under a legal duty to have regard to eliminating discrimination, advancing equality of opportunity, and foster good relations between those with protected characteristics and those without (see above). Both of the cases explained above demonstrate the vegan rights approach to changing workplace policy, practice, and culture in relation to the procurement of PPE, and the unquestioned assumption that everyone is happy to wear PPE made from the skin or hair of other animals.

Case Study 22: Discrimination During Recruitment

The next case in this section concerned a vacancy for an occupational therapist in eating disorders, which was advertised by a London NHS Trust. The Trust barred vegans from applying. The general principle that employers must not discriminate in recruitment is qualified by an exception on the grounds of a specific "occupational requirement," the application of which can be shown to be a proportional way of achieving a legitimate aim. The requirement must be crucial to the role, and applicants reasonably deemed not to meet the requirement can be rejected. Recruiters must be able to show that any exclusions meet the legal requirements.[69]

In this case, the NHS Trust merely assumed that a vegan would not be suitable for the role, referring to the unsuitability of applicant's eating "restrictive" diets, and did not ground the exclusion on a legitimate occupational requirement, as required under equality law. The challenge by the IVRA informed the Trust that vegans live according to moral convictions that are protected by law, that it had failed to explain the genuine occupational requirement, and that vegans do not eat a "restrictive" diet: the diet of vegan people is historically wholesome and nutritious and the British Dietetic Association states that "[p]lant-based diets can support healthy living at every age and life stage."[70]

The issue attracted significant media attention, and following the challenge presented by the IVRA, the Trust apologized and removed the restriction on vegan applicants.

Case Study 23: Vegans Accused of Extremism and Terrorism

The next issue discussed in chapter one concerns various applications of anti-terrorism measures to the lawful activities of vegans, and the guidance provided to public sector employees in training sessions by counter-terrorism educators, that vegans are a group to be aware of for the purposes of dealing with terrorism. Research conducted in relation to counter-terrorism measures found that "[n]either veganism or vegans are referred to in official published government counter terrorism policy documents, but innocent, law-abiding vegans have been caught up in the language of terrorism and processed under counter terrorism policy."[71]

A related issue concerns pre-employment screening services, some of which include investigating an applicant's involvement in animal welfare or protection. Research has identified that these services are a concern for the rights of vegans.[72]

Case Study 24: Vegan's Employment Contract Terminated

The next issue discussed in chapter one was about a case brought to an employment tribunal in 2020. The law applied in this case has already been explained. The research materials and support provided by the IVRA are publicly documented by both the litigant and their lawyer, Mr Peter Daly,[73] and celebrated within the vegan legal network as a measure of effectiveness and success.

With regard to the workplace pension issue referenced in this case, many vegans come across hurdles when enquiring about ethical pension options, from not being able to obtain informative responses about their investment options to enquiries taking an unreasonable time to be dealt with, and to being told that there are no ethical alternatives and the only option the vegan has is to opt out of contributing to the occupational pension scheme. Section 61 of the Equality Act 2010 specifies that an occupational pension scheme must be taken to include a non-discrimination rule.

Pension regulations and the various processes involved are notoriously complicated and, furthermore, it has not been easy to see how vegans can be adequately provided for, given the historical paucity of well-performing ethical investment funds. However, the issue of suitable occupational pension arrangements for vegans is an ongoing concern in the vegan legal network, and dedicated attention is currently being given to potential discrimination in a number of cases. Various ethical pension "guides" can be found online, including one by *The Times Money Mentor*.[74] However, vegan employees are encouraged to speak with the pension representative in their workplace and to seek specialist professional pension advice before taking any action in relation to their pension contributions.

Case Study 25: Complaints about Vegan Provisions in Military Service

The next issue noted a complaint about the lack of vegan food and vegan-friendly uniforms in the armed forces. Members of the armed forces are equal beneficiaries of the prohibition on discrimination[75] and the armed forces are also subject to the PSED. The IVRA supported a number of service personnel, and the recent establishment of a, now-thriving, Ministry of Defence (MOD) Vegan and Vegetarian Network[76] provides information and support to members and is also progressing workstreams in partnership with the MOD that support the adoption of new policies for vegan provisions.

Case Study 26: Complaints from Vegans Working in the Animal Care Sector

Case study 26 discussed the way vegans working in an animal welfare context feel in the workplace and considered complaints from vegans who were required to harm nonhuman animals to progress their workplace training. There is clearly a need for employers to consider the way vegans are made to feel in the workplace and create a more inclusive environment.

Under the Equality Act, an employment provision, practice, or criterion (PPC) that causes an individual with a protected characteristic a particular disadvantage can be challenged, and if the employer is unable to show an objective justification for the PPC, it will be deemed unlawful. In one case, out-of-court negotiations resulted in an employer agreeing that the training learning outcomes could be achieved using different methods, which were subsequently rolled out into training policy. The use of legal measures to protect vegans in this case supported vegans and directly facilitated a paradigm-shifting development of compassionate policy.

Case Study 27: Acknowledgment of Legal Protection for Vegans

The next issue discussed in chapter one is the way veganism featured in the decision-making process on mandatory vaccination during the COVID-19 pandemic compared to the way the concerns of people of religious faith were addressed. The information presented shows that the protected characteristic "religion or belief" continues to suffer from a problematic, disjointed approach.

Ultimately, government regulations on compulsory vaccination for people working in the health and social care sector were strict, and exemptions were permitted for certified medical reasons only. The regulations constituted a law that was required to achieve a legitimate aim, and any discrimination, in the wider context of jurisprudence on mandatory vaccination, is regarded to be proportional to meeting the aim of protecting public health and the rights of others. This view was considered appropriate across different nations and has since been supported by various employment tribunals.[77] In terms of compliance with the fundamental rights guaranteed under the ECHR, states are allowed to decide for themselves the measures required within their own territories,[78] and recent judgments confirm that a requirement for mandatory vaccination does not necessarily breach fundamental human rights.[79] The objective of this section is not to comment on the issues involved in mandatory vaccination, but to highlight the difference between the way religious worldview and veganism, as a protected non-religious worldview, are regarded in the political process.

This section included a reference to the case of *Ms T Owen* to illustrate the entrenched oppression of vegans and the demand on the vegan in this case to further prove that they objected to the consumption of animal products on ethical grounds before their claim of discrimination would be addressed. Given the law, legal guidance, and jurisprudence on mandatory vaccination, it is unlikely that a claim of discrimination on the grounds of veganism would have been successful. Nevertheless, the threshold requirements that were imposed on a vegan wishing to have the vaccination issue adjudicated, when considered in the light of the inadequate attention given to veganism as a protected belief in the mandatory vaccine equality assessment, further illustrate the oppressive "real-world" lived experiences of vegans.

Case Study 28: Unlawful Harassment in the Workplace

In the earlier case of *Reilly*,[80] the tribunal considered whether harassment under the Equality Act 2010 had taken place in relation to the conduct of the line manager, which included encouraging the vegan claimant to eat meat and waving meat products close to the claimant's face. The tribunal stated that:

> We were satisfied on the basis of the claimant's evidence that her belief in veganism perpetrates her life and how she lives her life. The claimant's evidence was that she does not use products which contain animal substances, or which have been tested on animals. She brings up her children as vegan. She is a peaceful activist for animal rights. She carries out 30 fundraising activities for animal charities. She provided an explanation for why she worked for the respondent, in a job which requires her to handle meat products. Her position was 'I'm not eating it or funding it' and that 'it was either that or no job and I had to pay my mortgage.' The claimant showed that her practice of veganism is a belief intrinsic to her sense of identity. We were satisfied that for the claimant, veganism is a philosophical belief within the meaning of section 10 of the Equality Act 2010 and is a protected characteristic for the claimant.

Applying the definition of harassment, the tribunal also stated that "[t]he claimant is a vegan for ethical reasons. She privately practises her belief in veganism by not eating or using animal products." And "[t]here was direct evidence of conduct toward the claimant which was related to the claimant's philosophical belief in veganism." Ms Reilly was awarded £10,000 (GBP) for injury to feelings.

This case observed that it was the perceptions of Ms Reilly that must be considered and confirmed that it was reasonable to conclude that the unwanted conduct would have created an intimidating, hostile, degrading, humiliating, or offensive environment that violated Ms Reilly's dignity.

CONCLUSION

This chapter has explored some of the research undertaken and how it features and has been applied in the campaign for vegan rights. It has shown how the use of legal measures to protect and accommodate vegans not only benefits vegans themselves, but can have significant value by facilitating and encouraging changes to policy and practice that help support, sustain, and normalize veganism, and, in turn, contribute to advancing veganism because they make veganism more accessible to non-vegans. These changing policy and social conditions support animal rights activity.

The case study examples referred to above involve vegans in the UK, where the prohibition on discrimination against vegans is now well known. However, there is still much work to be done. A vegan's access to justice, even in the UK, is not easy or straightforward,[81] and vegans frequently abandon valid and strong formal complaints due to stress, the time it takes to achieve a positive outcome, and, sometimes, the personal circumstances and costs involved.

The reasons for the struggle vegans face in accessing justice vary in different circumstances, but some relate to the widespread inadequate filtering-down of human rights standards. This is a complicated issue that is multi-faceted, involving, for example, government interpretations of international legal principles and law, the access to knowledge vegans have about their legal rights, and the partnerships governments have with national organizations and public bodies who are required to participate in implementing human rights and equality provisions but who might not have adequate guidance or policies in place: the case of Mr Roberts is a case in point.

Moreover, the "real world" conditions for veganism and vegans, as alluded to repeatedly in *Hashman*, continue to manifest in prejudice and work against veganism. Whether overt or covert, they are oppositional to veganism and entrenched in the social fabric of everyday life.

There is also much more work to be done in different countries around the world to achieve more favorable conditions for the practice of veganism and for vegans themselves. The next chapter provides brief insights into some of the successes of the campaign for vegan rights, the scope of protection for vegans in the UK, and information about developments in Germany, Italy, France, Switzerland, Denmark, and Canada. The next chapter also includes a "real world" account of personal experience of prejudice and difficulties accessing justice from a vegan firefighter in Canada, whose case was heard by a human rights tribunal in Ontario.

NOTES

1. *W. v. The United Kingdom*, No. 18187/91, Eur. Comm'n H.R. 1993.

2. Human rights law concerns the relationships of individuals with state bodies. The principle is to curtail potential abuses of power by government entities. Equality law, however, is applicable to both the public and private sectors. The British Government owns almost 40 percent of NatWest, but an argument that NatWest is a public body for the purposes of equality law was not advanced in this case.

3. Since the start of the campaign for vegan rights, further research has uncovered evidence of historical judicial respect for people with "vegetarian" convictions, as they would have been known prior to the introduction and explanation of "veganism." See, for example, Maureen O'Sullivan, "Veganism in the Irish Court of Appeal in 1898: Is This our Oldest Case?" The Vegan Society, March 15, 2022, accessed November 27, 2023, https://www.vegansociety.com/get-involved/international-rights-network/international-rights-network-blog/veganism-irish-court-appeal-1898-our-oldest-case.

4. [2005] UKHL 15, 2 A.C. 246.

5. *Hashman v. Milton Park (Dorset) Ltd. (t/a Orchard Park),* UKET 3105555/2009 [2011].

6. Northern Ireland has devolved power to establish its own equality law. It broadly aligns with the Equality Act and grounding principles emanating from the Convention and the EU Equality Directive. The Equality Commission confirms that veganism is protected by law.

7. This section does not intend to provide a comprehensive and detailed account of equality measures but merely show how the general principles can be applied to cases involving vegans.

8. See Schedule 19. EA 2010.

9. Equality and Human Rights Commission, "Equality law Banks and other Financial Services Providers," updated February 19, 2019, accessed October 10, 2023, https://www.equalityhumanrights.com/en/advice-and-guidance/equality-law-banks-and-other-financial-services-providers.

10. A claim of harassment is not available in the provision of services, but the complaint can be raised as direct discrimination.

11. Equality And Human Rights Commission, "How to Work out the Value of a Discrimination Claim: A Guide to Quantifying Discrimination Claims in Access to Services Cases," April 2018, accessed October 10, 2023, https://www.equality-humanrights.com/sites/default/files/quantification-of-claims-guidance.pdf. Updates to the scales can be obtained from the Courts and Tribunals Judiciary website. In respect of claims presented on or after April 6, 2023, the "Vento bands" shall be as follows: a lower band of £1,100 to £11,200 (less serious cases); a middle band of £11,200 to £33,700 (cases that do not merit an award in the upper band); and an upper band of £33,700 to £56,200 (the most serious cases), with the most exceptional cases capable of exceeding £56,200, accessed October 10, 2023, https://www.judiciary.uk/wp-content/uploads/2023/03/Vento-bands-presidential-guidance-April-2023-addendum.pdf.

12. See above, Equality and Human Rights Commission, "How to Work out the Value of a Discrimination Claim: A Guide to Quantifying Discrimination Claims in Access to Services Cases," 3.

13. This would partly be because the bank suffered reputational damage and would want to ensure robust staff training.

14. Council of the European Union. "Council Directive 2000/78/EC: Establishing a General Framework for Equal Treatment in Employment and Occupation." *Official Journal* L 303 (2000).

15. Ralf Müller-Amenitsch, *Vegan im Recht: Das Handbuch für juristische Fragen des vegetarischen und veganen Lebensstils*, (Mainz: Ventil Verlag UG & Co. KG, 2016).

See also, in English, Ralf Müller-Amenitsch, "Vegan Legal Issues in Germany," in *Law and Veganism: International Perspectives on the Human Right to Freedom of Conscience*, eds. Jeanette Rowley and Carlo Prisco, 71–89 (London: Lexington Books, 2022).

16. Marie Laffineur-Pauchet, "The Growth of Veganism in France," in *Law and Veganism: International Perspectives on the Human Right to Freedom of Conscience*, eds. Jeanette Rowley and Carlo Prisco, 143–168 (London: Lexington Books, 2022).

17. UNESCO, Intangible Cultural Heritage, "Decision of the Intergovernmental Committee: 5.COM 6.14," 1992–2023, accessed October 12, 2023,https://ich.unesco.org/en/decisions/5.COM/6.14.

18. It is acknowledged that the principles of equity apply and differences in treatment can be justified to meet the aims of equality law. The point being made is that the prohibition on discrimination applies equally.

19. The Equal Rights Trust, "Declaration of Principles on Equality 2008," accessed December 12, 2023, https://www.equalrightstrust.org/ertdocumentbank/Pages%20from%20Declaration%20perfect%20principle.pdf.

20. Dimitrina Petrova, Executive Director, The Equal Rights Trust, "Commentary on The Declaration of Principles on Equality: A Contribution to International Human Rights," accessed, December 12, 2023, https://www.equalrightstrust.org/ertdocumentbank/Pages%20from%20Declaration%20perfect%20croped%2016%20Oct%20dimitrina%20comment.pdf.

21. *Law v. Canada (Minister of Employment and Immigration)*, 1999 CanLII 675 (SCC), [1999] 1 S.C.R. 497, https://canlii.ca/t/1fqh9.

22. Learning Outside the Classroom, "What is the LOtC Quality Badge?" accessed October 16, 2023, https://www.lotc.org.uk/providers/lotc-quality-badge-2/.

23. The passage of time helps vegans heal, but these events are seldom forgotten.

24. United Kingdom Consumer Rights Act 2015, ss.11 and 49.

25. https://www.food.gov.uk/contact/consumers/find-details.

26. Andrew Seymore, "Police Informed of Death Threats against Chef Embroiled in Vegan 'Spiking' Row," *Food Service Equipment Journal,* (January 3, 2018), accessed October 15, 2023, https://www.foodserviceequipmentjournal.com/police-informed-death-threats-chef-embroiled-vegan-spiking-row/.

27. United Kingdom Food Safety Act 1990.

28. See also, Food and Drink Federation, "Guidance on 'Allergen'-Free & Vegan Claims," last reviewed August 2023, accessed October 16, 2023, https://www.fdf.org.uk/globalassets/resources/publications/fdf-guidance-allergen-free-and-vegan-claims.pdf.

29. Food Standards Agency, "Vegan Food and Allergens," last updated August 22, 2023, accessed, October 16, 2023, https://www.food.gov.uk/safety-hygiene/food-allergy-and-intolerance#vegan-food-and-allergens.

30. *Ms T Owen v. Willow Tower Opco 1 Ltd,* [2023] UK ET 2400073/2022.

31. *C. v. United Kingdom*, No. 10358/83, Eur. Ct. H.R. Dec. 15, 1983.

32. *W. v. The United Kingdom*, No. 18187/91, Eur. Comm'n H.R. 1993.

33. Council of Europe, European Court of Human Rights, "Guide on Article 9 of the European Convention on Human Rights: Freedom of Thought, Conscience and Religion," updated August 31, 2022, accessed August 22, 2023.

34. *R (Williamson) v. Secretary of State for Education and Employment,* [2005] UKHL 15, 2 A.C. 246.

35. *M Forstater v. CGD Europe and others,* [2022] UK ET 2200909/2019.

36. See further, Jeanette Rowley, "Defining Ethical Veganism," The Law Society Gazette, July 7, 2023, https://www.lawgazette.co.uk/practice-points/defining-ethical-veganism/5116582.article.

37. Para. 58.

38. On the issue of errors of judgment and scope for judicial training, see Maureen O'Sullivan, "Vegetarian and Vegan Rights in Europe: Chickening Out or Egging Them On?" *Forum of Animal Law Studies,* (2020), and "Vegetarian and Vegan Rights in Europe: Chickening Out or Egging Them On? dA. Derecho Animal (Forum of Animal Law Studies) 11, no 4 (2020), DOI https://doi.org/10.5565/rev/da.517.

39. See, Vegetarian for Life, "Dietary Diversity in the Care Sector: A Guide to Catering for People with Allergies, Intolerances, and Religious, Philosophical and Cultural Dietary Beliefs," 2019, accessed November 26, 2023, https://vegetarianfor-life.org.uk/resources/publications/dietary-diversity-in-the-care-sector.

40. Jade Elliott-Archer provides an insight into veganism and mental capacity in "Treatment for Disordered Eating in England: Balancing Vegan Rights and Treatment Requirements," in *Law and Veganism: International Perspectives on the Human Right to Freedom of Conscience*, eds. Jeanette Rowley and Carlo Prisco, 221–243, (London, Lexington Books, 2022).

41. Council of Europe, "Convention for the Protection of Human Rights and Fundamental Freedoms" (European Convention on Human Rights, ECHR), November 4, 1950, accessed July 15, 2023, https://www.echr.coe.int/Docuemnts/Convention_ENG.pdf. This right is made available under the United Kingdom Human Rights Act 1998.

42. United Kingdom The Welfare Food Regulations 1996, s.2, https://www.legislation.gov.uk/uksi/1996/1434/regulation/2/made

43. Department of Health and Social Care, "The Nursery Milk Scheme," Frequently asked Questions-Claiming Milk, What Types of Milk can I Claim for? accessed July 17, 2023, https://www.nurserymilk.co.uk/frequently-asked-questions.

44. Department for Education, "Statutory Framework for The Early Years Foundation Stage: Setting the Standards for Learning, Development and Care for Children from Birth to Five," March 31, 2021, 33, accessed July 17, 2023, https://www.gov.uk/government/publications/early-years-foundation-stage-framework--2

45. HM Government, "Example Menus for Early Years Settings in England, Part 1, Guidance" (2017), accessed July 17, 2023, https://assets.publishing.service.gov.uk/government/uploads/system/uploads/attachment_data/file/658870/Early_years_menus_part_1_guidance.pdf.

46. HM Government, "Example Menus for Early Years Settings: in England Part 2: Recipes," (2017), accessed July 17, 2023, https://assets.publishing.service.gov.uk/government/uploads/system/uploads/attachment_data/file/658872/Early_years_menus_part_2_recipes.pdf#:~:text=Week%201%3A%20Example%20spring%2Fsummer%20menu%20for%20early%20years,with%20milk%20and%20sliced%20banana%20Crumpet%20and%20spread

47. The Vegan Society, International Rights Network, "Department of Health Nursery Milk Scheme Legal Opinion," September 24, 2019, accessed October 19, 2023, https://www.vegansociety.com/sites/default/files/uploads/downloads/Legal%20Opinion%20Nursery%20Milk.pdf.

48. See Committee on Toxicity and SACN, "Final Minutes of the 1st Meeting: Joint SACN/COT Working Group on Plant-Based Drinks," December 2, 2021, Teleconference, accessed October 19, 2023, https://app.box.com/s/zimfu4icea4mstkpqiv30t1inoml7bae/file/929247556951.

49. More information from the Scientific Advisory Committee on Nutrition can be found at https://app.box.com/s/zimfu4icea4mstkpqiv30t1inoml7bae.

50. Scientific Advisory Committee on Nutrition (SACN), "Feeding Young Children Aged 1 to 5 years," July 2023, accessed October 19, 2023, https://assets.publishing.service.gov.uk/government/uploads/system/uploads/attachment_data/file/1167077/SACN-Feeding-young-children-aged-1-to-5-full-report.pdf.

51. Scottish Government, "Milk and Healthy Snack Scheme," https://www.gov.scot/policies/maternal-and-child-health/milk-and-healthy-snack-scheme/. https://www.gov.scot/publications/scottish-milk-healthy-snack-scheme-statutory-guidance-local-authorities-participating-registered-day-care-settings/.

52. A "responsible body" of an educational institution has legal duties and is liable for breaches of equality law.

53. The Vegan Society, "Primary School Forced to Change 'Cow's Milk or Water' Rule after Vegan Dad Fights Discriminatory Policy," June 24, 2021, accessed July 20, 2023, https://www.vegansociety.com/news/news/primary-school-forced-change-cows-milk-or-water-rule-after-vegan-dad-fights-discriminatory-policy.

54. Unreported. Discussed with permission from the vegan parent involved.

55. Laura Chepner is now the current Education Officer and chair of The Vegan Society's Education Network. Laura is a qualified teacher and is known for coining and promoting the phrase "vegan-inclusive education."

56. See chapter 3. In addition, the human right to food imposes a non-discriminatory duty on state bodies.

57. IVRA, "Open letter to: Priestlands School in Lymington, Hampshire County Council and Parents of Vegan Children Attending the School," The Vegan Society, January 22, 2018, accessed October 23, 2023, https://www.vegansociety.com/about-us/international-rights-network/international-rights-network-blog/open-letter-priestlands-school-lymington-hampshire-county-council-and-parents-vegan-children-attending-school.

58. Amy Packham, "Priestlands School Cancels Pig Slaughter Project After Mass Criticism," *Huffpost*, January 23, 2018, accessed July 22, 2023, https://www.huffingtonpost.co.uk/entry/priestlands-school-pig-project-slaughtered_uk_5a670350e4b0e56300730236.

59. This issue was the theme of a workshop presented by the author at the 2022 Education Conference, hosted by The Vegan Society. See The Vegan Society's International Rights Network, "The BIG Veganism in Education Conference Programme," accessed October 21, 2023, https://www.vegansociety.com/get-involved/international-rights-network/international-rights-conference-2022/big-veganism-education-conference-programme.

60. In this regard, see a discussion of the legal issues in Jeanette Rowley and Edie Bowles, "Veganism, Law and Education in the United Kingdom," in *Law and Veganism: International Perspectives on the Human Right to Freedom of Conscience*, eds. Jeanette Rowley and Carlo Prisco, 197–219, (London: Lexington Books, 2022).

61. A vegan rights approach to veganism in education links to critical animal and vegan education pedagogy. See, for example, and for a wide variety of references to other sources, works by Karin Gunnarsson Dinker, Helena Pederson, Matthew Cole, and Richard Twine.

62. A vegan rights approach to vegan advocacy in education was introduced at The Vegan Society by Dr Jeanette Rowley, see Research Advisory Committee, https://www.vegansociety.com/about-us/research/who-we-are/dr-jeanette-rowley.

63. See The Vegan Society, "Our Impact, 2022," accessed October 21, 2023, https://www.vegansociety.com/sites/default/files/uploads/downloads/2022%20Impact%20Report.pdf.

64. The Vegan Society, "Vegan-Inclusive Education," https://www.vegansociety.com/lifestyle/vegan-inclusive-education.

65. https://www.acas.org.uk/.

66. https://www.citizensadvice.org.uk/work/discrimination-at-work/discrimination-at-work/.

67. See, for example, The Vegan Society, "Supporting Veganism in the Workplace," accessed November 4, 2023, https://www.vegansociety.com/sites/default/files/uploads/downloads/The%20Vegan%20Society%20Employer%20Booklet.pdf.

68. The Health and Safety Executive recognizes that under equality law, the provision of PPE should take into account protected characteristics. See, "Personal Protective Equipment at Work, The Personal Protective Equipment at Work Regulations 1992 (as amended): Guidance on Regulations," 2022, accessed November 2, 2023, https://www.hse.gov.uk/pubns/priced/l25.pdf.

69. See Equality Act 2010, schedule 9. Provisions for genuine occupational requirements derive from Council Directive 2000/78/EC. See Preamble (23) and Article OJ 4 L 303/16.

70. The Association of UK Dietitians (BDA), "Vegetarian, Vegan and Plant-Based Diet," accessed November 4, 2023, https://www.bda.uk.com/resource/vegetarian-vegan-plant-based-diet.html.

71. Jeanette Rowley, "The Expert Series Spring 2021: Veganism, Counter Terrorism Strategy and Policing," The Vegan Society, 2021, accessed November 25, 2023, https://www.vegansociety.com/get-involved/research/research-news/expert-series-spring-2021-veganism-counter-terrorism-strategy-and-policing.

72. See Jeanette Rowley, "Veganism and Animal Rights Activism Employment Screening," The Vegan Society, 2022, accessed November 28, 2023, https://www.vegansociety.com/get-involved/research/research-news/veganism-and-animal-rights-activism-employment-screening.

73. See, The Vegan Society, "Veganism in the Workplace," *YouTube*, video, September 17, 2020, accessed October 26, 2023, https://www.youtube.com/watch?v=V1VfIr0yRgA and VegFest, "Ethical Veganism, The Inside Story," *YouTube*, video, accessed October 26, 2023, https://www.youtube.com/watch?v=OwjO9IJr-MM.

74. Rosie Murray-West, "Ethical pensions: How to Choose Investments that Make a Positive Impact," *Times Money Mentor*, April 20, 2023, accessed November 4, 2023, https://www.thetimes.co.uk/money-mentor/article/guide-to-ethical-pensions/.

75. Serving members of the armed forces must raise a work-related issue internally prior to bringing a claim to an employment tribunal.

76. https://www.facebook.com/modvegnetwork/. As recognized by the Ministry of Defence, https://www.gov.uk/guidance/mod-diversity-networks.

77. A search on the UK's tribunal decisions will reveal a large number of results: https://www.gov.uk/employment-tribunal-decisions.

78. A "margin of appreciation." See. *Handyside v. United Kingdom*, App. No. 5493/72, Eur. Ct. H.R. Dec. 7, 1976.

79. See, for example, *Vavřička and Others v. The Czech Republic*, Nos. 47621/13 and 5 others, Eur. Ct. H.R. Grand Chamber, Apr. 8, 2021.

80. *Ms K Reilly v. RT Management Bridgeton Limited,* [2022] UKET 4107984/2020.

81. The applicant in *Casamitjana* was involved in litigation for two years.

Chapter 5

The Successes, Additional Inroads, Still Listening

So far, I have commented on the negative social and political conditions in which veganism exists, explored some of the ways in which vegans have reported feeling unfairly treated or discriminated against, and examined how the law can protect vegans, help shape policies and practices, and support the transition to compassionate living and animal protection.

This chapter highlights some of the successes of the IVRA, summarizes the scope of legal protection for vegans in the UK, discusses some cases involving vegans in other parts of the world,[1] and gives space for a vegan voice—that of Adam Knauff, who recently lost their case for protection from discrimination at the Human Rights Tribunal of Ontario.

THE IMPACT AND INFLUENCE OF THE ORIGINAL INTERNATIONAL VEGAN RIGHTS ALLIANCE

By 2019, the representatives of IVRA and its associates[2] had become known round the world as the leading voice on vegan rights. Members had, individually and in collaboration with high-profile organizations, given presentations on vegan rights at various high-profile events, given interviews in the media, spoken on national radio channels, collaborated with external agencies and each other, published useful blogs, and uploaded resources online. Representatives had dealt with numerous complaints from vegans and had been involved with unimagined early successes, including bringing model cases to court in Germany and helping vegans bring about changes to food policies in schools, accommodation for the needs of vegans in educational settings, and employment contexts.

The influence of the IVRA had inspired three more surveys exploring the experiences of vegans: one in Scotland, one in Canada, and one undertaken by Crossland Employment Solicitors in the UK. All these later surveys confirmed that unfair treatment and discrimination against vegans were rife.[3]

In the UK, a number of cases had been settled out of court, and a number of others could have been escalated to an employment tribunal but were abandoned by the complainants due to the stress of, and time involved with, the process. Notwithstanding the prevailing problematic issue of vegan access to justice, these cases brought about changes to training and inclusion policy: for example, as a result of IVRA activity, veganism was on the customer service training agenda of a prominent high street bank, and IVRA cases involving the provision of vegan-suitable personal and protective equipment in the workplace brought about changes to standard provisions in many different employment contexts.

The IVRA message had been taken around Europe and presented in Canada, America, and Australia. Representatives had given presentations on vegan rights[4] and hosted informative professional symposia and conferences, including co-hosting with high-profile organizations. The IVRA had been represented in *The Law Society Gazette*,[5] the *International Business Times*,[6] *The Independent*,[7] *The Local*,[8] *The Washington Post*,[9] *Metro*,[10] *Vegconomist*,[11] and *Vegan Food and Living*.[12] It had contributed written evidence to the UK Parliamentary Human Rights Committee,[13] given oral evidence at the formation of the All-Party Parliamentary Group on Veganism and Vegetarianism,[14] been cited in academic publications,[15] contributed to health care practice guidance,[16] used to endorse campaign material published by The Vegan Society,[17] and grounded effective change making workstreams,[18] including contributing to a transformation of food provision in the public sector.[19] It had been referenced on the websites of law firms,[20] referred to in posts by account holders on LinkedIn,[21] and cited on *UnchainedTV*.[22] Its knowledge base and assertions have been shared and utilized in the campaign materials of other prominent organizations.[23]

Ultimately, its chair was called upon to provide information and materials to potential litigants and their legal teams. In the UK in 2020, a litigant, Jordi Casamitjana, had the courage and tenacity to endure the long and difficult legal process to bring their case before a tribunal.

The IVRA and its message were established, respected, and valued. It had demonstrated the strength and logic of its rationale and that its aims could be fulfilled. The genie was out of the bottle, and the vegan community now understood and could articulate veganism as a belief in law. Vegans were empowered and had the knowledge to advocate for themselves and frame their valid complaints in legal terms when they felt unfairly treated because they were vegan. They became aware that articulating their rights in the face of unfair treatment and discrimination against them was a legitimate manifestation of their right to practice their compassionate values for other animals.

Disseminating and sharing information have started to *shift the balance*. Policies and practices in education and workplaces were being adjusted to accommodate individual vegans, which made their lives easier and, at the same time, made it possible for people to adopt veganism and remain vegan. Academic researchers had started to engage with the rationale and campaign for vegan rights, and there was widespread acceptance—and some understanding—of the legal protection that could be used to protect vegans.[24] Requests for assistance were flooding in, collaboration proposals had to be put on hold, and more conference partners were scheduled.

Later Developments

The social media page Vegan Equality Non-Discrimination (VEND) was moderated by a volunteer administrator and was a self-contained, manageable activity until the volunteer could no longer offer their free time. VEND is no longer active.

On the basis of the success of the IVRA, offers to partner or merge with other organizations were considered, and a decision was finally taken in 2019 to gift the IVRA to The Vegan Society.[25] The decision was announced at the next vegan rights conference held at the Università degli Studi di Milano (University of Milan),[26] and announced in *The Vegan*.[27]

From 2019, the rebranded International Rights Network continued its work, supported by the infrastructure and resources of The Vegan Society. Its ongoing influence and impact are well-documented on the website of The Vegan Society, including through the successful cases of a Gloucestershire college student[28] and Mr Paul Roberts.[29]

The network retains collaborative links with around thirteen countries and has co-hosted further events with partners, including in Estonia and Portugal.[30] Following the introduction of a rights approach to vegan education at The Vegan Society, the first international vegan rights in education conference was hosted in the UK in 2022.[31]

Ongoing achievements include (among others) changes to food and milk policy in schools, access to vegan alternative medications where possible, changes to training programmes that require students to harm nonhuman animals, adjustments in the workplace when vegans experience a particular disadvantage as a result of apparently neutral policy requirements, and changes to policy so that vegan-friendly personal and protective equipment is now issued as standard for all vegan firefighters.[32] Out-of-court settlements have been achieved for vegans claiming discrimination in the workplace, policies on diversity and inclusion have been amended, and guidance on human rights and equality measures supporting vegans has been provided to a number of professional bodies, organizations, and health trusts.

The Network has also released a "legal opinion" on the exclusion of plant-based milk alternatives under government-run milk schemes in a call for legislation to be changed.[33] It has already successfully argued for changes to government-run milk schemes in Scotland, which now provides funding for plant-based alternatives to dairy milk to those who choose not to consume dairy for ethical reasons.[34] It has provided material for an amicus curiae (intervention) to assist judges at the European Court of Human Rights. The chair has given evidence in a vegan case at the Human Rights Tribunal of Ontario, provided a submission to the call for comments on new authoritative guidance drafted by the United Nations Committee on the Rights of the Child in relation to the environment and climate catastrophe, and, with other members, has provided content for submissions of evidence for various other consultations. Members also continue to publish academic materials,[35] and the chair and other members have supported the All-Party Parliamentary Group on Veganism and Vegetarianism.[36]

THE SCOPE OF LEGAL PROTECTION FOR VEGANS IN THE UK

As I have already noted, vegans in the UK are recognized as having protection under both human rights law and equality law. Protection under human rights law can be involved when vegans are in relationships with government bodies; for example, when they are in the care and control of state bodies, schools, hospitals, and prisons. Under human rights law, it is unlawful to interfere with a vegan's practice, unless there are overriding needs, but overriding needs are strictly limited: there must be a law that is required in a democracy for an important reason—examples being to protect public health or public order, and for reasons of health and safety. In addition, there must be a legitimate aim to be met, and any restriction on a vegan's practice must be shown to be proportional to meeting the legitimate aim. We have seen how this principle has been applied in the case of *W. v. the United Kingdom,* where judges found that the rules requiring a vegan prisoner to work in the prison print shop were in place to protect good order in the prison. In this case, the prison rules were the law required, the legitimate aim was to ensure good order in the prison, and any restriction on the practice of the vegan was proportional to meeting the legitimate aim.

We have also seen how this principle has played out in the recent COVID-19 pandemic. In the UK, legislation was in place mandating health and social care workers to be vaccinated against the virus, and the UK government undoubtedly relied on the legitimate aim of protecting public health. Any subsequent impact on the rights of vegans would have been rationalized as proportional to meeting the legitimate aim.[37]

Ethical vegans have a protected characteristic for the purposes of the Equality Act 2010. As such, it is prohibited to discriminate against vegans in the provision of goods and services, in education,[38] and in employment.

There is no defense for direct discrimination, which can be claimed when a vegan is treated in a worse manner than other people, simply because they are vegan. In a claim of indirect discrimination, however, where a policy applicable to everybody particularly disadvantages a vegan, a defense of "objective justification" is available. However, any restriction on a vegan's practice must be proportional to meeting the specified aim. In claims of indirect discrimination, if amending a policy to include vegans does not cause unreasonable hardship, then it should be amended to accommodate the needs of vegans.

Claims of "harassment" are limited to employment contexts and can be challenged as "direct discrimination" in other contexts. The definition of harassment is broad enough to cover jokes and "banter," and in cases of harassment, it is the complainant's subjective feelings that have legal significance.

If a vegan is treated badly or worse for raising an issue related to their rights, there could be a claim for "victimization" under the Act.

In the UK, the Public Sector Equality Duty requires public bodies to go further than avoiding discrimination. They are required to give due regard to the needs of vegans at the point of decision-making. The requirement for this kind of equality/inclusion assessment looks to eliminate discrimination, create conditions in which there is equality of opportunity, and help to create positive social conditions between vegans and non-vegans to deal with prejudice and promote understanding. Overall, public bodies must give due regard to vegans by assessing the impact of decisions they make and taking steps to meet their needs.

Protection for vegans is considered on a case-by-case basis, and it is the individual beliefs of the vegan complainant that are assessed against the legal test set out in *Grainger.* The legal test does not require the complainant to explicitly compare their vegan beliefs to the "status" and "cogency" of a religion.[39]

In terms of whether a complainant genuinely believes in ethical veganism, following the recent case of *Owen v. Willow Tower*, vegan complainants are reminded of the need to provide sufficient evidence of their vegan practice to satisfy the tribunal that they hold a "genuine belief" in ethical veganism.

The Vegan Society's definition of veganism has been helpful in legal proceedings[40] and in accordance with the "as far is practicable and possible" element of the definition, the scope of protection in the UK permits accidental or unavoidable transgressions.[41] In addition, the scope of protection for vegans extends to promoting the belief; this is included as an element of the protected belief itself.[42]

If the individual vegan explains their belief as including a criminal element, the belief will be deemed not to meet the legal test. In *Ms S Free Miles v. The Royal Veterinary College*,[43] Ms Free Miles explained their ethical vegan belief as that " . . . animals' lives have innate value and that humans should not eat, wear, use for sport, experiment on or profit from animals and that humans have a moral obligation to take positive action to reduce or prevent the suffering of animals, which includes trespass on private property to expose animal suffering and the removal of suffering animals."[44] While the tribunal did accept that the first part of the belief "that humans should not eat, wear, use for sport, experiment on or profit from animals" would amount to a philosophical belief, it did not accept that criminal activity constituted manifestation of the belief in law.[45] In terms of the legal test to be met, the tribunal stated that:

> We considered the Claimant's belief and manifestation of it together as the belief took the form of an obligation to act in a specific way, and it is, therefore, difficult to separate the acts done from the belief itself. The actions are an integral part of the belief. The manifestations of a belief are restricted both under Article 9 of EHCR [*sic*] and the Grainger criteria. We concluded that a belief to take actions that are unlawful (either contrary to civil or criminal law) and to interfere with the property rights of others does not satisfy the fifth element of the Grainger test. It cannot be worthy of respect in a democratic society. The laws of this country are made by its democratically elected representative and have to be observed by all citizens. It is not open to individuals to decide which laws are worthy of respect and which are unjust and can be disobeyed. Any belief that advocates or makes such actions obligatory is not worthy of respect in a democratic society. We concluded that the Claimant's belief that she was morally obliged to take positive action to prevent or reduce the suffering of animals, which included trespass and removal of animals and its manifestation was not a philosophical belief under section 10 of the Equality Act 2010.[46]

It now seems accepted that veganism is an excellent example of a "philosophical belief," and it has been used as such in other tribunal proceedings which considered the legal status of a complainant's beliefs. In *Mr E McClung v. Doosan Babcock Ltd and others*,[47] employment judge L. Wiseman considered whether support for a football club could be a protected philosophical belief under the Equality Act 2010. The judge recognized that a qualifying belief must be one of great seriousness and importance which influences decisions and behavior and stated, "I was not persuaded however that support for

Rangers Football Club invoked the same respect in a democratic society as matters such as ethical veganism."[48]

The campaign for vegan rights has been very influential in the UK, and early IVRA website statistics and correspondence demonstrate its global reach.[49] In 2016, a newsletter produced by the IVRA shared research showing that vegans around the world experienced a lack of understanding, prejudice, and contempt:[50]

- A vegan reported being forced by a court, to provide and cook meat for their child.
- An Italian MP singled out veganism as a dangerous diet and blamed parents for imposing their "moral crusade" on their children.
- Vegans reported being refused vegan food from public authorities while in their care.
- There are cases in which vegan parents have had their children taken from them because their "vegan diet" was deemed dangerous for their children.
- Legal cases show that veganism has been referred to by members of the medical profession as an "extreme diet" and accused of being a contributing factor in the malnourishment and death of an infant.
- In Canada, a teenager requested vegan food, and the request was labelled by a doctor as a "likely manifestation of mental instability."[51]

DEVELOPMENTS FOR THE LEGAL PROTECTION OF VEGANISM IN OTHER COUNTRIES

The development of legal protection for vegans in other parts of the world has gained momentum and is developing independently of any direct involvement with the original campaign or its members, associates, and supporters.[52] The case updates discussed below are brief examples of developments. Vegans can now benefit from legal protection in Italy, Germany, and Denmark, and vegan complainants in Switzerland are awaiting decisions from the European Court of Human Rights.

Legal Cases Involving Vegans in Switzerland

In 2016, the *International Business Times* reported that the Swiss military had declared a nineteen-year-old vegan, Mr Da Campo, unfit for military service because they refused to wear boots made from the skin of nonhuman animals (leather).[53]

Army authorities had deemed Mr De Campo potentially ineffective if they were unable to wear the standard-issue boots. Mr De Campo also requested vegan food but was informed that their vegan dietary needs could not be accommodated for logistical reasons, despite the army being able to accommodate the dietary needs of individuals on other, including religious, grounds. Military service is mandatory in Switzerland for adult males between 18 and 30, and the news report states that an individual deemed unfit for military service is required to pay a tax amounting to three percent of their income each year until the age of 30.

In October of the same year, *The Independent* reported that following Mr De Campo's legal challenge on the grounds that the army's decision went against their human right to maintain their personal convictions, the army had reversed its decision, had declared Mr De Campo fit for service, and had entered into negotiations with them about how to accommodate their vegan needs.[54] The automatic provision of vegan food, army boots, uniform (including uniform shoes) and other personal and protective equipment are an example of the policy developments hoped for by the IVRA.

In October 2022, the European Court of Human Rights posted details of two cases involving veganism and anti-speciesism. The complaints were that the Swiss authorities had refused to provide the complainants with an appropriate vegan diet while they were in prison and in a hospital psychiatric unit respectively. Both cases are being heard (partly) under Article 9 (the right to freedom of thought, conscience, and religion).[55] A successful outcome in either of these cases will be binding on Switzerland and influential across the remainder of the forty-seven member states. In terms of the original IVRA objectives, a positive outcome will bolster the case for the mandatory provision of vegan food for those in the care or control of state bodies, thus making veganism more sustainable and easier to adopt.

Legal Cases Involving Vegans in Italy

Attorney Carlo Prisco (PhD) has stated that "[d]iscrimination against vegans in Italy is widespread" and has published on the relationship between veganism and Italian law.[56]

In 2020, a judge of the Court of Bologna, Italy, Dr Filippo Palladino, ruled on the case of an applicant who felt discriminated against in their employment because their vegan dietary needs were not catered for. The case concerned a vegan primary school teacher in Bologna who made repeated, but unsuccessful, attempts to obtain vegan food at work. Vegan pupils, on the other hand, were accommodated under a school catering policy. Feeling discriminated against, the teacher took legal action against their employer, the Ministry of Education.[57]

In awarding compensation of 800 Euros plus litigation costs, the judge stated that "[i]t should be noted that the vegan diet appears determined by beliefs of a philosophical or religious nature, that appear deserving of protection within the broad scope of the right to freedom of thought recognized by the Italian Constitution."[58] It is likely that this outcome will support requests for accommodation of needs from other vegans in employment and, potentially, other contexts.

Legal Cases Involving Vegans in Germany

Long-standing IVRA member for Germany, attorney Ralf Müller-Amenitsch, has published on vegan rights in Germany and has raised successful legal challenges for vegan clients.[59]

In 2022, the Administrative Court of Münster, Germany, heard a case involving a vegan military officer who claimed that they were unconstitutionally discriminated against and financially burdened by the military's food provision and daily subsistence policy.[60] The officer argued that while subsistence payments made to personnel while they were living away from home were generally reduced if a catering facility was made available, they should not be reduced in this case; the officer was unable to eat in the communal catering facility because vegan meal options were not available and, furthermore, it was not possible to create a vegan meal from the food items available because they were not adequately labelled as being free from animal products.

It was established that the officer was not obliged to participate in communal catering and was free to decide whether to participate or not, but the officer argued that, due to their vegan dietary needs, they had no real choice because they were forced to self-cater. The officer argued that the reduced subsistence rate forced them to participate in a catering system which they could not use on account of their vegan convictions and, as a result, alleged that they were unconstitutionally discriminated against and that they were financially burdened.

The judgment recognized that the dietary needs of the plaintiff were an expression of a solidified, consistent, and ethically justified comprehensive vegan lifestyle.

This case is particularly significant in terms of the IVRA's original objectives. It not only provides guidance for the development of public catering policy but, importantly, it also breaks through a pre-existing anthropocentric barrier for judicial understandings of the intersection of human freedom of conscience and the vegan response to the suffering of other animals. As noted in chapters 2 and 4, the scope of protection for *weltanschauung* (worldview) was narrowly defined. To qualify for legal protection, a complainant's worldview:

> must functionally take the place of religion by asserting a comparable holistic claim to explanation. Positions that are limited in content and function—such as

> purely political convictions—are not sufficient to assume a worldview with the weight of a religious position. The worldview must present itself as a more or less coherent image of the world, at least identifiable to an (outsider) observer.[61]

In this case, it was noted that an "appeal to a decision of conscience is very close to the core of the personality captured by the dignity of the human person"[62] and that the plaintiff:

> has justified and explained in detail his worldview and his consequent comprehensively vegan lifestyle and on the basis of numerous concrete examples—for example regarding the treatment of cows in dairy farming, to the conviction that the plaintiff did not accept vegan communal catering because of his ideologically justified and also in the respective individual case "situationally" in the sense of a mandatory decision of conscience subjectively, as a commandment of unconditional thought, a vegan diet that is perceived as absolutely binding and does not only correspond to personal preferences.

The case recognized that:

> The plaintiff's worldview is based on the exercise of the required right to freedom of expression under Art. 4 secs. 1 and 2 GG also presents a sufficiently coherent picture of the world, at least identifiable to an outside observer, based in the beginning on the evolutionary development of all living beings. In accordance with the principles established in the settled case-law of the Federal Constitutional Court, the plaintiff is also free to base his entire conduct, including his eating habits, on the principles of his worldview that are perceived as binding.[63]

And:

> In the light of the foregoing, the plaintiff has also demonstrated to the satisfaction of the court that an actual use of the non-vegan catering offer would plunge him into a serious distress of conscience.[64]

Further:

> The fact that it is a deliberate decision on the part of the plaintiff does not alter the fact that it is precisely his right to freedom of expression guaranteed by Art. 4.1 and 4.2 of the Basic Law, and this decision is an expression of his conscience, which is also protected by this fundamental right.[65]

Novel judicial reasoning such as this, in previously restrictive contexts, points to the transformation originally envisaged at the outset of the campaign for vegan rights, in which the convictions of vegans will be routinely recognized as relevant to the human dignity entrenched in the human right to freedom of conscience. According to Mr Müller-Amenitsch, the court sufficiently linked freedom of belief, conscience, and ideology, in Article 4 Paragraphs 1 and 2 of the Basic Law, to bring veganism within the promising scope of protection of the fundamental right. Müller-Amenitsch considers that the Münster Administrative Court's decision illustrates judicial support for ethical vegans being protected in Germany.[66]

Legal Cases Involving Vegans in France

Marie Laffineur-Pauchet has discussed the issues for the development of veganism in France in relation to human rights and consumer law.[67]

In 2023, trainee dietician and ethical vegan, Astrid Prevost, was required to use animal products in class or risk failing their assessment. Ms. Prevost asked to be given the opportunity to use vegan alternative ingredients to the animal ingredients specified and submitted a note from their doctor to support the request, which was provided on relevant health care grounds. Ms Prevost's request for accommodation of needs was rejected, and they are currently involved in legal proceedings claiming discrimination.[68] Securing the recognition of vegans' rights in education was one of the original campaign objectives. A positive outcome in the case will influence equality policy and support French vegans in education and training contexts.

Legal Cases Involving Vegans in Denmark

In February 2024, a lower court in Hjorring, Denmark, ruled that vegans are protected under Article 9 of the ECHR. The case involved a Danish kindergarten that refused to provide vegan food to a vegan pupil and, at the same time, implemented a policy of refusing to allow the child to take a packed lunch. In this case, the court decided that the child was treated worse than their non-vegan peers and that, in order to attend the kindergarten, the child would be required to recant veganism. The court ruled that the child was subjected to indirect discrimination that was not reasonable or justified and, was, therefore, a breach Article 14 of the ECHR in conjunction with Article 9 (respectively, the principle of equality and the human right to freedom of belief). The court reiterated that those with vegan convictions have the right to not be "treated worse than people without vegan convictions who are in a similar or comparable situation."[69] The responsible Municipality was ordered to pay 10,000 Danish kroner and legal costs amounting to 17,750 Danish kroner.

At the time this book is going to print, it is also reported that a case concerning a pregnant person who was denied a vegan meal and instructed to bring a packed lunch for childbirth will be heard by a Danish court in April 2024. The outcome will no doubt be reported by Dansk Vegetarisk Forening.[70]

Legal Cases Involving Vegans in Canada

In 2017, Canadian vegan firefighter Adam Knauff contacted the IVRA about their complaint of employment discrimination. In publicly available news reports, Mr Knauff explains that their employer, the Ontario Ministry of Natural Resources and Forestry, discriminated against them by failing to accommodate their vegan dietary needs. Mr Knauff explained that they had to push through hunger and exhaustion because they were not adequately fed while fighting huge forest fires over many hours a day, despite their employer knowing about their dietary needs via the standard food employee information form. Mr Knauff explained that there were days when there was no suitable food at all, or when whatever they might be able to eat was contaminated with animal products. Mr Knauff was also suspended after repeated complaints and expressing their frustration about the circumstances they were subjected to, day in and day out. Mr Knauff eventually complained to the Human Rights Tribunal of Ontario (HRTO), stating:

> The Ontario Ministry of Natural Resources and Forestry discriminated against me and failed to accommodate my sincerely held ethical beliefs (creed) when it failed to provide me with food that accommodated my personal commitment to ethical veganism, and then disciplined me and suspended me because I attempted to assert my right to accommodation of that sincerely held ethical belief.[71]

Mr. Knauff's case was heard by the HRTO six years later in September 2023. On November 29, 2023, Mr Knauff received news from the tribunal that the case had been unsuccessful.[72]

In this case,[73] Mr Knauff claimed that they had been unlawfully discriminated against in their employment on the grounds of ethical veganism, their "creed." In deciding whether ethical veganism constitutes a creed for the purposes of the relevant Code, the tribunal referred to the determining characteristics of creed that form the legal test to be met. An applicant must provide evidence that the belief under consideration:

- Is sincerely, freely, and deeply held.
- Is integrally linked to a person's identity, self-definition, and fulfilment.

- Addresses ultimate questions of human existence, including ideas about life, purpose, death, and the existence or non-existence of a Creator and/or a higher or different order of existence.
- Is a particular and comprehensive, overarching system of belief that governs one's conduct and practices.
- Has some nexus or connection to an organization or community that professes a shared system of beliefs.

Adjudicator Karen Dawson accepted that ethical veganism satisfies the first and second parts of the test but stated that:

> I find that on the evidence presented, ethical veganism does not address the existence or non-existence of a Creator and/or a higher or different order of existence, as required by the third part of the test. Accordingly, I find that ethical veganism does not constitute a creed within the meaning of the Code.

The third element of the legal test can, in fact, accommodate ethical veganism as a belief that addresses human existence and offers ideas about human life and a different order of existence. Ethical veganism is relevant to the concept of humanity and addresses ultimate questions of human existence because it raises questions and invokes discussions about our shared morality, ethical duties and duties toward other animals, and about how these issues intersect with other social justice issues. These questions concern our interconnectedness with other living beings who share Earth's resources, the true nature of human existence, what it means to be human, and how we should organize our social systems and systems of justice. They clearly concern a higher or different order of existence.

The view that veganism does not meet the third element of the criteria for protection under the Code, arguably, does not align with the principles of the international right to freedom of belief and seems out of step with the approach adopted under the European system of human rights in its various jurisdictions and in the UK. Mr Knauff's legal team invited the tribunal to apply the legal test in conjunction with additional insights from foreign and international law. However, the adjudicator stated that they saw "no reason to resort to international law and foreign case law in order to interpret the Code, an Ontario statute, and I decline to do so."

The details of Mr Knauff's case link back to the explanation of the "real-world" context for the existence of veganism, as discussed in this book's introductory chapter. Descriptions of anti-vegan attitudes, hostility, "veganophobia," dismissal and trivialization all feature in Mr Knauff's explanation of their experience, as does the difficulty of accessing justice.

The remainder of this chapter gives space for Mr Knauff to give a firsthand account of their experience, convictions, and employment circumstances and their long struggle to access tribunal services.[74] The author's further comments on the failed case are provided in the conclusion to this book.

LITIGATING FOR VEGAN ETHICS: PULLING BACK THE CURTAIN

Adam Knauff

CONNECTING THE DOTS

My name is Adam. I was born and grew up in Thunder Bay, Ontario, Canada.

The first decade of my life was a fascinating time just before cellular phones, the internet, and thus worldwide information sharing became ubiquitous. International news via our local syndicate: *The Chronicle Journal,* would take a few days to reach us. Status quo and social norms came from sitcoms with laugh tracks and from weekly religious outings.

Despite coming of age tucked far away on the western shores of Lake Superior, at twelve or thirteen years old, I figured it out. The chicken "fingers," the fish "sticks," the "bacon," the rump "roast" . . . they all used to be *alive*. They all used to breathe and see and had undoubtedly had babies of their own. Therefore, there must be love and communication and community and interaction. And they were dead now. And on my plate. I stopped eating animal flesh and eggs then, in the early nineties.

A decision like this—a change like this—isn't easy. Especially in Thunder Bay. Especially in the nineties. Especially while having no role models; no support at all. I didn't know any other vegetarians in real life. It was rarely discussed in mainstream pop culture at the time. When it was, it was done in derogatory negativity. A joke. A punchline. Even on television's *Blossom*, the main character (along with the entire supporting cast) goads their dad "Nick" on the one episode where Nick "goes vegetarian". It's blessedly ironic that the lead actor, Mayim Bialik, has been vegan for over a decade now. But imagine a thirteen-year-old me, a fledgling vegetarian, watching the sitcom in early 1994 and seeing all these characters rip apart their fictional father for trying a vegetarian life. This was my first memory of another vegetarian, and it was not supportive. In October the following year, Lisa Simpson became a vegetarian—again to much relentless taunting. I think the little jingle: "*You Don't Make Friends with Salad*" probably set us back a decade. But Marge's epitomizing of the general Western stereotype with: "I didn't mean to take sides, I just got caught up in the rhythm" is *Simpsons* satirical genius. At least Lisa remains an ally today.

I definitely did not feel or see support from TV, my school, my peers, or my family. My close friends were curiously supportive, if for no other reason than that it seemed weird or rebellious.

After being duped for years by the highly subsidized Canadian dairy industry, at the age of eighteen I made the conscious decision to stop consuming dairy. I was no longer going to be a part of anything that used, abused, or killed animals. I became an ethical vegan. It was 1997, and the only other ethical vegans I knew of at the time were Bryan Adams and Apu Nahasapeemapetilon.

I never looked back.

I left home young. I began travelling the world at twenty years old. I worked piece-rate jobs in the silviculture industry to get around the globe—mainly tree-planting—for seven seasons. Doing manual labor in the wilds of Canada and abroad let me see a world beyond what I already knew. It allowed me to see things I never knew I could.

It isn't easy traveling around the world as an ethical vegan. Cultures, traditions, language barriers, availability; when you travel, you release control of so many aspects of your life. That is part of traveling and should be embraced. But that doesn't mean you must abandon your ethics or do things you don't want to do. Animals don't need to suffer for humans to see the world. Sometimes it's easy, and sometimes it's very difficult to remain steadfast to yourself. Peer pressure is real—even, or perhaps more—with new acquaintances. Staying ethically vegan and seeing and experiencing—and enjoying—the world is completely possible and getting better all the time.

OUT OF THE FRYING PAN

I became a forest firefighter in 2008, stationed in Kenora, Ontario. It was a natural progression from planting trees—in essence, "protecting" the forests I'd been planting for years. Another seasonal gig, I could still globe-trot in the winter.

It's a provincial government position. Canada is still a Commonwealth country, so I would be an employee of "the Crown".

Veganism and vegetarianism are welcome, accepted, and basically a *part* of the tree-planting world. At most tree-planting camps I've worked with, vegetarians and vegans make up at least half of the population, if not more.

Fire is different.

Working in forest firefighting as an ethical vegan is not easy or common. This came as an unwelcome surprise. The vegans and vegetarians at each fire base could be counted on one hand in the Northwest Region of Ontario (where employee numbers ranged from sixty to eighty at each base) when I joined.

Even then, these people were more likely to be base support staff and not direct fireline ranger personnel—thus making the crew ranks even more isolating. But I had survived as an ethical vegan without any support before. I would be fine.

Despite all the challenges, there was a safety net. In my immediate training on the standard operating procedures of forest firefighting, I discovered the intricacies of meals and food supply. In Ontario, we camp directly on the fireline and prepare meals ourselves (during unpaid hours) with food and cooking supplies provided by the Ministry. Although it is ultimately the crew leader's decision to make and submit food requests, for the most part, the entire crew has a voice in what is requested for meals. Food kits are usually requested and supplied in 48-hour turnaround times. As a crew, you share duties for cooking, cleaning, tool maintenance, etc. Everyone has certain tasks, and a hierarchy exists. The idea is to be self-sufficient on location, with resources supplied as needed until the fire is out.

There are protocols specific to meals and eating allowances as to portions per person per day. Specific food order forms vary from base to base, but portion allotments per person are the same everywhere. Each crew person is allowed portions or a dollar value for daily meal requirements. These portions or dollar values are the same for everyone. So, in transit, we may source our own meals and get reimbursed for those expenses. When we are deployed on massive project fires, living out of base camps, that dollar value will be represented by grams of nourishment to all staff equally, regardless of dietary differences or position.

This framework, in which employees are enabled to make or receive their meals (on an equal basis, off the clock), exists because it's a government job in which employees are working in an emergency service away from normal access to the food/meals they would provide themselves. The framework existed long before I was an employee with the Ministry. There should never be a need for anyone to advocate for themselves for this contractual supply of food to occur. It is part of the collective working agreement. It is an employee right, regardless of seniority or position. The right to food. And dietary requirements—including being vegan, which is known about and accepted—are covered under these contracts and protocols. Again, this existed before I was an employee of the Crown.

I was habituated to being provided with meals after working on location in forests, or rather clear-cuts, across Canada and Australia, where there was no other access to food and preparation facilities, let alone the time to prepare it. I had never had to think about the specifics before, as I had never had an issue when eating at most of the tree-planting camps I'd been employed with over my seven-year career.

Again, fire is different.

I worked my way through the ranks as a crew member, senior crew member, and finally crew leader in 2013. It was tough as an ethical vegan being a crew member and a senior crew member because I had to rely on the "chain of command" and thus my crew leader to speak for me. When we were on fires or deployments, I had to rely on my crew leader to alert the cooking staff/management that there was a vegan on the crew and to order vegan items on resource orders. There is written documentation that goes with each exported crew which explicitly states this and other pertinent details of each crew person, but somehow these documents go unnoticed.

Having your ethics in the hands of others is never easy.

Relying on someone else to enable you to stay true to yourself requires the utmost trust.

It was extremely difficult at times.

But I managed. I could tell stories for days of outright hatred, belittling, teasing, and bullying during those years of fire. Crew leaders who made my life harder. Cooking and logistics staff who went out of their way to make my being an ethical vegan extremely difficult. All seemingly "just because". I would plead with cooks to simply not put cheese on the vegetarian options, and in reply I would get smiles and direct eye contact as they covered everything in processed dairy. I could never understand why.

I stuck it out because fire was exciting and challenging and new. I didn't want my ethical veganism to be a reason I couldn't do things. Ethics should never have to be compromised for me to be successful at something that doesn't inherently contribute to animal abuse and death. We were out in the forests of Canada, fighting raging wildfires on the frontline of conservation; where does killing and eating animals need to get involved?

But clearly, this was a different work environment, and if I wanted to survive, I needed to keep my head down and get by without support. I always assumed my ethical veganism was my "cross to bear". An "inconvenience". A "problem." My "fault." It was how I'd dealt with it at home as a teen, and it's how general society expects vegans and vegetarians to coexist; so you just go with it. You just try to get by. It's amazing that you have to try so hard in this life not to kill anyone.

So, on becoming crew leader in 2013, I was finally in charge of my own voice. I would be the first point of contact with cooks, logistics, and supply chain providers. I thought things would get better; be easier.

I was wrong.

Many of my deployments and fires as a crew leader were difficult specifically because of how I was treated over my ethical veganism—sometimes they were difficult *only* because of my ethical veganism. People seemingly sought out confrontation over the word itself.

So I continued to desperately try to fly under the radar. To not "cause waves" Not "rock the boat." I wouldn't disclose my ethical veganism to anyone except those who needed to know, such as the cooking staff on deployments or management and logistics for submitting food orders when on fires. Unprovoked debates, drama, negativity, and discrimination follow closely when the word “vegan” is muttered in fire. It was much easier to “fit in” when I didn’t disclose my ethical veganism to my colleagues. And so, I continued accepting the standard discrimination and challenges of trying to gain the same access to food as everyone else. I did so quietly and discreetly for years.

TOUR DE FARCE

During the fire season of 2017, my crew was deployed to the province of British Columbia (BC) to fight ongoing project fires. We were stationed at Williams Lake.

This was my fifth season as a crew leader. I am extremely good at what I do—and I was at the peak of my career. Despite the contentious fire situation in the province, I felt confident and prepared for this deployment.

More and more regulations have been put into place during my career in fire, and typically forest firefighters are now restricted to twelve-hour workdays. On this deployment, we were working fourteen- to sixteen-hour days throughout the stint. Deployments had already been reduced to fourteen consecutive fireline days from the nineteen days we had previously worked. A standard deployment or “tour” was a fortnight on location, fire or incident, followed by a mandatory two-day break. And then you did it all over again. And again and again. As necessary, of course.

We live out of tents directly in the bush when working on fires in Ontario. BC has different regulations, but we were still living out of tents on this deployment, just not directly on the fireline. Instead, we were stationed in a sprawling basecamp. We lived in a “tent city” with some basic facilities and were never too far from the helicopter landing zones, food and resource supplies, washing facilities, and general operations headquarters. Paramilitary in nature, these basecamps do resonate as a military operation. These basecamps are a hum of activity nearly 24/7, and this one in Williams Lake in 2017 was no exception.

Forest firefighting is as dangerous, intense, and demanding as you can imagine. This was one of “those” tours.

Briefings, objectives, resources, and maps are distributed and reviewed with the crew leaders, sector bosses, and technicians on day one. As everyone else began situating themselves and preparing for objectives, I needed to perform my next objective and make contact with the cooking staff to ensure I would receive adequate sustenance during the deployment.

Quite quickly and alarmingly, the lack of sustenance provided to vegans at this camp became apparent and glaring.

The "menu board" by the hand-washing station in the queue for meals was always varied, with copious options written in various colors of dry-erase marker. There was a section, however, that read "vegan/vegetarian/celiac," with one, maybe two, listings under it. Reading this on the first day, I was puzzled and worried. Although a vegetarian eating a vegan diet really isn't a big deal, a celiac is not necessarily on a vegan diet, and vegans and vegetarians don't necessarily avoid gluten.

It was a sad and lazy way to group "annoying" dietary requirements together by this basecamp, yes, but if it was nutritionally balanced and adequate (considering our job and workday duration), then there wasn't much to be done about it.

But it wasn't nutritious or adequate.

So I began the arduous mission I had undertaken so many times previously, where I befriended the cooking staff, logistics personnel, even the supply chain personnel—whoever is necessary to ensure that I can get some grub that didn't used to be alive while I worked relentlessly for two weeks.

I did not realize how hard I would have to work for this.

My packed lunches—insufficient in general for a fourteen- to sixteen-hour workday—were 50 percent filled with items that contained animals in them every day. This would leave two or three pieces of fruit, one or two 200ml juice boxes, and a very small cellophane-wrapped bunch of vegetables (think carrot sticks or mini broccoli heads). The "wrap" I was given most days would literally consist of only a few shreds of iceberg lettuce and cheese—not acceptable for my ethical veganism, and not sufficient as a meal anyway. Or a peanut butter and jam sandwich on buttered bread—again unacceptable. The granola bars would have dairy or honey. The trail mix would have dairy and candies coated in shellac.

Breakfast was perhaps the only meal during which I acquired some sustenance—the porridge, realistically gruel, was like solidifying cement, but I'm sure it had some protein, and no one was killed to prepare it. My colleagues warned me they had witnessed bacon and sausage bits dripping or falling into the baked beans while they were being served (I witnessed several instances of cross-contamination throughout the deployment). Mushrooms were soaking in butter. Everything that was deep-fried was fried together with animals.

Vegan meals and therefore eating were dire at this camp.

I was not the only one suffering. Vegetarians, celiacs, and other vegans would gather at the smoking section (surprisingly right beside the dining mess tents) to furiously complain about how our nutritional needs were going unmet. We exchanged protein bars, nut mixes, and anything else we could acquire on our own. No one else seemed to be actively trying to make things better. And I get it: no one wants to be noticed. No one wants to stand out. No one wants to be "that person."

But then, nothing changes.

So I tried. Every day I spoke to the cooking staff and logistics. Every day.

They admitted, every day, that they were failing and that what was being provided was insufficient. Flimsy excuses were paraded day after day. Nothing improved.

Never was it called what it actually was; it was discrimination.

Discrimination is treating someone or a group of similar persons differently than "everyone else" for illegitimate reasons.

If we usher the devil's advocate out of the room, may I ask: for what reasons is it okay to treat someone or a group of people differently than everyone else?

And so, I continued to try.

I will admit, I was getting more and more hangry every day. Frustration was obviously mounting. Long days as a crew leader on a very contentious fire meant I was doing physically demanding work all day in considerable heat and smoke. I was constantly making huge decisions: for my crew, the fire, safety, time constraints, topography, and resources—and all with no fuel to make it happen. It was increasingly difficult to be "nice" or "patient" as my food situation remained stagnant, my job demands remained constant, and all I was receiving was apathetic lip service.

Meal examples: a single black bean, placed atop a rice-filled red pepper—like a garnish—as my protein source. I was refused a second one when I asked for more. An entire plate of boiled broccoli in a sweet chili sauce. A spinach salad with cherry tomatoes. This wasn't one entire meal—this is three separate examples of what this basecamp thought was acceptable and sufficient to feed all those living as vegan, vegetarian, or celiac as their entire dinner meal.

These are not meals. This is not sustenance for a forest firefighter on a two-week deployment of fourteen- to sixteen-hour workdays.

I acquired foodstuffs myself and supplied the cooking staff with them in the hope of getting better-balanced meals. I never saw those foodstuffs again.

Even on "BBQ night," when I thought I might receive some sustenance via a veggie burger or veggie dog, I watched as the cook, who was preparing both veggie and meat burgers right next to one another, touched the meat burgers with his hand and then instantly touched the veggie burger with the same hand. Was this to check the temperature? I am still confused by this action. I instructed him that he couldn't do that. It is basic food-handling practice—not exactly a "vegan concern." He told me off. I swore at him. He swore at me.

I had no dinner.

And now I couldn't trust any prepared food coming from this basecamp.

I was told by management the next morning that my behavior had been unacceptable.

After a breakfast of oatmeal gruel, I got my packed lunch. I accepted the plastic bag with "VEGAN" written on the side in black permanent marker. This time I spilled the contents on the table in front of the lunch packers and showed them all the non-vegan items in my lunch. They looked back at me with blank stares. They cared not.

Shortly thereafter, I was addressed by management and told that my behavior, again, was unacceptable.

I was sent home.

This is the biggest *faux pas* you can make in a fire.

I was mortified.

ME. I was sent home. I was so dedicated to my job. I had so much to do on the fireline that day. I was an integral part of this operation. I followed protocol. I followed the chain of command. I trained my crew to the utmost tier, season after season. I trained at least one rookie—if not two—every season. I am really good at my job. And I was sent home.

When I asked why I was sent home, I was told it was because of my "attitude."

A person having a bad attitude is not an acceptable excuse to send them home, especially in my case, given how well I had been performing my duties on the tour despite the meal situation. One of the managers who was telling me I was going home was the same chief of logistics whom I had been speaking to every day about how dire the food was. He had admitted multiple times that it was unacceptable. He had told me multiple times that he was personally working on it. And now he was saying that how I had approached him about the situation was also unacceptable. I was being scapegoated as the problem at the basecamp. The situation itself was apparently not the problem.

But I understand now.

It was much *easier* to send me home than to provide vegan meals to personnel on this fire. It was much *easier* to make one meal for three groups of dietary requirements that had no nutritional value than to provide what is laid out in contracts and use basic common sense and dignity.

So one would think: Okay, that's it then.

He was sent home.

But it didn't end there. For the next 36 hours, I was more or less sequestered in "custody." I had no control, and I was actively kept without food during this time. I had restricted internet access and only managed to acquire one basic meal during this time. I was dumped at a post-secondary school housing area where evacuees from the fire were being housed. My "chaperone" retired to a hotel room. The campus was sprawling with evacuees, who were wandering everywhere. I had no idea where I was. I had no point of contact. I slept on the floor of a school room for the night. The next morning, my "chaperone" picked me up and offered to stop "at a grocery store" for breakfast an hour before my flight. He kept repeating: "I don't even know what a vegan breakfast *is*," over and over. I explained I couldn't pick up breakfast from a grocery store, and he smiled and said it was my choice not to eat. I realize now that even that was a false offer; we barely had enough time to make it to the airport for my flight, so we couldn't possibly have stopped anywhere for breakfast.

This same person was the "A-rep," or agency representative, for me. He was supposed to be looking out for me. That's the actual job—make sure your personnel are okay while on tour. I should have been briefed and given contact information. I should have had access to proper meals. I should have had knowledge of my sleeping arrangements and safety protocols. Instead, he kept me from food, laughed at me, belittled me, and told me that if I had allergies, he would "bend over backward," but he would not do so for my "preferences". He seemed to derive pleasure from my discomfort. He genuinely believed I should be punished for what I "did." He continued to say that no one would care about this. He had neglected to identify himself as the Ministry A-rep, and he did not leave his contact number when he dumped me at the school. He treated me with genuine disdain for the duration of our time together, despite the fact that it was the beginning of his fourteen-day deployment, and we had never met before.

It was after two or three flights that I landed in Winnipeg, Manitoba. I asked my driver to stop somewhere for a meal, which meant I finally did eat. Kenora is a two-hour drive east from there.

"WE'RE NOT BEING UNPROFESSIONAL—YOU'RE BEING UNPROFESSIONAL!"

And still, it didn't stop there.

Upon my arrival back in Kenora, I was greeted with rumors and a completely destroyed professional reputation.

I was already a laughingstock when I was presented with disciplinary action.

I was to be punished for trying to eat as an ethical vegan on a forest firefighting deployment as an employee of "the Crown" and for standing up for myself when I was prevented from doing so.

Remember, providing vegan meals was already in the existing contracts. This was already an accepted thing. I wasn't asking for or demanding anything that wasn't already in written protocols. It was just that no one actually did what is required. No one actually cares if it's done. And no one did anything about it when it was identified and agreed that it was not being done. I was working under a false narrative of inclusion and provision by my employer for my entire career.

This was why I had to stand up for myself.

This was why I submitted a grievance with my union against my employer.

And this was why I ended up litigating against them via the HRTO.

If they hadn't punished me, I don't think I would have done anything. I just would have kept plugging along, maybe kept my head further down. Stayed even more quiet. Shouldered the burden more silently still. It seemed ludicrous to me that they were going to the lengths they were to punish me. They conducted and concluded a "fact-finding" inquiry into my deployment. They never talked to me, my crew, or the many co-workers who witnessed the meals and staff interactions during the deployment. They never talked to the other vegans, vegetarians, and celiacs on the tour. The Ministry is obviously very thorough and pragmatic in its fact-finding missions.

They decided I was at fault for unprofessionalism—under the grounds of breaking the Workplace Discrimination and Harassment Policy (WDHP) and the Workplace Violence Policy (WVP).

The irony is not lost on me.

Using accusations of discrimination to legitimize discriminating against me.

So, in retrospect, I'm glad they punished me for my ethical veganism. If they hadn't, I might still be their employee.

(I encourage anyone who wants to know more minute details of the entire ordeal, which became my application to the HRTO in 2018, to read it at the website provided in the endotes.[75])

My punishment was three unpaid days suspension, and a suspension from performing my duties outside Ontario for the remainder of the 2017 season and the entirety of the 2018 season. Further, the whole ordeal was to be put on my permanent record. I was basically being grounded, with extreme prejudice.

Not only was this embarrassing, but out-of-province deployments are a huge fiscal boost to a seasonal position with outdated and underfunded remuneration. My punishment was a destroyed reputation and then a huge attempt at hitting my wallet for a season and a half.

And really, I just couldn't understand why.

I couldn't understand what I had done wrong. How could I be at fault? What had I done?

I still don't understand. My confusion is only compounded when you break it down and ask the players involved: Is this an acceptable meal? No. Okay. So why do I keep having to go through this every day? Why do I keep having to speak up and address this as a problem if everyone seems aware and in agreement that it's wrong? Every day.

I don't understand how people can eat animals. But I *really* can't understand how it's a problem for them if I don't.

And so, the reality that everyone just wanted it—me—ethical veganism—to just go away started to sink in.

I lost all faith in my employer. They didn't protect me. They didn't support me when I was doing my job to the highest level of professionalism, risking my health and life day in and day out. They couldn't provide me with grub that didn't include death and suffering when they said they would? Unacceptable. And then I'm punished because I stand up for myself? When everyone is agreeing with me that it's wrong the whole time? Nonsensical. I don't know what they expected me to do.

My professional life was destroyed. I used to be seen as excellent at my job—credible. Someone you would want to have working on a fire or deployment. I followed protocol. I have trained many firefighters—so many rookies learned the ropes with me. And my employer just hung me out to dry.

And then punished me for it.

A depression started to sink in like thick black smoke around me as the majority of forest firefighting staff across the province accepted the rumors and jumped on the bullying bandwagon. A conglomeration of amplified hate was being hurled at me in my workplace. All the time.

You could go crazy trying to figure out why.

I reached out to my local union representative while I was en route from BC back to Ontario. I had written everything that had occurred during the deployment on my ride from the camp to the airport and on my flights over those days: meals, interactions, broken promises, the explanation that my "attitude" was the rationale for my expulsion, and the harrowing treatment at the hands of my A-rep.

Everyone that I shared the events with confirmed they thought what had happened to me was wrong. The director of the Ministry responded with shock and sympathy. And then he quickly changed his tune and suggested dealing with "the situation" through the union would be best. Going to a higher level still, I got the same response: first shock and sympathy, and then stubborn silence and a finger in the direction of union representation.

My union representative was putting together the grievance form, but he, and everyone else seemed confused over "on what grounds" discrimination had occurred.

For those of you who don't know, our "human rights" aren't as simple—or as agreed-upon—as you might assume.

As with everything in humanity, there are *rules*.

And ethical veganism falls into a grey zone of these rules.

Needless to say, by fall of 2018 I knew my union was about as useful as a water gun on a rank five wildfire.

My frustration brewed over the credibility, preparation, and conviction of my union to actually defend me against my employer.

I pulled back the curtain on this giant conglomerate: a farce of worker representation. Funnelling money in and producing bureaucracy and nugatory positions. It is so sad that the thousands of dollars I had been forced to donate to this entity was doing so little for me, providing no credibility in my time of need.

I knew I needed better representation. Professional representation.

I needed to formally concede my grievance with the union to allow for legal representation to present my case before the HRTO.

And so I did.

WHAT'S CREED GOT TO DO WITH IT?

Sometimes, the biggest connections seem so small and insignificant when they happen.

It was October of 2017, a few months after I had been sent home from the BC tour and thus after the start of my punishment and the grievance process with my union.

I had been laid off for the season, and I was internet-sleuthing my favorite subject as of late: vegan human rights.

The International Vegan Rights Association (IVRA) was an obvious landing pad.

As international as they are, they had no Canadian representative at the time, and thus no "local" contact for me to bounce my grievance off.

Regardless of—or perhaps because of—this, I reached out to Jeanette Rowley, the founder and director of the Association, to connect.

Given that I had no legal background or knowledge, she wondered how useful I could be to the organization as a Canadian representative. I agreed that I was not an expert, but I explained my recent experience to more or less bolster myself as an ally.

This was far more intriguing to the IVRA.

Jeanette put me in touch with the director of Animal Justice, Camille Labchuk, here in Canada.

Camille also found my situation very intriguing.

The IVRA and Animal Justice agreed: they wanted to help.

Animal Justice connected with the law firm Ross and McBride, whose specialty is human rights law. Then the Animal Justice team set up my GoFundMe to raise the funds needed for such an endeavor. Ross and McBride agreed to take on the case.

Over the years, many junior lawyers were attached to my case, worked with me, and then moved on. Wade Poziomka would be the lead lawyer attached to the case from start to present.

And so I entered the world of litigation; a begrudging delegate to the vegan campaign. An unlikely ambassador hoping to win this case for ethical vegans everywhere, and thus for *animals* everywhere.

I've never thought I can change the world. It seems like such a daunting, consuming task. I just want to do my thing. See as much of the world as I can and have some fun while I do that. All without hurting anyone. I always knew I could see the world without hurting or killing anyone. Honestly, I couldn't imagine much more beyond that. Beyond doing "my bit."

I never thought that a conflict against that—against me—would force me into a position where I had to do something like this: to try to make a change.

As with Jeanette at the IVRA, I began by outlining all the events that took place on the deployment in Williams Lake to Camille and then to Wade. I am blessed that I wrote everything down when I did—in near real-time—as the details would be reviewed over and over. Everyone wants to paraphrase or literally change the events, and again, I appreciate having my detailed documentation. I know what happened to me. I know what was happening to all the vegans and vegetarians (and somehow the celiacs) at that basecamp for the duration of my deployment.

I aided in the writing and revising of my application to the HRTO, stating that my employer discriminated against me under the Ontario Human Rights Code. We had to choose the "ground" under which the discrimination occurred. We chose the ground of "Creed" in May 2018.

Ethical veganism is in a grey zone for a "ground" or rule under which our human rights are protected. To push it out of the grey zone and into the light, we had to quantify it under an existing ground.

"Creed" seems easily identifiable as religion, but the reason it's covered separately under the Ontario and Canadian Human Rights Code is that a creed can go beyond the boundaries of religion as long as it is represented by these annotations:

A creed:

- Is sincerely, freely, and deeply held.
- Is integrally linked to a person's self-definition and spiritual fulfilment.
- Is a particular, comprehensive, and overarching system of belief that govern one's conduct and practices.
- Addresses ultimate questions of human existence, including ideas about life, purpose, death, and the existence or non-existence of a creator and/or a higher or different order of existence.
- Has some "nexus" or connection to an organization or community that professes a shared system of belief.

Any ethical vegan can relate to these annotations, head nodding, and feel a connection—a sense of belonging; maybe even acceptance.

Now we needed the tribunal to agree that ethical veganism is a creed and thus covered as a human right under the Human Rights Code.

It would be a precedent-setting case.

If we won.

ENTER INTO "THE PROCESS"

Paperwork in the form of responses and applications goes back and forth between the lawyers for the Ministry ("The Crown") and mine ("The Applicant") and the HRTO. The timelines seem so far away for each submission.

Patience is a virtue. Even if you don't have it, you still have to wait.

It seems that justice is not only blind, but she takes her sweet time to make up her mind as well.

The HRTO timeline does not "normally" take this long—indeed, it's a point in their mission statement: "The HRTO resolves claims of discrimination and harassment brought under the *Human Rights Code* in a fair, just, and timely way."

But there was something going on in the background that would potentially undermine this statement.

In June 2018, a provincial Conservative government had been voted into office, a month after we submitted our application to the HRTO. As soon as the new premier took office, monkey wrenches were hurled at my case with unrelenting accuracy.[76]

It took a year before a brief mini-media whirlwind, from May 2019 until about July, made my case into headlines around the world. And then things got quiet.

And slow.

Huge swathes of time passed where I heard nothing. Some days, I even managed to forget I was in this "precedent-setting" case altogether. That I had been discriminated against by my employer; the employer that I still went in and risked my health and life for on a daily basis.

I was allowed to resume out-of-province deployments in 2019—still with no resolution from the HRTO from the 2017 events.

It was not until February 2020 that a mediation with an HRTO mediator finally happened.

I was deep in the Sahara Desert when the mediation occurred. I connected across the globe from the quiet, sandy streets of the Siwa Oasis.

All parties knew an agreement would not be reached. But we had to go through the steps.

It's called "the process."

All the applications, responses, responses to responses. The responses to the responses' responses! It was all part of "the process." With "right honourable this" and "respectfully that." Again, the deadlines between these documents seemed achingly long.

The mediation lasted hours, using an array of communication venues across Canada and the globe.

No resolution occurred. The mediator said the case would go to the next step: the hearing.

No dates were given.

There was a vague assurance that the next part of "the process" would transpire. Without much else, I was astonished that it had taken nearly two years to get to this preliminary stage. Nothing had really happened. Just stages in the process.

Before all parties left the virtual meeting, the mediator spoke directly to me, saying I should consider returning to Canadian soil before I might not be able to.

"I'm watching the situation," I replied, making reference to a novel virus that was making headlines on every media outlet.

A month later, the world changed.

In March 2020, I was standing in the queue to board my flight at Cairo International Airport, a week earlier than my original scheduled flight. With desert sand still invading most crevices of my shoes, I took slow, shuffling steps with the masses, trying to "get somewhere" before we couldn't. It was the first time I started to see pandemic garbage in the form of masks and gloves. I stared at a discarded mask littering the polished floor of the departures lounge as we passengers slowly embarked the plane. I knew that this, whatever "this" would be, couldn't possibly be good for the case.

The mediator was right—I needed to get home sooner rather than later. Waiting those few extra days could have gotten me marooned. The border I had crossed just a few weeks earlier was now closed. I had to get home while I could.

Within days of my landing back in Toronto, in mid-March of 2020, the pandemic officially began shutting the world down. As borders were closed, curfews were instated, and martial law became commonplace, I marvelled at the thought that I had been inside one of the Great Pyramids of Giza a few days earlier.

Equally marvellous: everything had simply shut down.

Work. Government. Transportation.

Even *justice* had shut down.

Huge swathes of time now passed, and I got no update on the case. The pandemic, coupled with the Conservative government continuing its slash-and-burn tactics on the HRTO, meant that sometimes as long as nine months would transpire without any word whatsoever.

Was this still part of "the process"?

PULLING BACK THE CURTAIN

I must preface this statement with my previous belief in the Canadian legal system, in Canadian Justice—and its inherent infallibility. I believed law speech or speak to be a complicated, untouchable affair controlled and navigated by lawyers and judges who have spent so much time in school and in practice. It's not until you are entrenched in the documentation—proofreading pages and pages with points and sub-paragraphs and labels instead of names—that you realize something you have already realized before.

Pulling back the curtain, you have the epiphany that your parents are just people; they aren't infallible, and they make mistakes. They make bad decisions sometimes. Similarly, I deduced that the legal system is also made up of "just people"—not necessarily *just* people.

These people, however, do have their own language and intricate rituals and vernaculars that most laypeople do not understand.

Without alienating the lawyers and judges out there who are fighting for justice (of whom there are many), I must say that the legal system is rife with posturing and time-consuming pompous formalities, ultimately giving those in control more respect and reverence than necessary. I understand the need for formalities, deadlines; your response to the response, submissions of evidence, and so on. But all the posturing and unrealistic timelines drag out these litigations and cost so much money. The dates for these deadlines seem arbitrary and act as postponements, delays, and extensions that are generously welcomed; a form of active procrastination. All of which just costs more money.

And draws out justice.

Justice is not available to those without money. Nor time. Nor the perseverance to continue from beginning to end. I think the HRTO knows this. The "justice" system knows this. It's a tactic used by the system to "lighten the load" of cases; simply by making them unaffordable or so painful to continue that people simply do give up and walk away. Not that walking away after trying so hard is simple.

The time delay itself is one problem. But from it, other problems are born.

It was early 2022 when the latest junior lawyer to work on my case wanted to work with me on an update to the application. It had now been four years since the original submission and over two years since our official mediation.

We still had no hearing date and no relevant communication from the HRTO of any kind since the mediation, really.

Since nothing had changed *vis-à-vis* ethical veganism discrimination in my workplace, the update would be an amendment to the application, either as an extension or a new application.

This is one of the major instances that rang alarm bells for me and shattered my confidence in the HRTO and "the process" itself.

I had been instructed to document ongoing discrimination by way of what was offered to me as meals while I continued my career with the Ministry.

This was extremely distressing. I was expected to knowingly accept meals that had animals in them for the sake of documentation, to put that forward as evidence in an application amendment to show ongoing discrimination, when no one was addressing the original discrimination from the 2017 incidents.

It was preposterous.

I argued regularly with my counsel that I didn't want to be a part of it anymore. If there was any way I could knowingly extract myself from the stress at work, I would rather do that than document otherwise. With my existing reputation, it only furthered the extent of discrimination in my workplace. And the delays with the HRTO made everything worse.

Now I was being instructed that if I didn't submit documentation of continuing discrimination on an annual basis to the HRTO, the documentation itself would be inadmissible.

I couldn't believe what I was hearing.

This inherently flawed instruction from the HRTO meant only one thing to me: the HRTO knew and was aware of discrimination or possible discrimination that was occurring and ongoing. It was not only cognizant of this, but was further expecting me to endure it, to document it, and to submit this documentation within an annual deadline—or else it would not take it into consideration as evidence. How long did they expect me to do this without a resolution to the submitted 2018 application? And the annual deadline could only insinuate the expectation this case would go unresolved for several years. I can't help but feel that the HRTO is now complicit in the discrimination.

Just as we finalized the second application, the HRTO dropped a bombshell on the case. They required proof that our case was worth hearing, or else it would be dismissed in its entirety.

We had already gone through mediation with an HRTO mediator. We already had loads of documentation going back and forth. We were already in "the process." A case had already been established; it had just stagnated. And it had stagnated at the hands of the HRTO. How could stagnation equal irrelevance? They were saying they wanted documentation of discrimination on an annual basis, but now they were saying they didn't know why this case was before them. The HRTO had already recognized that "something" had occurred which needed their intervention. Why now, after the case had been sitting on the shelf for years, were we being asked to prove relevance again? Were we to submit the original documentation all over again? Perhaps with highlighter or big arrows at certain sections?

Our timeline was unnecessarily short—a fortnight. After so many years, this also comes across quite unseemly. We needed to scramble to reproduce documents and legitimize our case, or else it would be thrown out. Emphasized in this request from the HRTO was an explicit statement that the Ministry needed to provide nothing at this time.

My faith in the justice system continued on its downward trajectory.

My lawyers told me they were including a document stating how inappropriate this situation was. With legal vernacular—all delicately tiptoeing around egos and exemplifying respect for the system—we needed to voice to the deciding authority of Ontario justice that this situation was wrong and insulting.

The credibility of the omnipotent framework of the tribunal was crumbling before me.

Ross and McBride presented the existing documentation justifying our original application before the tribunal, along with the delicately worded "what's your damage?" letter regarding the inappropriateness of their request for such documentation. The separate, new application (to be heard with the existing one), which cited evidence of continued discrimination from 2018 to 2022 under the same grounds as the 2018 application, was also ready.

All three documents were submitted within the fortnight timeline the tribunal gave us to justify a case they already knew needed a hearing.

Despite the fervor and the acute deadline given by the tribunal, we were met with silence.

And the silence continued. We reached out in the months that followed.

They confirmed they had received all the documentation.

Silence.

Finally, September 12th, 2023, would be the hearing date for my case. It would be virtual.

As we prepared, I pulled back the curtain even further. I learned that arbitrators on the tribunal can be conservative or liberal. This, in itself, is a very problematic conundrum.

An oxymoron.

I knew there was such a thing in the American system, even on the so-called Supreme Court. But here in Canada?—part of the Commonwealth?—it seems so bizarre, so contradictory.

How can a judicial arbitrator sway one way or another?

Shouldn't judgment come from rationally acquiring all the information and evidence in a case and providing a just decision on the basis of that research?

How can there be predisposition in justice? Why would the framework exist in the first place?

Knowing what outcome your case will have based solely on the person presiding seems like such a waste of time.

Canadians—all citizens—should be aware that justice has a side. Justice is skewed because it relies on humans to make these judgments on justice.

SEARCHING FOR THE COAST GUARD

For brief moments, there has been support and representation. The International Vegan Rights Alliance, Animal Justice, and Ross and McBride have been unwavering supporters.

I spoke at the Canadian Animal Law Conference in 2019. Everyone was thinking we were so close to a decision.

I gave impromptu interviews here and there.

I became wary of these: of how the media will skew inflection in words to tell the story they want, not necessarily the truth. It is difficult to gain access to fundamentally neutral news outlets, even here in Canada.

Impacts from my litigation included direct and constant discrimination in the workplace and an intensity of belittlement, rumors, and horrible treatment from colleagues. The snail's pace of the process only provided more room for my mistreatment because no one had officially agreed that what had happened to me was wrong. This was a green light for the treatment to continue.

The years from 2018 onward were an extremely rough time of brutal discrimination, almost directly resulting from the HRTO application—and maybe because it was unresolved for so long.

Mistreatment due to my ethical veganism continued unabated as it had before 2017, only now it was louder.

Other impacts were more tedious. Losing faith in my employer, who just happened to be my government, was a hard reality to face. Continuing to work for them became more and more unacceptable. Continuing to pay into a union that didn't assist me was unacceptable as well.

We had our say on September 12th, 2023.

The fact that we were arguing our case before a relatively new adjudicator appointed by the chugging machine of a conservative provincial government did not sit well with me. The hearing lasted most of the day.

I spoke. My expert witnesses spoke.

I was disappointed with the distracted detachment created by the hearing being virtual. I felt speakers lost their emphasis and power. The screens did not capture the weight of the wait to get us all there on that day. The issues didn't command the same respect or attention as they would have if we had all actually been sitting in a room.

When we finished for the day, it was back to waiting. We were all so good at it by now, but still, it seemed achingly slow.

On November 29th, I woke up and made coffee. I began my morning routine and noticed the subject line of an email. I sat down and read the nine-page decision from the HRTO adjudicator.

I had lost.

After five and a half years. So much waiting. So much mistreatment. And apparently, there had never been discrimination.

During this same timeline, very similar—if not identical—cases arising over ethical vegan human rights appeared across the world. Those cases began *after* and were resolved *before* my case was even heard here in Canada. Those other cases were decided in favor of ethical veganism being recognized as a human right. It made this decision from the HRTO more difficult to accept.

It's so ignorant.

And predictable.

And so, this will continue.

All my documents and correspondence will continue to pile up. I was hoping to have a cathartic—and controlled—bonfire with them, but instead, I will retain them. For there will be more trudging along and discovering new avenues of "the process."

Vindication after the events of 2017—let alone my fifteen-year career as a forest firefighter—is still awaited.

With 20–20 Hindsight-brand glasses, I can say now I should have done things differently. After the events at the basecamp in Williams Lake, I should have quit my position immediately upon my return to Kenora. No one should be treated like I was, and I shouldn't have continued to work for them after those events. I should have let go of the Ministry and the umbrella of the Crown and sought a new career; I should have moved on with my life. I should not have listened to my union telling me I had a better chance of winning if I remained an employee. I should have continued with the grievance, but also, I should have quit. Staying in fire and putting my faith in the hands of the union and then the HRTO to right those wrongs started a journey that only led to prolonged misery and mistreatment.

All for not wanting to kill anyone.

I want to assist the vegan movement. I tried to help. I gave six years of my life to trying to litigate for change. But it's not enough.

And it's not over. Just like an exasperated Lisa Simpson asks Homer:"I mean, if you're the police, who will police the police?"Homer just shrugs: "Coast guard?"So here I stand, searching for the coast guard.Reaching out to my union was futile. Reaching out to the HRTO seemed to be more of an exacerbating problem than a solution.

I have been desperately looking around with my hands up, imploring someone—anyone—with common sense to recognize how wrong something is and do something about it.

Who do you turn to when you have received this response from Ontario's highest level of justice for human rights?

It is difficult to accept and understand.

This decision is a missed opportunity for Canada to recognize and legislate for a sustainable and more peaceful future. We can see other legal decisions across the country that are negatively impacting nonhuman animals and the humans who are advocating for them. It seems that in every opportunity Canada is given to make the world a better place for non-human animals, it consciously chooses the opposite.

In October 2022, two animal rights activists, Amy Sorano and Nick Schafer (part of the "Excelsior Four"), were found guilty of breaking and entering and mischief after obtaining and sharing video proof of obscene, torturous treatment of pigs at the "Excelsior Hog Farm" in BC. The "farm" itself did not bear any repercussions for the blatant animal abuse these activists exposed.

In March of 2023, the driver of a lorry that killed animal rights activist Regan Russell in 2020 was sentenced to a year's probation and a $2,000 fine. The life of an ethical vegan animal rights activist seems to have little value in the Canadian judicial system.

Bill C-275 passed another vote toward full implementation in the federal government at almost the exact same time that I received the decision from the HRTO on my case. This legislation imposes severe punishments and limitations upon anyone exposing or getting near the nonhuman animal industries across Canada. These punishments are far more severe than those imposed on the untouchable mega-industries found guilty of any animal abuses. Now animal abuse will be nearly impossible to uncover and is controlled and regulated by those in the "industry" itself. The government should be promoting more transparency and communication between these industries that "feed" the country, but instead, it does the opposite.

The protection and strengthening of nonhuman animal institutions in Canada—via subsidies, outright legislation, and promoting blatant propaganda (the Canadian food guide)—by the Canadian government illustrates obvious bias.

Not recognizing attempts to live in greater harmony with this world as a human right is so strange. So disingenuous of a country to its citizens, especially now—and by Canada, of all countries.

We have applied to the HRTO for a judicial review via a reconsideration, basically appealing this decision. A judicial review will have more than one person making the decision.

It's all part of "the process."

Whatever we have to do. Whatever I have to do. But I'm tired.

How am I supposed to have faith in my country after these events? In justice? In humanity? It all seems so unnecessary and brutal and ridiculous. To live in a country where it has been deemed that ethical veganism is NOT my human right makes me feel unwelcome. Like I don't belong here.

All for not wanting to kill anyone.

NOTES

1. The genie is out of the bottle. The indirect reach of the campaign for vegan rights is unknown. Vegans defending their rights are no longer necessarily linked to the campaign or members of the campaign's legal network. Given the website statistics of the former IVRA, which gave detailed information about the number of visits from different countries around the world, it can only be assumed that there is a degree of ongoing indirect influence.

2. The IVRA collaborated with a number of associates who were unable to be publicly associated with the IVRA or be publicly profiled for various "real-world" reasons: for example, negative stereotyping, discomfort in social settings, and employment reasons, such as negative professional or personal consequences. This is still the situation in 2024.

3. Crossland Employment Solicitors, "Nearly Half of Vegans Feel Discriminated Against at Work," May 9, 2019, accessed October 3, 2023, https://www.crosslandsolicitors.com/site/hr-hub/nearly-half-of-vegans-feel-discriminated-against-at-work. The Vegan Society, "The Results are In: Here's What Canadian Vegans Said in Our Vegan Rights Survey," January 8, 2020, accessed October 3, 2023, https://www.vegansociety.com/get-involved/international-rights-network/international-rights-network-blog/results-are-here%E2%80%99s-what-canadian-vegans-said-our-vegan-rights-survey. Go Vegan Scotland, "Results of Survey on Vegan Provision in Scotland," 2017, accessed October 3, 2023, https://docs.wixstatic.com/ugd/d95b36_f4bccc9845854533ba8aea3cf8e590b2.pdf.

4. See for example, Petr Kudelka, "Vegan Rights," CARE-2017, *YouTube*, video, accessed November 21, 2023, https://www.youtube.com/watch?v=d1FgBX9W6Tk.

5. Monidiper Fouzder, "Vegan Challenges Discriminatory Job Ad," *The Law Society Gazette*, July 3, 2017, accessed October 2, 2023, https://www.lawgazette.co.uk/lawyer-in-the-news/vegan-challenges-discriminatory-job-ad/5061773.article.

6. James Tennent, "Italian Vegans Outraged over Law that Could Jail Parents for Imposing Diet on Children, "*International Business Times*, August 16, 2016, accessed October 2, 2023, https://www.ibtimes.co.uk/italian-vegans-outraged-over-law-that-could-jail-parents-imposing-diet-children-1576323.

7. Lizzie Dearden, "Italy's Proposed Law to Jail Vegan Parents for up to Four Years Criticised as 'Discriminatory' Attack on Human Rights," *The Independent*, August 16, 2016, accessed October 2, 2023, https://www.independent.co.uk/news

/world/europe/italy-s-proposed-law-to-jail-vegan-parents-for-up-to-four-years-criticised-as-discriminatory-attack-on-human-rights-a7193496.html.

8. The Local Italy, "Backlash over Italy's Proposal to Punish Vegan Parents," August 15, 2016, accessed October 2, 2023, https://www.thelocal.it/20160819/vegans-protest-italys-unfair-law-proposal-parents-backlash.

9. Isaac Stanley-Becker, "Veganism? His 'creed.' Access to vegan food? This firefighter claims it's his human right," *The Washington Post*, May 22, 2019, accessed October 3, 2023, https://www.washingtonpost.com/nation/2019/05/22/vegan-firefighter-adam-knauff-canada-human-rights/.

10. Miranda Larbie, "The Vegan Society Launches a Book of Nutritional Advice for Vegan Prisoners," Monday, July 9, 2018, accessed October 3, 2023, https://metro.co.uk/2018/07/09/vegan-society-launches-book-nutritional-advice-vegan-prisoners-7694569/.

11. Vegconomist, "Lawyers Gather at Conference to Discuss Vegan Rights," May 31, 2019, accessed October 3, 2023, https://vegconomist.com/society/lawyers-gather-at-conference-to-discuss-vegan-rights/.

12. Justine Butler, "Vegan Hospital Food: Is it a Basic Human Right?," *Vegan Food and Living* (October 17, 2018), accessed October 3, 2023, https://www.veganfoodandliving.com/features/vegan-hospital-food-is-it-a-basic-human-right/

13. The IVRA, Written Evidence from The Vegan Society and The International Vegan Rights Alliance (HRB0019), October 2016, accessed October 2, 2023, https://committees.parliament.uk/writtenevidence/73344/html/.

14. Jeanette Rowley, "What Does Brexit Mean for Vegetarians and Vegans," December 6, 2016, accessed October 2, 2023, https://vegappg.org.uk/. See also, "Is it time for a legal definition of veganism?" https://vegappg.org.uk/wp-content/uploads/2018/05/Minutes.pdf, and Vegetarian for Life, "Is it Time for a Legal Definition of Veganism," July 19, 2018, accessed October 3, 2023, https://vegetarianforlife.org.uk/blog/post/is-it-time-for-a-legal-definition-of-veganism.

15. See, for example, Oscar Horta, "Discrimination Against Vegans," *Res Publica* 24 (2018), 359–373, accessed October 3, 2023, https://link.springer.com/article/10.1007/s11158-017-9356–3.

16. Sarah Fuller, Dr Graeme O'Connor, Heather Russell, and Sarah Elder, in association with the BDA (The Association of UK Dietitians) Mental Health Specialist Group, "Practice Guidance: Veganism and Eating Disorders," ResearchGate, July 2019, accessed October 3, 2023. https://www.researchgate.net/publication/334792429_Practice_Guidance_Veganism_and_Eating_Disorders.

17. The Vegan Society, "Catering for Everyone: Guide for Vegan Prisoners," September 4, 2018, accessed October 3, 2023, https://www.vegansociety.com/sites/default/files/C4E_12pp%20Booklet_SPREADS.pdf.

18. The Vegan Society, "Vegan-Inclusive Education," https://www.vegansociety.com/lifestyle/vegan-inclusive-education.

19. In 2019, there were endless complaints from parents about the lack of vegan food options on school menus. In 2023, The Vegan Society research revealed that most councils do now provide vegan food. The Society's catering campaign included information provided by the IVRA from 2018. However, there is still work to do.

See, The Vegan Society, "Catering for Everyone," accessed October 21, 2023, https://www.vegansociety.com/get-involved/campaigns/catering-everyone.

20. MLP Law, "Are Vegans Protected From Discrimination?" October 4, 2018, accessed October 3, 2023, https://www.mlplaw.co.uk/are-vegans-protected-from-discrimination/. Gareth Dando, "Employment Tribunal Finds that Ethical Veganism is a Protected Characteristic," Ramsdens Blog, January 6, 2020, accessed October 3, 2023, https://www.ramsdens.co.uk/blog/employment-tribunal-finds-ethical-veganism-protected-characteristic. Amy Wren, "Sacked Vegan Claims Discrimination—a "Landmark Case"?" Farrer & Co, Blog, December 14, 2018, accessed October 3, 2023, https://www.farrer.co.uk/news-and-insights/blogs/sacked-vegan-claims-discrimination---a-landmark-case/. Slater and Gordon, "Ethical Veganism as a Protected Philosophical Belief," December 20, 2019, updated January 3, 2020, accessed October 3, 2023, https://www.slatergordon.co.uk/newsroom/ethical-veganism/.

21. Tania De Bruler, "Are You A Vegan in the Workplace? Do you know your rights?" *LinkedIn*, June 20, 2018, accessed October 3 2023, https://www.linkedin.com/pulse/you-vegan-workplace-do-know-your-rights-tania-de-bruler-mcipd/.

22. Jordi Casamitjana, "The Vegan Rights Movement is Happening Now!" *UnchainedTV*, February 24, 2021, accessed October 3, 2023, https://unchainedtv.com/2021/02/24/the-vegan-rights-movement-is-happening-now/.

23. Go Vegan World, for example, https://goveganworld.com/international-vegan-rights/.

24. Including support from Professor Gary Francione.

25. The Vegan Society, "International Rights Network Launches at a Vegan Rights Conference," May 31, 2019, accessed October 3, 2023, https://www.vegansociety.com/whats-new/news/international-rights-network-launches-vegan-rights-conference. See, also, interest on Reddit, "The International Vegan Rights Alliance (IVRA) Has Now Been Absorbed into The Vegan Society as 'The Vegan Society's International Rights Network'," accessed December 13, 2023, https://www.reddit.com/r/VeganRights/comments/cu6odb/the_international_vegan_rights_alliance_ivra_has/.

26. https://www.vegansociety.com/about-us/international-rights-network/international-rights-network-blog/international-rights-network-conference-milan-2019.

27. https://issuu.com/vegan_society/docs/2019_issue_3_single_pages.

28. The Vegan Society, "Vegan Student Forced to 'Study Unit on Farming or Fail' Wins Case Against College," April 12, 2021, accessed October 3, 2023, https://www.vegansociety.com/news/news/vegan-student-forced-%E2%80%98study-unit-farming-or-fail%E2%80%99-wins-case-against-college.

29. The Vegan Society, "Primary School Forced to Change 'Cow's Milk or Water' Rule after Vegan Dad Fights Discriminatory Policy," June 24, 2021, accessed July 20, 2023, https://www.vegansociety.com/news/news/primary-school-forced-change-cows-milk-or-water-rule-after-vegan-dad-fights-discriminatory-policy.

30. https://www.vegansociety.com/international-rights-conference-2022/international-rights-conference-2022/international-rights-conference-2020.

31. https://www.vegansociety.com/get-involved/international-rights-network/international-rights-conference-2022.

32. Information was supplied to the author in a meeting with the Diversity Inclusion Cohesion and Equality (DICE) Lead for a UK regional fire service.

33. https://www.vegansociety.com/sites/default/files/uploads/downloads/Legal%20Opinion%20Nursery%20Milk.pdf.

34. Scottish Government. "Scottish Milk and Healthy Snack Scheme: Statutory Guidance." https://www.gov.scot/publications/scottish-milk-healthy-snack-scheme-statutory-guidance-local-authorities-participating-registered-day-care-settings/. Accessed September 1, 2023.

35. See, for example, the work of Maureen O'Sullivan, The Vegan Society's Research Network, https://www.vegansociety.com/get-involved/research/researcher-network/dr-maureen-osullivan

36. See, for example, The Vegan Society, "Veganism in the Workplace APPG," *YouTube*, video, September 17, 2020, accessed October 3, 2023, https://www.youtube.com/watch?v=V1VfIr0yRgA.

37. This does not mean that employees were to be vaccinated against their will. The alternative was to be redeployed, if that course of action was at all possible, or to leave their employment.

38. Discrimination cannot be claimed in relation to curriculum content.

39. The requirement stated in *Grainger*, that "[t]he belief must be of a similar cogency or status to a religious belief," is related to the definition of "belief" in earlier equality legislation and was discussed at length in *Grainger* but does not appear in the legal test itself. The "requirement" does not appear to have been discussed in cases involving vegans following *Grainger.*

40. *Casamitjana Costa v. The League Against Cruel Sports*, [2020] UK ET 3331129/2018.

Para. 13.

41. See *Casamitjana*, para. 34.

42. See Casamitjana, para. 36.

43. *Ms. S Free Miles v. The Royal Veterinary College,* [2022] UK ET 2206733/2020.

44. See *Ms. S Free Miles,* paras. 2.1 and 18.

45. See *Ms. S Free Miles,* para. 65.

46. See *Ms. S Free Miles,* para. 64.

47. *Mr. E McClung v. Doosan Babcock Ltd and others,* [2022] UK ET 4110538/2019.

48. *Mr. E McClung*, para. 79.

49. Its influence is explained in chapter 2.

50. On file with the author.

51. The research at the time included news reports and legal cases, some of which were later discussed in Jeanette Rowley, *Towards a Vegan Jurisprudence: The Need for a Reorientation of Human Rights* (PhD diss., 2017; London: Lexington Books, 2020).

52. For previous information on veganism and law from the United States of America, Canada, Portugal, France, Germany, the UK, and Italy, see Jeanette Rowley and Carlo Prisco, eds., *Law and Veganism: International Perspectives on the Human Right to Freedom of Conscience* (London: Lexington Books, 2022).

53. Christopher Harress, "Vegan Soldier Rejected by Swiss Army for Refusing to Wear Leather Boots," *International Business Times*, January 26, 2016, accessed

August 7, 2023, https://www.ibtimes.com/vegan-soldier-rejected-swiss-army-refusing-wear-leather-boots-2280206.

54. Charlotte England, "Vegan Allowed to Serve in Swiss Army in Landmark Case," *The Independent*, October 25, 2016, accessed August 7, 2023, https://www.independent.co.uk/news/world/europe/switzerland-vegan-serve-swiss-army-landmark-case-a7379621.html.

55. *G.K. and A.S. v. Switzerland*, (communicated), App Nos. 55299/20 and 31515/22, Eur. Ct. H.R. The "communicated" cases can be found at https://hudoc.echr.coe.int/#{%22fulltext%22:[%22vegan%22],%22itemid%22:[%22002-13855%22]}. The page has links to Swiss Federal Court judgments.

56. See for example, Carlo Prisco, "Veganism and Law in Italy," in *Law and Veganism: International Perspectives on the Human Right to Freedom of Conscience*, edited by Jeanette Rowley and Carlo Prisco, 91–105 (London: Lexington Books, 2022).

57. LAV, "Bologna: the Teacher has the Right to the Vegan Meal," *LAV*, April 14, 2020, accessed August 9, 2023, https://www.lav.it/news/bologna-maestra-ha-diritto-al-pasto-vegano.

58. Giudice Del Lavoro—Tribunale Di Bologna—Sentenza N. 2359/2020 Del 9 Aprile 2020. "*Occorre Rilevare Che Il Regime Alimentare Vegano Appare Determinato Da Convinzioni Di Natura Filosofica E/O Religiosa Che Appaiono Meritevoli Di tutela nell'ambito di ampio riconoscimento del diritto alla libertà di Firmato di pensiero riconosciuto dalla Costituzione italiana.*"

59. For example, see Ralf Müller-Amenitsch, "Vegan Legal Issues in Germany," in *Law and Veganism: International Perspectives on the Human Right to Freedom of Conscience,* edited by Jeanette Rowley and Carlo Prisco, 71–89 (London: Lexington Books, 2022).

60. *VG Münster*[Verwaltungsgericht Münster], Urteil [Judgment] of February 9, 2022, Case No. 5 K 2576/20, openJur 2022, 3746 (Germany).

61. *VG Münster*, para. 51.

62. *VG Münster,* para. 55.

63. *VG Münster,* para. 63.

64. *VG Münster,* para. 64.

65. *VG Münster,* para. 65.

66. See Dr Vera Christopeit, "Success is Relative—and Veganism is a Human Right," PETA Blog, August 17, 2022, accessed November 18, 2023, https://tierrechtsblog.de/deutschland/vgmuenster-veganismus-art4gg/.

67. Marie Laffineur-Pauchet, "The Growth of Veganism in France," in *Law and Veganism: International Perspectives on the Human Right to Freedom of Conscience*, eds. Jeanette Rowley and Carlo Prisco, 143–168 (London: Lexington Books, 2022).

68. Astrid Prevost, "It's All About Food- Jeanette Rowley, PhD; Astrid Prevost; Tamara Bedić, Esq., Vegan Discrimination Cases, Part 2," *It's All About Food.* Hosted by Caryn Hartglass, Progressive Radio Network, October 4, 2023, accessed November 18, 2023, https://itsallaboutfood.podbean.com/e/it-s-all-about-food-jeanette-rowley-phd-astrid-prevost-tamara-bedic-esq-vegan-discrimination-cases-part-2/.

69. Law report on file with author. See Dansk Vegetarisk Forening, "A Milestone Win: Vegans are Protected by Human Rights, Danish Court Rules," February 12, 2024, accessed February 14, 2024, https://vegetarisk.dk/milestone-win-vegans-are-protected-by-law-danish-court-rules/.

70. Dansk Vegetarisk Forening https://vegetarisk.dk/.

71. Liam Casey, "Vegan Ontario Firefighter Files Human Rights Complaint Over Food Served While Battling B.C. Wildfire," *Global News*, May 21, 2019, accessed August 7, 2023. https://globalnews.ca/news/5299333/vegan-firefighter-human-rights-complaint/. This case was initially referred to the IVRA, was processed according to the mission of the IVRA, and was referred to Camille Labchuk of Animal Justice in Canada. It has been discussed at IVRA conferences, and a chapter about the case was published by Krystal-Anne Roussel and Camille Labchuk, "A Single Black Bean: Discrimination and the Protection of Ethical Vegans in Canada," in *Law and Veganism: International Perspectives on the Human Right to Freedom of Conscience*, eds. Jeanette Rowley and Carlo Prisco, 27–44 (London: Lexington Books, 2022).

72. See Animal Justice, "Human Rights Tribunal of Ontario Rejects Protections for Ethical Vegans," December 11, 2023, accessed December 11, 2023, https://animaljustice.ca/media-releases/human-rights-tribunal-of-ontario-rejects-protections-for-ethical-vegans and report, https://animaljustice.ca/wp-content/uploads/2023/12/2023-HRTO-1729-Knauff-Final-29-Nov-2023.pdf.

73. *Knauff v. Ontario* (Natural Resources and Forestry), 2023 HRTO 1729.

74. Personal correspondence, February 2024.

75. https://www.canadianlawyermag.com/staticcontent/AttachedDocs/Adam%20Knauff.pdf.

76. https://www.theglobeandmail.com/opinion/article-justice-delayed-the-decline-of-the-ontario-human-rights-tribunal-under/.

Conclusion

In bringing this book to a close, the key message is that our mission to protect other animals, bring about animal freedom, grant nonhuman animals rights, facilitate liberation–however we frame our responsibility and duty to other animals—is bound up with the social, political, and legal conditions in which veganism exists. Predominantly, veganism is reviled, and the concerns of vegans are often seen to be trivialized and dismissed. Being vegan in a non-vegan world can and does present difficulties. Political and institutional support for veganism is inadequate, which creates problems and issues for vegans, and domestic legal systems can be resistant to recognizing the legitimate status of vegan convictions under the international human right to freedom of conscience and belief.

As Gary Francione has long insisted, the conditions for other animals are in our hands, and the world can be vegan, but it is us who must create that world. Creating the vegan world does not only depend on vegans advocating for and non-vegans adopting veganism; it also depends on critical assessments, evaluations, and exposés of issues in the "real world," including a critical assessment of the operation and function of law and advocating for top-down support for veganism and vegans. However we choose to frame and discuss the primary human right to freedom of belief or conscience, and however it features in different types of legislation, such as equality law, employment law, law on education, et cetera, we can make use of the protections we have been afforded as human beings to bring our concerns for other animals within the framework of human rights and to challenge the policies and practices that negatively impact our right to practice veganism.

One of the reasons for writing this book was to share knowledge and learning acquired over years of campaigning and advocating for the rights of vegans. It is rare for the issues affecting vegans to be discussed publicly. As already noted, most vegans don't want to be thought of as "making a fuss," they don't look for trouble, they don't want to be engaged in disputes, and they don't want the popular press disregarding their concerns and disrespecting them by misreporting and sensationalizing the issues they face. The vegans who do share their stories publicly are immensely courageous because they are aware that they are vulnerable to ridicule and mockery. Although the number of issues concerning vegans in a wide range of contexts, such as in schools, colleges, and universities, in different employment environments, as consumers of goods and services, in detention or prison, or in hospitals and other health care settings, is high, complaints are necessarily processed behind closed doors and in silence. This is revealing.

In 2012, the campaign for vegan rights was presented in Stream Five at the fifth Equality, Diversity and Inclusion International Conference in Toulouse. The stream title was *Hear Me Roar: Views from the Edge.* The header quote for consideration and reflection was "*Silencing" is "a measure of the exclusion of such an experience from the dominant society and the stories it allows*".[1] It was a stream for papers that "traverse uncharted contexts," that "shift conversations" beyond mainstream thinking, papers that "dared to explore spaces and places inhabited by people whose voices are often silenced or undervalued," including in research. The idea was to provoke "edgy" thinking. The stream's inclusive approach allowed for diverse views, challenging conversations, connections, and openings that embrace complexity, plurality, and messiness in all its forms. We were "dared to engage."

The stream's header quote, under which I presented the idea of vegan rights, never left my mind: "*Silencing" is "a measure of the exclusion of such an experience from the dominant society and the stories it allows.*" A second key message in closing this book, therefore, is that prejudice impacts vegan people much more than we can document. In the dominant "real world" of animal exploitation and prejudice, the issues vegans face, and the reluctant complaints they make, are unreported because vegans are, effectively, silenced. They are silenced by dismissal, mockery, ridicule, contempt, bullying, so-called banter, and disrespect, and made to feel that they and their concerns are unimportant or trivial in comparison to other pressing issues. The function of this silencing is, of course, to invalidate veganism, vegans, and the issues they raise. Regarding the above quote for reflection, in the case of veganism, silencing is a measure of excluding their negative experiences from the range of complaints accepted as valid and legitimate in the dominant society and the stories it allows. This was evident thirteen years ago, when the Draft Code of Practice was published by the UK's Equality and Human Rights Commission, and, despite the progress of the campaign for vegan rights, it remains relevant today. When Vegan Equality Non-Discrimination

(VEND) was formed, its slogan was "Vegan Loud and Proud." Collectively, we are not there yet.

In this book's introduction, I briefly noted the adverse social conditions for vegans. In chapter 1, I explored some of the difficulties vegans face. In chapter 2, I explained how the dedicated campaign for rights created an international body committed to identifying, using, and developing legal measures to protect vegans and support the growth of veganism, and how, through its activities and research, this body provided and disseminated much-needed information to support and build on existing efforts by advocates in different parts of the world. In chapter 3, I explored the validity of veganism in law, the value of using the human right to freedom of conscience and belief, and the development of protection for non-religious beliefs and convictions. In chapter 4, I examined how research and law have been applied to the issues some vegans in the UK have faced, and identified some of the benefits that have resulted. In chapter 5, I noted some of the successes of the dedicated campaign for vegans' rights and the work of the International Vegan Rights Alliance (IVRA), its popularity within the vegan movement, and how the concept of legal rights for vegans gained pace and became entrenched in the animal protection movement.

I have also considered the difficulties, frustrations, and negative impacts associated with accessing justice as vegans.

As can be seen in the case of Adam Knauff, policies and domestic legal systems in the "real world" have gate-keeping functions. They can harbor restrictive interpretations of the human right to freedom of belief and remain resistant to the idea that vegans, as a vulnerable minority in a non-vegan world, need and are entitled to the protection of law.

In Adam's case, the HRTO decided that veganism doesn't offer a perspective on human life that deals with the "big questions" and ruled against recognizing ethical vegans as a creed under the Human Rights Code. Despite historical information about the needs of vegans presented to the Ontario Human Rights Commission by Camille Labchuk, and subsequent policy developments concerning protection for "creed," there was, in the view of the adjudicator, no evidence that veganism "addresses ultimate questions of human existence, including ideas about life, purpose, death, and the existence or non-existence of a Creator and/or a higher or different order of existence." This view is flawed.

An issue for consideration, following this decision, is that protection for religion or belief obviously offers protection for beliefs other than those that are religious. Therefore, a requirement to reference religious principles when providing evidence for the validity of a non-religious belief seems out of step with the protection offered. Regardless of this, however, veganism does, in fact, meet the third element of the legal test because it raises important questions about human existence and what veganism means for our system of justice. This evidence was presented to the tribunal to show that veganism clearly concerns a higher or different order of existence, but, obviously, it was not accepted.

The decision in this case represents a lack of understanding of (or willingness to understand) how ethical veganism is important to discussions about human life. Veganism opposes prejudice, exploitation, and oppression, and looks to an anti-anthropocentric humanity that opposes violence and suffering. It seeks to include, not exclude, other animals in our system of justice in recognition that compassion is an element of, or intrinsic to, human dignity.

As explained in these pages, authoritative guidance from the Human Rights Committee reminds us that the human right to freedom of belief is far-reaching and profound, concerns non-religious beliefs on an equal basis to religious beliefs, and can protect new and emerging beliefs.

Readers will recall that veganism was recognized under the ECHR in 1993, and, since the start of the dedicated campaign for vegan rights, it has been recognized under the constitutions of Germany, Italy, recently in Denmark and under equality law in the UK. I also explained, in chapter 3, that judges at the European Court of Human Rights have acknowledged that defending our human right to freedom of conscience is important because it is directly related to animal protection. It is, therefore, well-established that veganism is a valuable belief contributing to a different order of existence, and the view that veganism does not meet the third element of the criteria for protection in Ontario does not align with the principle laid down in international human rights materials. However, despite being able to do so, the adjudicator stated that they would not look to international law or foreign case law in order to interpret legislation in Ontario. The tribunal's decision not to recognize veganism in law is clearly controversial.

Denying vegans the benefit of legal protection has significant ramifications. First, vegans remain vulnerable to discrimination. Second, access to veganism is constrained and unsupported because it remains difficult to bring about policy changes. Third, the challenge of sustaining veganism persists because vegans have limited access to suitable food and other items that meet their needs. Fourth, and importantly, the mission to acknowledge and establish that protection for nonhuman animals is an issue for human rights is hindered at least and stunted at worst.

This case reminds us of our ongoing struggle, but it emboldens our efforts. Moreover, there is hope. Ralf Müller-Amenitsch has explained the historical restrictive German concept of *weltanschauung*, but, as seen in chapter 4, there are now new judicial understandings recognizing the need for vegans to be protected from unlawful acts and supporting the validity of veganism in law.

Any instances of unfairness toward vegans on account of their valid complaints must be regarded as issues of and for justice because negative responses to their complaints originate in the non-vegan "real world": the world of entrenched animal oppression and prejudice, which can so easily manifest in prejudice toward vegans and dismissal and trivialization of their concerns. In this regard, British equality law makes provision for "protected acts" and prohibits "victimization": the act of treating someone badly or worse because they have raised an issue relating to their equality rights. My view is that we must capitalize on every opportunity provided by law to promote veganism and support and protect vegans. But we must also be critical and creative in our use of law, keeping in mind the limitation that law provides protection for human individuals. Our goal is social, political, and legal transformation, and to get there we must also use whatever legal tools we have.

My work advocating for vegan rights and with vegans has enriched my personal knowledge and understanding beyond expectation. I was already committed to, and empathetic toward, the issues vegan people faced, but I came to realize that I had limited awareness of the extent of the unfairness and the real impact of discrimination on the lives of vegans and, sometimes, on the lives of their families.

Consider, for example, the loss of mental capacity or the potential impact of suffering a stroke. In these kinds of situations, members of a vegan's family will attempt to advocate for their loved one so that their vegan beliefs will be honored and respected, but in both of these contexts, vegans have been disrespected, as if their moral convictions don't matter, and they and their families have been made to feel "inconvenient" and as though they have no choice but to adopt/accommodate a non-vegan lifestyle.

Another example arises in education. Imagine a nine-year-old vegan child, happily vegan from birth but, following yet another negative experience at school, telling their parent or guardian that it's horrible being vegan.

Similarly, imagine vegans in employment who, after struggling with workplace banter and bullying, explain that they are no longer able to face going to work due to the physical manifestations of stress and anxiety. They take sick leave but are unable to explain the true reason because they are ignored and belittled.

Insights such as these are incredibly important, and the application of legal measures in such cases have proved not only useful, but vital for redress, as well as for encouraging support for veganism and bringing about impactful changes.

As I have shown in these pages, rights-based vegan advocacy has brought about a number of tangible benefits, both for individual vegans and for the growth and sustainability of veganism. For example, the inclusion of funding for plant-based alternatives to cow's milk on ethical grounds under Scottish legislation paves the way for the normalization of veganism in the provision of care for young children. Further, the campaign for vegan rights has achieved more than the accommodation of needs for vegan individuals. In alignment with its rationale, strategy, and function to counter prejudicial norms, we have seen in these pages how the funded supply of plant-based milk in a Solihull School brought with it a critical assessment of the appropriateness of the narrative of the "Cool Milk" cow's milk scheme in a UK school. This critical assessment of a long-standing, exploitative practice that violates the dignity of nonhuman animals can be regarded as relevant to the legal responsibility to teach a critical, objective, and plural curriculum.

Another example of how rights-based vegan advocacy has gone further than merely providing a tangible benefit for an individual vegan is the subsequent provision of vegan-friendly resources being purchased for a school library.

A further example is the programme of study at a Bristol college which now accommodates the needs of vegans in the way the programme is taught. These are highly impactful outcomes of the campaign for vegan rights because they not only provide tangible benefits for individual vegans involved; the policy changes required to accommodate the needs of individual vegan complainants bring the message of compassion and benefits of vegan inclusion to a large number of other people too.

These examples illustrate how the campaign for vegan rights has put veganism on the agenda of policy decision makers, as is now required by law in the UK. This validates and helps to normalize veganism and promotes further changes toward the goal of direct protection for nonhuman animals.

The learning provided by these examples, acquired over the years, includes valuable additional insights from different branches of the animal protection movement. There has always been a range of activity in the movement, from grassroots campaign groups to formally established organizations and charities, whose functions include representation in politics and who have the infrastructure and funds to operate internationally, or at least participate in international initiatives. The most important lesson is that to validate our convictions in the non-vegan world and bring about the changes we want to see, we are stronger when we work collaboratively.

With regard to the campaign for vegan rights and the progress and development of the IVRA, community acceptance was formative, and community participation was fundamental. The proposal for the community to adopt a rights-based approach to vegan advocacy and the creation of the IVRA were viewed by some with suspicion because the idea invoked human rights. Though there were dissenting voices, the campaign and the mission were ultimately blessed with respect and acceptance. The legacy is that, together, we have made inroads. But even after over a decade, we are only just getting started, and the more work we do, the more opportunities for further inroads we see.

As I have shown, vegans can and do experience unlawful discrimination, they suffer the consequences of bullying, their rights can be violated, and they can often find it difficult to be heard. In the UK, the everyday lawful activities of vegans can be reported to employers, who request applicant screening. Vegans have been accused of extremism under counter-terrorism measures simply for discussing veganism, and counter-terrorism policing lists the vegan flag in its list of "signs and symbols." Much more attention to these issues is needed in the future, especially in light of increasing police powers.

On the other hand, vegans have legal protection in some parts of the world, and there have been significant wins and there are regular small–but inspiring and motivating—policy changes that go unnoticed. These new and developing social, political, and legal contexts for veganism offer opportunities for further initiatives to help normalize veganism and make it much more accessible and sustainable. Consider, for example, the work of The Vegan Inclusion Co., a new initiative established in 2024. Its purpose is to provide information and to support and certify vegan-inclusive employers. Founder and Chief Executive Officer Jess Swallow explains:

> Many employers want to do the right thing by their people, but they don't fully understand the needs and legal rights of their vegan staff. The Vegan Inclusion Co. supports them in gaining an understanding of the vegan perspective and the profound impact that discrimination and harassment can have.
>
> We are eliminating the barriers that prevent vegans from feeling fully integrated at work by equipping organisations with the knowledge and tools they need to ensure a safe, respectful workplace for everyone, where all staff, including vegans, can thrive.
>
> Our certification scheme allows companies to proudly and publicly celebrate their vegan inclusivity. It lets current and prospective vegan employees know that they can expect to be treated with the same respect and understanding as anybody else, and that their ethical beliefs will be taken seriously in the workplace.[2]

The type of work being done by The Vegan Inclusion Co. is important for the development of vegan inclusion in workplace contexts, but it is also important because it helps employers act in recognition of their legal duties, avoid claims of discrimination, and show that they take veganism seriously. Of critical significance is that a vegan-inclusive certification scheme facilitates vegan visibility and, in doing so, further supports bringing the moral standing of nonhuman animals from the margins to the center of human concerns and activity.

The legal protection of vegans also offers opportunities to broaden further work to interconnected workstreams. For example, new United Nations authoritative guidance advocates a child-rights approach to the climate catastrophe and environmental degradation. This child-rights approach links to existing children's rights, and the child's right to be protected from violence now includes being protected from witnessing violence to other animals. In relation to the right to education, the guidance has established that children have the right to information about important issues that affect them, to help them make responsible decisions, including about sustainable lifestyles. It is clear to see that a rights-based vegan advocacy is well-grounded and intersects with the mission of the UN. Through creative collaborations, much more progress can be made.

In 2023, for example, the call for submissions by the United Nations to support its forthcoming guidance on the rights of the child in relation to the climate catastrophe and environmental degradation motivated a submission from The Vegan Society, explaining how the rights of vegan children were relevant to the mission of the UN.[3] The Vegan Society's International Rights Network member, Alexandra Cantarelli, who is a lawyer in Brazil, has summarized the submission and explains how the UN Committee on the Rights of the Child could have gone further in its guidance.[4] Individuals and networks must continue to collaborate, and knowledge and information must be freely shared to continue pushing forward against barriers, however seemingly insurmountable.

In addition, it is inspiring and motivating to see that professional legal activism is developing according to a "joined-up" approach that also accommodates the vegan rights message. Consider, for example, the powerful motivation of network lawyer, Marcelo Daidone Chalita:[5]

> As a Brazilian, and coming from the greatest biodiversity on Earth, I consider it my job to help to protect the natives, but also, all of us. I feel that the average Brazilian cares a lot about the Amazon rainforest, but they continue to eat meat and cannot see the relationship between diet and destruction. Many are activists for the forest, yet don't know that animal agriculture is responsible for up to 91 per cent of the destruction of the Amazon rainforest.[6] Furthermore, many people are unaware that the Brazilian corporation, JBS, the largest of all meatpackers in the world, slaughters nearly 14 million animals every day and has a turnover of $50 billion.[7]
>
> Furthermore, Brazil became the second largest exporter of meat, the largest exporter of beef, and the second largest producer of soybeans, used mostly as animal feed in Brazil and abroad.[8]

> Basically, we are sweeping our biomes, more specifically, our Amazon and Cerrado (the vast ecoregion of tropical savanna in eastern Brazil), to plant grains to feed cattle, cows, pigs, poultry and fish in other parts of the world, while there are 125.1 million Brazilians with insufficient food (more than half of the population), and 33.1 million hungry.[9]
>
> Around the world, more than enough food is produced to feed everyone, yet there are still 150 million people or 10% of the population hungry.[10]
>
> Gaining insights into the direct impact that farming animals has on the lives of animals, human health and global warming made working in this domain to help resolve issues the main priority in my life. Combining my law background with my passion for veganism, on a daily basis, I would be working towards saving and protecting fauna, flora and ecosystems, combating deforestation and land degradation, and, at the same time, standing up for vegans, other animals, the environment and climate change issues.
>
> My understanding is that everyone tends to be compassionate in their daily lives, but all of us need to understand that animals are holders of moral rights, regardless of formal state recognition.[11] As an animal advocate, if I had to choose only one option to give to animals, I would choose the basic right to not be treated as the property of others.
>
> Every vegan lives according to an important obligation in their daily routine, to honour the dignity of all nonhuman animals. For us, as vegan lawyers, we work in acknowledgement of the strands of interconnection, and arguing in favour of our human clients, including vegans, is the same as arguing for nonhuman animals and the environment. Animals are being killed every second, and thousands of hectares are being deforested every day. In every country, in addition to taking personal action, we need to educate for a change in speciesist mentality in a political way: recognizing in nonhuman animals the ability to feel and suffer (sentience), and extend to them an intrinsic dignity of not suffering and not being subjected to the violation of their integrity, is a first step. Our mission is urgent, and upholding the rights of vegans is an important aspect of the work to which we are committed.

Establishing the IVRA and developing its work have provided knowledge for enhanced understanding that can feed into this new era of joined-up vegan activism.

The campaign for vegan rights and its narrative do not displace nonhuman animals from the center of our moral concern. Rather, they promote a critical examination of exclusive protective rights; specifically, to identify those provisions that allow us to defend our right to live according to our vegan ethical convictions *in order to* show and foster respect for other animals. The use of the human rights framework, for this purpose, is not a self-centered endeavor, but a representation of the grossly exploited others who are denied their right to life, denied their autonomy, denied living in their natural habitats, denied fulfilling their natural and social urges, and suffer horrendous misery and brutality.

To that end, this book celebrates the revolution in the vegan community's understanding and articulation of the human right to freedom of conscience and belief and its offshoots. It celebrates every instance of a rights-based approach to vegan advocacy, every new supportive initiative, every policy adaptation to accommodate those who live with compassion, and every vegan challenging a failed request for accommodation of needs or legal case. It celebrates all these because they function as a revolt against the current oppressive social conditions that suppress veganism and, also, importantly, as seeds of change. They are catalysts for emboldened effort, more refined creative and critical comment, solidarity, and activism. This book, *Seeds of Change . . .*, celebrates all these because they chip away at the prejudicial, destructive social infrastructure that trivializes veganism, hinders its growth, and does appalling violence to other animals.

NOTES

1. Licops, D. "Rescripting History and Fairy Tales in Brigitte Rouan's 'Outremer,' *Women's Studies Quarterly* 30, no. 1/2 (Spring-Summer 2002): 103, https://www.jstor.org/stable/40004640.Cited by Irene Ryan and Barbara Myers Stream Convenors, "Hear me roar: Views from the Edge," accessed April 19, 2024, https://www.edi-conference.org/streams.php?past_conf_id=26.
2. Jess Swallow, personal correspondence, February 2024. See www.veganinclusion.co.uk.
3. "Comments on the Draft General Comment No 26 on Children's Rights and the Environment, With a Special Focus on Climate Change: Comments Submitted by The Vegan Society," accessed April 19, 2024, https://view.officeapps.live.com/op/view.aspx?src=https%3A%2F%2Fwww.ohchr.org%2Fsites%2Fdefault%2Ffiles%2Fdocuments%2Fhrbodies%2Fcrc%2Fgcomments%2Fgc26%2F2023%2Fcs%2FGC26-CS-vegan-society-2023-02-14.docx&wdOrigin=BROWSELINK
4. Alexandra Cantarelli, "Children's Rights, The Environment, Climate Disaster and Veganism: A Comment on new United Nations' Authoritative Guidance," The Vegan Society, December 15, 2023, accessed February 17, 2024, https://www.vegansociety.com/get-involved/international-rights-network/international-rights-network-blog/childrens-rights.
5. Marcelo Daidone Chalita, personal correspondence, December 2023.
6. Anne, "16 Facts That Show How Going Vegan Helps Stop Climate Change," Peta, November 29, 2015, accessed July 31, 2023, https://www.peta.org.uk/blog/how-going-vegan-helps-stop-climate-change/.

7. Ed Winters, *This is Vegan Propaganda (and other lies that the meat industry tells you)* (London: Vermilion, 2022), 43.

8. Cynthia Schuck Paim and Marly Winckler, "Food Animals in Brazil: Five Decades of Transformation," in *Animals in Brazil - Economic, Legal and Ethical Perspectives*, ed. Carlos Naconecy (Palgrave Macmillan, 2019), 10.

9. "A fome e a insegurança alimentar avançam em todo o Brasil" (Hunger and Food Insecurity Advance Throughout Brazil), Olhe Para a Fome, 2022, trans. Marcelo Daidone Chalita, accessed July 31, 2023, https://olheparaafome.com.br/.

10. Action Against Hunger, "World Hunger Facts, Action Against Hunger," 2023, accessed July 31, 2023, https://www.actionagainsthunger.org/world-hunger-facts-statistics.

11. Carlos Frederico Ramos de Jesus, "Cartilha Direitos Animais—Por Onde Começar?" (Animal Rights Booklet, Where to Start?), trans. Marcelo Daidone Chalita (GEDA USP, 2023), 21, accessed July 31, 2023, https://direito.usp.br/pca/arquivos/fdde35684ab3_cartilha-direito-animal-220701.pdf.

Appendix A

Table of Cases

Arrowsmith v. United Kingdom, App. No. 7050/75, Eur. Ct. H.R. (1980).

C. v. United Kingdom, No. 10358/83, Eur. Ct. H.R. Dec. 15, 1983.

Campbell and Cosans v. United Kingdom, No. 48 Eur. Ct. H.R. (Ser. A) (1982).

Casamitjana Costa v. The League Against Cruel Sports (2020) UK ET 3331129/2018.

Church of the New Faith v. Commissioner for Pay-roll Tax (Vict.), 154 CLR 120 (1983).

Conisbee v. Crossley Farms Ltd (2019) UK ET 3335357/2018.

Chassagnou and Others v. France, Grand Chamber Judgment, April 29, 1999, App. Nos. 25088/94, 28331/95, and 28443/95.

Friedman v. Southern California Permanente Medical Group, 102 Cal. App. 4th 39, 125 Cal. Rptr. 2d 663 (2002).

Giudice del Lavoro - Tribunale di Bologna - sentenza n. 2359/2020 del 9 Aprile 2020.

G.K. and A.S. v. Switzerland (communicated), App Nos. 55299/20 and 31515/22, Eur. Ct. H.R.

Grainger plc and others v. Nicholson (2010) IRLR 4.

Handyside v. United Kingdom, App. No. 5493/72, Eur. Ct. H.R. Dec. 7, 1976.

Hashman v. Milton Park (Dorset) Ltd. (t/a Orchard Park)(2011) UK ET 3105555/2009.

Herrmann v. Germany, No. 9300/07, Eur. Ct. H.R. Grand Chamber, June 26, 2012.

Jakobski v. Poland, No. 18429/06, Eur. Ct. H.R. Fourth Section, Dec. 7, 2010.

Knauff v. Ontario (Natural Resources and Forestry) (2023) HRTO 1729.

Law v. Canada (Minister of Employment and Immigration) (1999) CanLII 675 (SCC) (1999) 1 S.C.R. 497.

M Forstater v. CGD Europe and others (2022) UK ET 2200909/2019.

McClintock v. Department of Constitutional Affairs (2008) IRLR 29.

Mr. E McClung v. Doosan Babcock Ltd and others (2022) UK ET 4110538/2019.

Mr. M Ali v. Indian Cuisine Limited (2019) UK ET 2206359/2018.

Ms. K Reilly v. RT Management Bridgeton Limited (2022) UK ET 4107984/2020.

Ms. S Free Miles v. The Royal Veterinary College (2022) UK ET 2206733/2020.

Ms. T Owen v. Willow Tower Opco 1 Ltd (2023) UK ET 2400073/2022.

R (Williamson) v. Secretary of State for Education and Employment (2005) UKHL 15, 2 A.C. 246.

Vartic v. Romania (No. 2), No. 14150/08, Eur. Ct. H.R. Third Section, Dec. 17, 2013.

Vavřička and Others v. The Czech Republic, Nos. 47621/13 and 5 others, Eur. Ct. H.R. Grand Chamber, Apr. 8, 2021.

VG Münster [Verwaltungsgericht Münster], Urteil [Judgment] of Feb. 9, 2022, Case No. 5 K 2576/20, openJur 2022, 3746 (Germany).

W. v. The United Kingdom, No. 18187/91, Eur. Comm'n H.R. (1993).

Wisconsin v. Yoder, 406 U.S. 203, 215-16 (1972).

X. v. Germany, No. 8741/79, Eur. Ct. H.R. Mar. 1981.

Bibliography

Abbott, Diane. "Prevent Programme." *Hansard*. HC Deb., vol. 670, col. 304. January 22, 2020.

Adams, Carol, J. *The Sexual Politics of Meat*. Cambridge: Polity Press, 1990.

Agriculture and Horticulture Development Board. "Education." Accessed April 19, 2024. https://ahdb.org.uk/education.

Alexander, Stian. "Sneaky Lags Pretend to be Vegan in a Bid to Get Better Prison Dinners." *The Mirror*, November 5, 2022. https://www.mirror.co.uk/news/uk-news/sneaky-lags-pretend-vegan-bid-28417598.

All-Party Parliamentary Group on Vegetarianism and Veganism. "Respect for Religious and Philosophical Beliefs while Eating in Care." Accessed July 22, 2023. https://vegappg.org.uk/wp-content/uploads/2021/11/VegAPPG-beliefs-respect-report-1.pdf.

Alvim, Nuno. "The Protection of Vegans in Portugal: Law and Progress." In *Law and Veganism: International Perspectives on the Human Right to Freedom of Conscience*, edited by Jeanette Rowley and Carlo Prisco, 107–120. London: Lexington Books, 2022.

Angulo, Jazmine. "Alumnos de San Marcos piden en tribunales que se sirva comida vegana y rectora responde: "Es un absurdo"." *infobae,* May 1, 2024. Accessed May 7, 2024. https://www.infobae.com/peru/2024/05/01/alumnos-de-san-marcos-piden-en-tribunales-que-se-sirva-comida-vegana-y-rectora-responde-es-un-absurdo/.

Animal Justice. "Human Rights Tribunal of Ontario Rejects Protections for Ethical Vegans." Accessed December 11, 2023. https://animaljustice.ca/media-releases/human-rights-tribunal-of-ontario-rejects-protections-for-ethical-vegans.

Arrowsmith v. United Kingdom, App. No. 7050/75, Eur. Ct. H.R. [1980].

Balls, Ed. "Jobs and Growth." *Hansard*. HC Deb., vol. 545, col. 722. May 17, 2012.

BBC News. "NatWest Worker Told Customer 'Vegans Should be Punched'." February 18, 2019. Accessed July 8, 2023. https://www.bbc.co.uk/news/uk-england-bristol-47257996.

BBC News. "Vegan Parent Complains about Lymington School's Pigs." January 23, 2018. Accessed July 22, 2023. https://www.bbc.co.uk/news/uk-england-hampshire-42782437.

BBC News. "Vegan School Meal Options Promised After Mother's Campaign." November 5, 2019. Accessed July 29, 2023. https://www.bbc.co.uk/news/uk-scotland-50249679.

Bellingham, Lord. "Metropolitan Police: Criminality." *Hansard*. HL Deb., vol. 827, col. 663. February 1, 2023.

Benyon, Lord. "Food Strategy White Paper." *Hansard*. HL Deb., vol. 823, col. 1076. July 7, 2022.

Bishop, Lord of Manchester. "The. Food Strategy White Paper." *Hansard*. HL Deb., vol. 823, col. 1076. July 7, 2022.

Blencathra, Lord. "Queen's Speech." *Hansard*. HL Deb., vol, 801, col. 277. January 8, 2020.

BookTrust. "Milly Cow Gives Milk: Storytime and Craft with Julia Groves." *YouTube*. Video, July 30. 2021. Accessed August 5, 2023. https://www.youtube.com/watch?v=9IuzNT4DALI.

Buscombe, Baroness. "Online Safety Bill." *Hansard*. HL Deb., vol. 831, col. 405. June, 22, 2023.

Butler, Justine. "Vegan Hospital Food: Is it a Basic Human Right?" *Vegan Food and Living*, October 17, 2018. Accessed October 3, 2023. https://www.veganfoodandliving.com/features/vegan-hospital-food-is-it-a-basic-human-right/.

C. v. United Kingdom, No. 10358/83, Eur. Ct. H.R. Dec. 15, 1983.

Campbell and Cosans v. United Kingdom, No. 48 Eur. Ct. H.R. (Ser. A) (1982).

Cantarelli, Alexandra. "Children's Rights, The Environment, Climate Disaster and Veganism: A Comment on New United Nations' Authoritative Guidance." The Vegan Society, December 15, 2023. Accessed January 24, 2024. https://www.vegansociety.com/get-involved/international-rights-network/international-rights-network-blog/childrens-rights.

Casamitjana, Jordi. "The Vegan Rights Movement is Happening Now!." *UnchainedTV*, February 24, 2021. Accessed October 3, 2023. https://unchainedtv.com/2021/02/24/the-vegan-rights-movement-is-happening-now/.

Casamitjana Costa v. The League Against Cruel Sports, [2020] UK ET 3331129/2018.

Casey, Liam. "Vegan Ontario Firefighter Files Human Rights Complaint over Food Served While Battling B.C. Wildfire." *Global News*, May 21, 2019. Accessed August 7, 2023. https://globalnews.ca/news/5299333/vegan-firefighter-human-rights-complaint/.

Casimiro, Diego. "Alumnos de San Marcos piden en tribunales que se sirva comida vegana y rectora responde: Es un absurdo." *infobae*, April 12, 2024. Accessed May 7, 2024. https://www.infobae.com/peru/2024/04/12/pj-admite-demanda-para-que-el-comedor-de-la-unmsm-cuente-con-una-opcion-vegana/.

Charter of Fundamental Rights of the European Union. *Official Journal* C 364/01 (December 18, 2000).

Chassagnou and Others v. France, Grand Chamber Judgment, April 29, 1999, App. Nos. 25088/94, 28331/95, and 28443/95.

Christopeit, Dr Vera. "Success is Relative – and Veganism is a Human Right." *PETA Blog,* August 17, 2022. Accessed November 18, 2023. https://tierrechtsblog.de/deutschland/vgmuenster-veganismus-.

Church of the New Faith v. Commissioner for Pay-roll Tax (Vict.), 154 CLR 120 (1983).

Cole, M., and K. J. Morgan. "Vegaphobia: Derogatory Discourses of Veganism and the Reproduction of Speciesism in UK National Newspapers." *British Journal of Sociology* 62, no. 1 (2011): 134–153.

Committee on Toxicity and SACN. "Final Minutes of the 1st Meeting: Joint SACN/COT Working Group on Plant-Based Drinks." Teleconference, December 2, 2021. Accessed October 19, 2023. https://app.box.com/s/zimfu4icea4mstkpqiv30t1inoml7bae/file/929247556951.

Conisbee v. Crossley Farms Ltd, [2019] UK ET 3335357/2018.

Consolidated Version of the Treaty on European Union. *Official Journal* C326/1 (2012).

Council of Europe. "Convention for the Protection of Human Rights and Fundamental Freedoms." November 4, 1950. Accessed July 15, 2023. https://www.echr.coe.int/Docuemnts/Convention_ENG.pdf.

Council of Europe, European Court of Human Rights. "Guide to Article 2 of Protocol No. 1: Right to Education." Updated August 31, 2022. Accessed July 15, 2023. https://www.echr.coe.int/documents/604084/839313/Guide_Art_2_Protocol_1_ENG.pdf.

Council of Europe, European Court of Human Rights. "Guide on Article 9 of the European Convention on Human Rights: Freedom of Thought, Conscience, and Religion." Updated August 31, 2022. Accessed August 22, 2023. https://www.echr.coe.int/documents/d/echr/guide_art_9_eng.

Council of the European Union. "Council Directive 2000/78/EC: Establishing a General Framework for Equal Treatment in Employment and Occupation." Official Journal L 303 (2000).

Council of the European Union. "EU Guidelines on the Promotion and Protection of Freedom of Religion or Belief." June 24, 2013. Accessed August 27, 2023. https://www.eeas.europa.eu/sites/default/files/137585.pdf.

Council Regulation (EEC) No. 1898/87 of 2 July 1987 on the Protection of Designations Used in Marketing of Milk and Milk Products. *Official Journal* L 182 (July 3, 1987), pp. 36–38.

Courts and Tribunals Judiciary. "Presidential Guidance Employment Tribunal Awards for Injury to Feelings and Psychiatric Injury Following *De Souza v. Vinci Construction (UK) Ltd* [2017] EWCA Civ 879, Sixth Addendum to Presidential Guidance Originally Issued on 5 September 2017." Accessed October 10, 2023. https://www.judiciary.uk/wp-content/uploads/2023/03/Vento-bands-presidential-guidance-April-2023-addendum.pdf.

Crossland Employment Solicitors. "Nearly Half of Vegans Feel Discriminated Against at Work." May 9, 2019. Accessed October 3, 2023. https://www.crosslandsolicitors.com/site/hr-hub/nearly-half-of-vegans-feel-discriminated-against-at-work.

Dando, Gareth. "Employment Tribunal Finds that Ethical Veganism is a Protected Characteristic." Ramsdens Blog, January 6, 2020. Accessed October 3, 2023. https://www.ramsdens.co.uk/blog/employment-tribunal-finds-ethical-veganism-protected-characteristic.

Dansk Vegetarisk Forening. "A Milestone Win: Vegans are Protected by Human Rights, Danish Court Rules." February 12, 2024. Accessed February 14, 2024. https://vegetarisk.dk/milestone-win-vegans-are-protected-by-law-danish-court-rules/.

De Bruler, Tania. "Are You a Vegan in the Workplace? Do You Know Your Rights?" LinkedIn. June 20, 2018. Accessed October 3, 2023. https://www.linkedin.com/pulse/you-vegan-workplace-do-know-your-rights-tania-de-bruler-mcipd/.

Dearden, Lizzie. "Italy's Proposed Law to Jail Vegan Parents for up to Four Years Criticised as 'Discriminatory' Attack on Human Rights." *Independent*. August 16, 2016. Accessed October 2, 2023. https://www.independent.co.uk/news/world/europe/italy-s-proposed-law-to-jail-vegan-parents-for-up-to-four-years-criticised-as-discriminatory-attack-on-human-rights-a7193496.html.

Department for Education. "Statutory Framework for the Early Years Foundation Stage: Setting the Standards for Learning, Development and Care for Children from Birth to Five." March 31, 2021. Accessed July 17, 2023. https://www.gov.uk/government/publications/early-years-foundation-stage-framework--2#full-publication-update-history.

Department of Health and Social Care. "Making Vaccination a Condition of Deployment in Health and Wider Social Care Settings-Equality Impact Assessment." November 9, 2021. Accessed August 12, 2023. https://assets.publishing.service.gov.uk/government/uploads/system/uploads/attachment_data/file/1032203/making-vaccination-a-condition-of-deployment-in-the-health-and-wider-social-care-sector-government-response.pdf.

Department of Health and Social Care. "The Nursery Milk Scheme." Accessed July 17, 2023. https://www.nurserymilk.co.uk/.

Dobson, Charlotte. "Mum Wins Battle to Get Vegan Free School Meals for Her Daughter." *Manchester Evening News*, October 9, 2018. Accessed August 6, 2023. https://www.manchestereveningnews.co.uk/news/greater-manchester-news/vegan-free-school-meals-bury-15254775.

Douzinas, Costas. *The End of Human Rights: Critical Legal Thought at the Turn of the Century.* Oxford: Hart Publishing, 2000.

Elliott-Archer, Jade. "Treatment for Disordered Eating in England: Balancing Vegan Rights and Treatment Requirements." In *Law and Veganism: International Perspectives on the Human Right to Freedom of Conscience*, edited by Jeanette Rowley and Carlo Prisco, 221–243. London: Lexington Books, 2022.

England, Charlotte. "Vegan Allowed to Serve in Swiss Army in Landmark Case." *Independent*. October 25, 2016. Accessed August 7, 2023. https://www.independent.co.uk/news/world/europe/switzerland-vegan-serve-swiss-army-landmark-case-a7379621.html.

Equality and Human Rights Commission. "Employment Statutory Code of Practice: Draft for Consultation." Employment Lawyers Association. Accessed June 22,

2023. https://www.elaweb.org.uk/sites/default/files/docs/Draft%20Employment%20Code%20of%20Practice%201109798532.pdf.

Equality and Human Rights Commission. "Equality law - Banks and other Financial Services Providers." Updated February 19, 2019. Accessed October 10, 2023. https://www.equalityhumanrights.com/en/advice-and-guidance/equality-law-banks-and-other-financial-services-providers.

Equality and Human Rights Commission. "How to Work out the Value of a Discrimination Claim: A Guide to Quantifying Discrimination Claims in Access to Services Cases." April 2018. Accessed October 10, 2023. https://www.equalityhumanrights.com/sites/default/files/quantification-of-claims-guidance.pdf.

Equality and Human Rights Commission. "Religion or Belief Discrimination." Accessed November 2, 2023. https://www.equalityhumanrights.com/equality/equality-act-2010/your-rights-under-equality-act-2010/religion-or-belief-discrimination?return-url=https%3A%2F%2Fwww.equalityhumanrights.com%2Fsearch%3Fkeys%3Dclimate.

Food and Drink Federation. "Guidance on 'Allergen'-Free & Vegan Claims." Last reviewed August 2023. Accessed October 16, 2023. https://www.fdf.org.uk/globalassets/resources/publications/fdf-guidance-allergen-free-and-vegan-claims.pdf.

Food Standards Agency. "Vegan Food and Allergens." Last updated August 22, 2023. Accessed October 16, 2023. https://www.food.gov.uk/safety-hygiene/food-allergy-and-intolerance#vegan-food-and-allergens.

Foreman, Polly. "London Dungeon Apologizes After 'Banning Vegans' for January." *Plant Based News*, January 9, 2023. Accessed July 8, 2023. https://plantbasednews.org/culture/ethics/london-dungeon-apologizes-banning-vegans/.

Fuller, Sarah, Dr Graeme O'Connor, Heather Russell, and Sarah Elder, in association with the BDA (The Association of UK Dietitians) Mental Health Specialist Group. "Practice Guidance: Veganism and Eating Disorders." ResearchGate, July 2019. Accessed October 3, 2023. https://www.researchgate.net/publication/334792429_Practice_Guidance_Veganism_and_Eating_Disorders.

Fouzder, Monidiper. "Vegan Challenges Discriminatory Job Ad." *The Law Society Gazette*, July 3, 2017. Accessed October 2, 2023. https://www.lawgazette.co.uk/lawyer-in-the-news/vegan-challenges-discriminatory-job-ad/5061773.article.

Fraser, Murdo. "Budget (Scotland) Bill: Stage 1." Meeting of the Parliament, Chamber and Committees, February 2, 2017.

Friedman v. Southern California Permanente Medical Group, 102 Cal. App. 4th 39, 125 Cal. Rptr. 2d 663 (2002).

Gadenne, Donelle. "Veganism and the Veterinary Profession: An Incongruous Union? The Experiences of Vegan Veterinary Professionals Working in Small Animal Veterinary Practice in England." PhD diss., Edge Hill University, 2021. https://research.edgehill.ac.uk/ws/portalfiles/portal/48208175/Donelle_Gadenne_PhD_Thesis.pdf.

Gilliver, Liam. "Vegan Soldiers File Complaints against Armed Forces over Lack of Plant-Based Options." *Plant Based News,* May 13, 2021. Accessed August 12, 2023. https://plantbasednews.org/culture/ethics/vegan-soldier-armed-forces-plant-based-options/.

Giudice del Lavoro - Tribunale di Bologna - sentenza n. 2359/2020 del 9 Aprile 2020.

G.K. and A.S. v. Switzerland (communicated), App Nos. 55299/20 and 31515/22, Eur. Ct. H.R.

Go Vegan Scotland. "Results of Survey on Vegan Provision in Scotland." 2017. Accessed October 3, 2023. https://docs.wixstatic.com/ugd/d95b36_f4bccc98458 54533ba8aea3cf8e590b2.pdf.

Gorvett, Zaria. "The Hidden Biases that Drive Anti-Vegan Hatred." *BBC,* February 4, 2020. Accessed September 1, 2023. https://www.bbc.com/future/article/20200203 -the-hidden-biases-that-drive-anti-vegan-hatred.

Gove, Michael. "Topical Questions," *Hansard.* HC Deb., vol. 605, col. 149. January 26, 2016.

Grainger plc and others v. Nicholson, [2010] IRLR 4.

Gregson, Rebecca, Jared Piazza, and Ryan L. Boyd. "'Against the Cult of Veganism': Unpacking the Social Psychology and Ideology of Anti-Veganism." *Appetite* 178 (2022). https://www.sciencedirect.com/science/article/pii/S0195666322002343.

Haas, Michael. *International Human Rights: A Comprehensive Introduction*. 2nd ed. Oxon: Routledge, 2014.

Halpern, Phillip. "Preliminary Report of the Proposed Study on Discrimination in the Matter of Religious Rights and Practices." UN Doc., E/CN.4/Sub.2/162 (1954). Accessed December 11, 2023. https://digitallibrary.un.org/record/783698.

Handyside v. United Kingdom, App. No. 5493/72, Eur. Ct. H.R. Dec. 7, 1976.

Harress, Christopher. "Vegan Soldier Rejected by Swiss Army for Refusing to Wear Leather Boots." *International Business Times*, January 26, 2016. Accessed July 7, 2023. https://www.ibtimes.com/vegan-soldier-rejected-swiss-army-refusing-wear -leather-boots-2280206.

Hartglass, Caryn. "It's All About Food-Tamara Bedić, Jerold Friedman, Jordi Casamitjana: Vegan Discrimination Cases, Part I." Podcast, September 27, 2023. Accessed November 21, 2023. https://podcasts.apple.com/us/podcast/its-all-about-food -tamara-bedi%C4%87-jerold-friedman-jordi/id387958221?i=1000629378227.

Hashman v. Milton Park (Dorset) Ltd. (t/a Orchard Park), [2011] UK ET 3105555/2009.

Health and Safety Executive. Personal Protective Equipment at Work: The Personal Protective Equipment at Work Regulations 1992 (as amended): Guidance on Regulations. HMSO, 2022. Accessed November 2, 2023. https://www.hse.gov.uk/pubns /priced/l25.pdf.

Herrmann v. Germany, No. 9300/07, Eur. Ct. H.R. Grand Chamber, June 26, 2012.

HM Government, "Example Menus for Early Years Settings in England, Part 1, Guidance." 2017. Accessed July 17, 2023. https://assets.publishing.service.gov .uk/government/uploads/system/uploads/attachment_data/file/658870/Early_years _menus_part_1_guidance.pdf.

HM Government. "Example Menus for Early Years Settings: in England Part 2: Recipes." 2017. Accessed July 17, 2023. https://assets.publishing.service.gov .uk/government/uploads/system/uploads/attachment_data/file/658872/Early_years _menus_part_2_recipes.pdf#:~:text=Week%201%3A%20Example%20spring

%2Fsummer%20menu%20for%20early%20years,with%20milk%20and%20sliced%20banana%20Crumpet%20and%20spread.

Horta, Oscar. "Discrimination Against Vegans." *Res Publica* 24 (2018): 359–373. Accessed October 3, 2023. https://link.springer.com/article/10.1007/s11158-017-9356-3.

Human Rights Committee. General Comment No. 22: The Right to Freedom of Thought, Conscience, and Religion (Article 18 of the International Covenant on Civil and Political Rights). UN Doc. CCPR/C/21/Rev.1/Add.4, 1993.

Hunt, Elle. "Parents who Feed Children Vegan Diet Face Prosecution Under Proposed Italian Law." *The Guardian*, August 10, 2016. Accessed October 1, 2023. https://www.theguardian.com/lifeandstyle/2016/aug/10/parents-children-vegan-diet-prosecuted-italian-law.

Independent Monitoring Boards. "Annual Report of the Independent Monitoring Board at HMP Warren Hill for Reporting Year 1 June 2021 – 31 May 2022." October 2022. Accessed July 26, 2023. https://cloud-platform-e218f50a4812967ba1215eaecede923f.s3.amazonaws.com/uploads/sites/13/2022/10/AMENDED-Warren-Hill-AR-21-22-final-for-circulation-without-track-changes.pdf.

International Rights Network. "Department of Health Nursery Milk Scheme Legal Opinion." The Vegan Society, September 24, 2019. Accessed October 19, 2023. https://www.vegansociety.com/sites/default/files/uploads/downloads/Legal%20Opinion%20Nursery%20Milk.pdf.

International Rights Network. "The BIG Veganism in Education Conference Programme." The Vegan Society. Accessed October 21, 2023. https://www.vegansociety.com/get-involved/international-rights-network/international-rights-conference-2022/big-veganism-education-conference-programme.International Vegan Rights Alliance. "Written Evidence from The Vegan Society and The International Vegan Rights Alliance (HRB0019)." October 2016. Accessed October 2, 2023. https://committees.parliament.uk/writtenevidence/73344/html/.

International Vegan Rights Alliance. "Concluding Declaration of the 1st International Law Symposium on Vegan Rights." Accessed September 19, 2023. https://d3n8a8pro7vhmx.cloudfront.net/veganaustralia/pages/10064/attachments/original/1579571581/Concluding-Declaration-of-the-1st-International-Law-Symposium-on-Vegan-Rights.pdf?1579571581.

International Vegan Rights Alliance. "Open letter to Priestland's School in Lymington, Hampshire County Council and Parents of Vegan Children Attending the School." The Vegan Society, January 22, 2018. Accessed October 23, 2023. https://www.vegansociety.com/about-us/international-rights-network/international-rights-network-blog/open-letter-priestlands-school-lymington-hampshire-county-council-and-parents-vegan-children-attending-school.

ITV News. "Bristol Vegan Student Forces College into U-Turn on Making her do Farming Module." April 14, 2021. Accessed July 29, 2023. https://www.itv.com/news/westcountry/2021-04-14/bristol-vegan-student-forces-college-into-u-turn-on-making-her-do-farming-module.

Jakobski v. Poland, No. 18429/06, Eur. Ct. H.R. Fourth Section, Dec. 7, 2010.

Jamieson, Cathy. "Finance (No. 2) Bill." *Hansard.* HC Deb., vol. 579, col. 330. April 9, 2014.

Jenkins, Ruth. "Is There an Aspect of Inclusion Your School is Missing?" *Primary First*, no. 1 (June 1, 2021): 38–43. https://issuu.com/synergyprint/docs/primary_first_issue_31/45.

Kearns, Alicia. "Business of the House." *Hansard.* HC Deb., vol. 705, col. 1173. December 16, 2021.

Knauff v. Ontario (Natural Resources and Forestry), 2023 HRTO 1729.

Kudelka, Petr. "Vegan Rights." Presentation at CARE-2017. *YouTube*. Video. Accessed November 21, 2023. https://www.youtube.com/watch?v=d1FgBX9W6Tk.

Laffineur-Pauchet, Marie. "The Growth of Veganism in France." In *Law and Veganism: International Perspectives on the Human Right to Freedom of Conscience*, edited by Jeanette Rowley and Carlo Prisco, 143–168. London: Lexington Books, 2022.

Larbie, Miranda. "The Vegan Society Launches a Book of Nutritional Advice for Vegan Prisoners." Monday July 9, 2018. Accessed October 3, 2023. https://metro.co.uk/2018/07/09/vegan-society-launches-book-nutritional-advice-vegan-prisoners-7694569/.

LAV. "Bologna: the Teacher has the Right to the Vegan Meal." *LAV*, April 14, 2020. Accessed August 9, 2023. https://www.lav.it/news/bologna-maestra-ha-diritto-al-pasto-vegano.

Law v. Canada (Minister of Employment and Immigration), 1999 CanLII 675 (SCC), [1999] 1 S.C.R. 497, https://canlii.ca/t/1fqh9.

Learning Outside the Classroom. "What is the LOtC Quality Badge?" Accessed October 16, 2023. https://www.lotc.org.uk/providers/lotc-quality-badge-2/.

Lugassy, Hayley. "Vegan Young People in England: An Exploratory Study on their Identity, Relationships and Educational Experience." PhD diss., University of East Anglia, 2022. https://ueaeprints.uea.ac.uk/id/eprint/89352/.

M Forstater v. CGD Europe and others, [2022] UK ET 2200909/2019.

MacInnis, Cara, C. and Hodson, Gordon. "It ain't Easy Eating Greens: Evidence of Bias Toward Vegetarians and Vegans from both Source and Target." *SAGE Group Processes & Intergroup Relations*(December2015): 1–24. DOI: 10.1177/1368430215618253.

Mann, Tanveer. "Vegan, 12, Took His Own Life after Bullies Threw Meat at Him." *Metro*, September 29, 2017. Accessed July 20, 2023. https://metro.co.uk/2017/09/29/boy-12-hanged-himself-after-bullies-threw-meat-at-him-because-he-was-vegan-6964518/.

Marshall, John, Mr, "Creutzfeldt-Jakob Disease." *Hansard.* HC Deb., vol. 279, col. 674, June 18, 1996.

McCarthy, Kerry. "Agricultural Bill (Tenth Sitting)." *Hansard.* HC Deb., col. 354. November 13, 2018.

McClintock v. Department of Constitutional Affairs, [2008] IRLR 29.

McNeil, Daniel. "London Dungeon Announces They Will 'Ban' Vegans from Entering in January in Support of Beloved Character." *LondonWorld,* January 3, 2023. Accessed July 8, 2023. https://www.londonworld.com/whats-on/london-dungeon

-announces-they-will-ban-vegans-from-entering-in-january-in-support-of-beloved-character-3972614.

Ministry of Defence Police, "Diversity and Inclusion." Accessed July 31, 2023. https://www.mod.police.uk/diversity-and-inclusion/.

MLP Law. "Are Vegans Protected from Discrimination?" October 4, 2018. Accessed October 3, 2023. https://www.mlplaw.co.uk/are-vegans-protected-from-discrimination/.

Mr E McClung v. Doosan Babcock Ltd and others, [2022] UK ET 4110538/2019.

Mr M Ali v. Indian Cuisine Limited [2019] UK ET 2206359/2018.

Ms K Reilly v. RT Management Bridgeton Limited, [2022] UK ET 4107984/2020.

Ms S Free Miles v. The Royal Veterinary College, [2022] UK ET 2206733/2020.

Ms T Owen v. Willow Tower Opco 1 Ltd, [2023] UK ET 2400073/2022.

Müller-Amenitsch, Ralf. "Vegan Legal Issues in Germany." In *Law and Veganism: International Perspectives on the Human Right to Freedom of Conscience*, edited by Jeanette Rowley and Carlo Prisco, 71–89. London: Lexington Books, 2022.

Müller-Amenitsch, Ralf. *Vegan im Recht: Das Handbuch für juristische Fragen des vegetarischen und veganen Lebensstils*. Mainz: Ventil Verlag UG & Co. KG, 2016.

Murray-West, Rosie. "Ethical pensions: How to Choose Investments that Make a Positive Impact." *Times Money Mentor,* April 20, 2023. Accessed November 4, 2023. https://www.thetimes.co.uk/money-mentor/article/guide-to-ethical-pensions/.

O'Sullivan, Maureen. "Veganism in the Irish Court of Appeal in 1898: Is This Our Oldest Case?" The Vegan Society, March 15, 2022. Accessed November 27, 2023. https://www.vegansociety.com/get-involved/international-rights-network/international-rights-network-blog/veganism-irish-court-appeal-1898-our-oldest-case.

O'Sullivan García, M. "Vegetarian and Vegan Rights in Europe: Chickening Out or Egging Them On?" *dA. Derecho Animal (Forum of Animal Law Studies)* 11, no. 4 (2020). DOI: https://doi.org/10.5565/rev/da.517.

Packham, Amy. "Priestlands School Cancels Pig Slaughter Project After Mass Criticism." *Huffpost*, January 23, 2018. Accessed July 22, 2023. https://www.huffingtonpost.co.uk/entry/priestlands-school-pig-project-slaughtered_uk_5a670350e4b0e56300730236.

PETA. "Animal-Derived Ingredients List." PETA 2023. Accessed November 22, 2023, https://www.peta.org/living/food/animal-ingredients-list/.

Petrova, Dimitrina. "The Declaration of Principles on Equality: A Contribution to International Human Rights." *The Equal Rights Review*, The Equal Rights Trust, Volume Two, 2008, pp. 58–70. Accessed December 12, 2023. https://www.equalrightstrust.org/content/petrova-dimitrina-declaration-principles-equality-contribution-international-human-rights (Equal Rights Trust).

Piazza, Jared, Simpson, Victoria, and McGuire, Luke. "Why Children Moralise Harm to Animals but Not Meat." *Trends in Cognitive Sciences* 27, no. 8 (2023): 685–688. https://doi.org/10.1016/j.tics.2023.05.004.

Prevost, Astrid. "It's All About Food- Jeanette Rowley, PhD; Astrid Prevost; Tamara Bedić, Esq., Vegan Discrimination Cases, Part 2." *It's All About Food.* Hosted by Caryn Hartglass. Progressive Radio Network, October 4, 2023. Accessed

November 18, 2023. https://itsallaboutfood.podbean.com/e/it-s-all-about-food-jeanette-rowley-phd-astrid-prevost-tamara-bedic-esq-vegan-discrimination-cases-part-2/.

Priestlands School. "Walled Garden." 2023. Accessed July 22, 2023. https://www.priestlands.hants.sch.uk/general-information/extracurricular-activities/walled-garden.

Prisco, Carlo. "*The Right to Vegetarianism.*" Hamilton Books, 2017.

Prisco, Carlo. "Veganism and Law in Italy." In *Law and Veganism: International Perspectives on the Human Right to Freedom of Conscience*, edited by Jeanette Rowley and Carlo Prisco, 91–105. London: Lexington Books, 2022.

R (Williamson) v. Secretary of State for Education and Employment, [2005] UKHL 15, 2 A.C. 246.

Rea, Lord. "Complementary Medicine." *Hansard.*HL Deb., vol. 489, col. 1395. November 11, 1987.

Reddit. "The International Vegan Rights Alliance (IVRA) Has Now Been Absorbed into The Vegan Society as 'The Vegan Society's International Rights Network'." Accessed April 9, 2024. https://www.reddit.com/r/VeganRights/comments/cu6odb/the_international_vegan_rights_alliance_ivra_has/.

Roussel, Krystal-Anne, and Labchuk, Camille. "A Single Black Bean: Discrimination and the Protection of Ethical Vegans in Canada." In *Law and Veganism: International Perspectives on the Human Right to Freedom of Conscience*, edited by Jeanette Rowley and Carlo Prisco, 27–44. London: Lexington Books, 2022.

Rowley, Jeanette. "Celebrating 30 Years of Legal Recognition for Veganism." The Vegan Society, February 10, 2023. Accessed October 2, 2023. https://www.vegansociety.com/get-involved/research/research-news/celebrating-30-years-legal-recognition-veganism.

Rowley, Jeanette. "Dairy's Identity Crisis: Digesting the Socio-politico-legal Landscape." The Vegan Society, April 13, 2023. Accessed January 28, 2024. https://www.vegansociety.com/get-involved/research/research-news/dairy-identity-crisis-digesting-socio-politico-legal-landscape.

Rowley, Jeanette. "Defining Ethical Veganism." *The Law Society Gazette*, July 7, 2023. https://www.lawgazette.co.uk/practice-points/defining-ethical-veganism/5116582.article.

Rowley, Jeanette. "Human rights are Animal Rights: The Implications of Ethical Veganism for Human Rights." In *Critical Perspective on Veganism,* edited by Jodey Castricano and Rasmus Rahbeck, Simonsen, 67–92. Switzerland: Springer, 2016.

Rowley, Jeanette. "The Expert Series Spring 2021: Veganism, Counter Terrorism Strategy and Policing." The Vegan Society, April 29, 2021. Accessed November 25, 2023. https://www.vegansociety.com/get-involved/research/research-news/expert-series-spring-2021-veganism-counter-terrorism-strategy-and-policing.

Rowley, Jeanette. *Towards a Vegan Jurisprudence: The Need for a Reorientation of Human Rights*. London: Lexington Books, 2020.

Rowley, Jeanette. "Veganism and Animal Rights Activism Employment Screening." The Vegan Society, March 28, 2022. Accessed November 28, 2023. https://www

.vegansociety.com/get-involved/research/research-news/veganism-and-animal-rights-activism-employment-screening.

Rowley, Jeanette. "Veganism and Equality Research (2013-2014)." Lancaster University Research Directory (2015). Accessed July 20, 2023. https://www.research.lancs.ac.uk/portal/en/publications/veganism-and-equality-research(f7c7c455-d6b6-49a2-9766-863fc7a92213).html.

Rowley, Jeanette. "What Does Brexit Mean for Vegetarians and Vegans." Presentation to the All-Paty Parliamentary Group on Vegetarianism and Veganism, December 6, 2016. Accessed October 2, 2023. https://vegappg.org.uk/.

Rowley, Jeanette, and Bowles, Edie. "Veganism, Law and Education in the United Kingdom." In *Law and Veganism: International Perspectives on the Human Right to Freedom of Conscience*, edited by Jeanette Rowley and Carlo Prisco, 197–219. London: Lexington Books, 2022.

Rowley, Jeanette, and Carlo Prisco, eds. *Law and Veganism: International Perspectives on the Human Right to Freedom of Conscience.* London: Lexington Books, 2022.

Scientific Advisory Committee on Nutrition (SACN). "Feeding Young Children Aged 1 to 5 Years.". July 2023. Accessed October 19, 2023. https://assets.publishing.service.gov.uk/government/uploads/system/uploads/attachment_data/file/1167077/SACN-Feeding-young-children-aged-1-to-5-full-report.pdf.

Scotland, Baroness of Asthal. "Equality Bill. "*Hansard*,. HL Deb., vol. 673, col. 1109. July 13, 2005.

Scottish Government. "Scottish Milk and Healthy Snack Scheme: Statutory Guidance." https://www.gov.scot/publications/scottish-milk-healthy-snack-scheme-statutory-guidance-local-authorities-participating-registered-day-care-settings/. Accessed September 1, 2023.

Scottish Government. "The Milk and Healthy Snack Scheme (Scotland) Regulations 2021." https://www.legislation.gov.uk/ssi/2021/82/schedule/1.

Seymore, Andrew. "Police Informed of Death Threats against Chef Embroiled in Vegan 'Spiking' Row." *Food Service Equipment Journal* (January 3, 2018). Accessed October 15, 2023. https://www.foodserviceequipmentjournal.com/police-informed-death-threats-chef-embroiled-vegan-spiking-row/.

Simpson, Vicky, and Jared Piazza. "Vegan-Inclusive Education: An Interview with Ruth Jenkins." PHAIRSociety, October 23, 2022. Accessed October 23, 2023. https://phairsociety.org/2022/10/23/vegan-inclusive-education-an-interview-with-ruth-jenkins/.

Slater and Gordon. "Ethical Veganism as a Protected Philosophical Belief." December 20, 2019, updated January 3, 2020. Accessed October 3, 2023. https://www.slatergordon.co.uk/newsroom/ethical-veganism/.

Slawson, Nicola. "Head Chef Resigns Over 'Spiking' Vegan Meal Comments." *The Guardian*. January 3, 2018. Accessed July 15, 2023. https://www.theguardian.com/lifeandstyle/2018/jan/03/head-chef-gets-death-threats-over-spiking-vegan-food-claim.

Soifer, Sarah. "Vegan Discrimination: An Emerging and Difficult Dilemma." *Loyola of Los Angeles Law Review* 36, no. 4 (2003): 1709–1731. Available at: https://digitalcommons.lmu.edu/llr/vol36/iss4/17/.

Solihull Observer. "Solihull School's U-Turn after Vegan Dad's Campaign to Get Soya Milk on the Menu." July 2, 2021. Accessed July 17, 2023. https://solihullobserver.co.uk/news/solihull-schools-u-turn-after-vegan-dads-campaign-to-get-soya-milk-on-the-menu/.

Sparks, Tom. "Protection of Animals Through Human Rights: The Case-Law of the European Court of Human Rights." In *Studies in Global Animal Law*, edited by Anne Peters, Beiträge zum ausländischen öffentlichen Recht und Völkerrecht 290, Berlin, Heidelberg: Springer, 2020. https://doi.org/10.1007/978-3-662-60756-5.

Spencer, David, Chris Donaldson, and Paul Stott. "'Blurred Lines: Police Staff Networks – Politics or Policing?'" Foreword by Rt Hon Priti Patel MP. Policy Exchange, 2023. Accessed December 4, 2023. https://policyexchange.org.uk/wp-content/uploads/2023/01/Blurred-Lines.pdf.

Stanley-Becker, Isaac. "Veganism? His 'creed.' Access to Vegan Food? This Firefighter Claims it's his Human Right." *The Washington Post*, May 22, 2019. Accessed October 3, 2023. https://www.washingtonpost.com/nation/2019/05/22/vegan-firefighter-adam-knauff-canada-human-rights/.

Taylor, Paul, M. *Freedom of Religion: UN and European Human Rights Law and Practice*. Cambridge: Cambridge University Press, 2005.

Tennent, James. "Italian Vegans Outraged over Law that Could Jail Parents for Imposing Diet on Children". *International Business Times*, August 16, 2016. Accessed October 2, 2023. https://www.ibtimes.co.uk/italian-vegans-outraged-over-law-that-could-jail-parents-imposing-diet-children-1576323.

The Association of UK Dietitians (BDA). "Vegetarian, Vegan and Plant-Based Diet." Accessed November 4, 2023. https://www.bda.uk.com/resource/vegetarian-vegan-plant-based-diet.html.

The Equal Rights Trust. "Declaration of Principles on Equality 2008." Accessed December 12, 2023. https://www.equalrightstrust.org/ertdocumentbank/Pages%20from%20Declaration%20perfect%20principle.pdf.

The Local Italy. "Backlash over Italy's Proposal to Punish Vegan Parents." August 15, 2016. Accessed October 2, 2023. https://www.thelocal.it/20160819/vegans-protest-italys-unfair-law-proposal-parents-backlash.

The Vegan Society. "Catering for Everyone." Accessed November 28, 2023. https://www.vegansociety.com/get-involved/campaigns/catering-everyone.

The Vegan Society. "Catering for Everyone: Guide for Vegan Prisoners." September 4, 2018. Accessed October 3, 2023. https://www.vegansociety.com/sites/default/files/C4E_12pp%20Booklet_SPREADS.pdf.

The Vegan Society. "Definition of Veganism." Accessed July 3, 2023. https://www.vegansociety.com/go-vegan/definition-veganism.

The Vegan Society. "International Rights Network Launches at a Vegan Rights Conference." May 31, 2019. Accessed October 3, 2023, https://www.vegansociety.com/whats-new/news/international-rights-network-launches-vegan-rights-conference.

The Vegan Society. "Our Impact, 2022." Accessed October 21, 2023. https://www.vegansociety.com/sites/default/files/uploads/downloads/2022%20Impact%20Report.pdf.

The Vegan Society. "Primary School Forced to Change 'Cow's Milk or Water' Rule after Vegan Dad Fights Discriminatory Policy.". June 24, 2021. Accessed July 20, 2023. https://www.vegansociety.com/news/news/primary-school-forced-change-cows-milk-or-water-rule-after-vegan-dad-fights-discriminatory-policy.

The Vegan Society. "Prison Guards Impose an Oppressive Dietary Regime and Refuse to Allow Prisoners to Become Vegan, says Vegan Society Rights Advocate." November 10, 2022. Accessed July 26, 2023. https://www.vegansociety.com/news/news/prison-guards-impose-oppressive-vegan-dietary-regime.

The Vegan Society. "Supporting Veganism in the Workplace." Accessed November 4, 2023. https://www.vegansociety.com/sites/default/files/uploads/downloads/The%20Vegan%20Society%20Employer%20Booklet.pdf.

The Vegan Society. "The Results are in: Here's What Canadian Vegans Said in Our Vegan Rights Survey." January 8, 2020. Accessed October 3, 2023. https://www.vegansociety.com/get-involved/international-rights-network/international-rights-network-blog/results-are-here%E2%80%99s-what-canadian-vegans-said-our-vegan-rights-survey.

The Vegan Society. *The Vegan.* Issue 3. 2019. Accessed September 20, 2023. https://issuu.com/vegan_society/docs/2019_issue_3_single_pages.

The Vegan Society. "Veganism in the Workplace APPG". *YouTube.* Video. September 17, 2020. Accessed October 3, 2023. https://www.youtube.com/watch?v=V1VfIr0yRgA.

The Vegan Society. "Vegan-Inclusive Education." Accessed October 21, 2023. https://www.vegansociety.com/lifestyle/vegan-inclusive-education.

The Vegan Society. "Vegan Student Forced to 'Study Unit on Farming or Fail' Wins Case against College." April 12, 2021. Accessed July 29, 2023. https://www.vegansociety.com/news/news/vegan-student-forced-%E2%80%98study-unit-farming-or-fail%E2%80%99-wins-case-against-college.

The Vegan Society. "Vegans Welcome to Apply – it's the Law." June 13, 2017. Accessed August 12, 2023. https://www.vegansociety.com/whats-new/news/vegans-welcome-apply-%E2%80%93-it%E2%80%99s-law.

Traynor, Sian and Hanlon, Tim. "Vegan Furious over Rude Note Written on Restaurant Menu after Meatless Enquiry." *The Mirror*, June 1, 2021. Accessed July 8, 2023. https://www.mirror.co.uk/news/uk-news/vegan-furious-over-rude-note-24225814.

United Kingdom. Food Safety Act 1990. https://www.legislation.gov.uk/ukpga/1990/16/contents.

United Kingdom. The Welfare Food Regulations 1996. https://www.legislation.gov.uk/uksi/1996/1434/contents/madehttps://www.legislation.gov.uk/uksi/1996/1434/regulation/2/made.

UNESCO. "Decision of the Intergovernmental Committee: 5.COM 6.14." *Intangible Cultural Heritage*, 2010. Accessed October 12, 2023. https://ich.unesco.org/en/decisions/5.COM/6.14.

United Kingdom. Consumer Rights Act 2015, various sections. Accessed July 15, 2023. https://www.legislation.gov.uk/ukpga/2015/15/contents.

United Kingdom. Equality Act 2010, various sections. Accessed April 21, 2024. https://www.legislation.gov.uk/ukpga/2010/15/contents/england.

United Kingdom Parliament. "Employment Equality (Religion Or Belief) Regulations 2003." *Hansard* HL Deb. Vol 649. June 17, 2003. https://hansard.parliament.uk/Lords/2003-06-17/debates/db7cf612-a1d2-40a2-bd46-f8686f74f7ef/EmploymentEquality(ReligionOrBelief)Regulations2003.

United Nations. Convention on the Rights of the Child. Committee on the Rights of the Child "General Comment No. 26 (2023) on Children's Rights and the Environment, with a Special Focus on Climate Change." https://docstore.ohchr.org/SelfServices/FilesHandler.ashx?enc=6QkG1d%2FPPRiCAqhKb7yhsqIkirKQZLK2M58RF%2F5F0vHrWghmhzPL092j0u3MJAYhyUPAX9o0tJ4tFwwX4frsfflPka9cgF%2FBur8eYD%2BEeDmuoVnVOpjkzwB9eiDayjZA. Accessed September 1, 2023.

United Nations. "International Covenant on Civil and Political Rights." G.A. Res. 2200 A, 21 UN GAOR, Supp. (No 16) 53, UN Doc. A/6316 (1966).

United Nations General Assembly. "Declaration on the Elimination of All Forms of Intolerance and of Discrimination Based on Religion or Belief." GA Res. 36/55, November 25, 1981. UN Doc. A/36/51.

United Nations General Assembly. "Interim Report of the Special Rapporteur on Freedom of Religion or Belief." A/69/261 (5 August 2014).

United Nations General Assembly. "Interim Report of the Special Rapporteur on Freedom of Religion or Belief." A/71/269 (2 August 2016).

Vartic v. Romania (No. 2), No. 14150/08, Eur. Ct. H.R. Third Section, Dec. 17, 2013.

Vavřička and Others v. The Czech Republic, Nos. 47621/13 and 5 others, Eur. Ct. H.R. Grand Chamber, Apr. 8, 2021.

Vegan-Inclusive Education. https://vieducation.co.uk/.

Vegconomist. "Lawyers Gather at Conference to Discuss Vegan Rights." May 31, 2019. Accessed October 3, 2023. https://vegconomist.com/society/lawyers-gather-at-conference-to-discuss-vegan-rights/.

Vegetarian for Life. "Dietary Diversity in the Care Sector: A Guide to Catering for People with Allergies, Intolerances, and Religious, Philosophical and Cultural Dietary Beliefs." 2019. Accessed November 26, 2023. https://vegetarianforlife.org.uk/resources/publications/dietary-diversity-in-the-care-sector.

Vegetarian for Life. "Is it Time for a Legal Definition of Veganism." July 19, 2018. Accessed October 3, 2023. https://vegetarianforlife.org.uk/blog/post/is-it-time-for-a-legal-definition-of-veganism.

VegFest. "Ethical Veganism, The Inside Story," *YouTube*. Video. Accessed October 26, 2023. https://www.youtube.com/watch?v=OwjO9IJr-MM.

VG Münster[Verwaltungsgericht Münster], Urteil [Judgment] of February 9, 2022, Case No. 5 K 2576/20, openJur 2022, 3746 (Germany).

W. v. The United Kingdom, No. 18187/91, Eur. Comm'n H.R. 1993.

Walker, Kirsty. "Now Vegans are Covered by Harman's Equality Law." *Mirror Online,* March 8, 2010. Accessed September 2, 2023. https://www.dailymail.co.uk/news/article-1256264/Harriet-Harmans-equality-law-cover-vegans-teetotallers-atheists.html.

Warsi, Baroness. "Equality Bill". *Hansard.* HL Deb., vol. 718, col. 852–854. March 23, 2010.

Winters, Ed. "Stop Priestlands School from Sending Pigs to Slaughter!" Change.org. January 20, 2018. Accessed July 22, 2023. https://www.change.org/p/priestlands-school-stop-priestlands-school-from-sending-pigs-to-slaughter.

Wisconsin v. Yoder, 406 U.S. 203, 215–216 (1972).

Wren, Amy. "Sacked Vegan Claims Discrimination - a 'Landmark Case'?". *Farrer & Co, Blog*. December 14, 2018. Accessed October 3, 2023. https://www.farrer.co.uk/news-and-insights/blogs/sacked-vegan-claims-discrimination---a-landmark-case/.

X. v. Germany, No. 8741/79, Eur. Ct. H.R. Mar. 1981.

Index

Note: Page locators followed by 'n' refer to notes.

Abbott, Diane, 15n18
Adams, Carol, 60
All-Party Parliamentary Group on Vegetarianism and Veganism, 27, 146, 148
Alvim, Nuno, 73n28
Arrowsmith v. the United Kingdom, 91
Australia, 68, 74n38, 146, 160
Austria, 69, 74n38

balance of power, shifting the, 2, 11, 14n1, 67, 68, 147. *See also* strapline
Basque Country, the, 2
Baxi, Upendra, 101n5
BBC News, 4, 20, 29
Bellingham, Lord, 16n21
Benyon, Lord, 16n19
Bishop, Lord, 16n20
Blencathra, Lord, 5
Bowles, Edie, 103n32, 142n60
Boyd, Ryan, L., 15n6
British Dietetic Association (BDA), The Association of UK Dietitians, 133, 180n16
Buscombe, Baroness, 15n16

C. v. the United Kingdom, 140n31
Campbell and Cosans v. UK, 91, 95, 97, 107
Canada, 2–4, 60, 74n38, 137, 146, 156, 156–79; creed, xiii, xiv, 60, 156, 157, 169–71, 180n9, 187; Ontario Human Rights Commission, xiii, xiv, 60, 187
Cantarelli, Alexandra, 192
Casamitjana Costa v. The League Against Cruel Sports, 15n14, 16n25, 39, 47n59, 72n12, 104n63, 123, 143n81, 146, 181n22, 182nn40–42
Charter of Fundamental Rights of the European Union, 93
Chassagnou and Others v. France, 79, 83, 102nn13–14
Chepner, Laura, 31, 128, 141n55
Children's Food Trust for Public Health England, 126
Church of the New Faith v. Commissioner for Pay-roll Tax, 103n37
Cole, Matthew, xvinn5–6, 15n7, 142n61
Committee on Toxicity and SACN, 141n48
compassion, as value and an issue for law, 8, 10–11, 13, 55, 59, 63, 77, 78, 100, 101, 118, 135, 147, 188, 190, 193

conference: Fifth International Equality, Diversity, and Inclusion Conference, 55; Second International Animal Rights Conference, 55
Conisbee v. Crossley Farms Limited, 47n59
Consumer Rights Act 2015, 139n24
Council Directive 2000/78/EC, 71n4, 104n49, 139n14, 143n69
Council for Learning Outside the Classroom, 118

Dansk Vegetarisk Forening, 156, 184nn69–70
Declaration of Principles on Equality, The, 117, 139nn19–20
Declaration on the Elimination of All Forms of Intolerance and of Discrimination Based on Religion or Belief, 87
Denmark, 2, 3, 137, 151, 155–56
Department for Education, 141n44
Department for Health and Social Care, 127
discrimination, concealed forms of, 99
Douzinas, Costas, 73n33, 101n5

Early Years Foundation Stage, 126
Education: Article 2 of Protocol 1, ECHR, and, 89–90; International Bill of Rights, and, 84–85, 87; meaning, of, 90; religion or belief, and, 88; rights of parents, and, 91–92; social responsibility, in, 118; United Nations, and, 192; vegan rights approach, to, 147, 152, 155
Elder, Sarah, 180n16
Elliott-Archer, Jade, 140n40
Equality: Directive 2000/78/EC, 93, 94; Employment Equality (Religion or Belief) Regulation, 94; principle of non-discrimination, 87, 93; right to, 3, 117
Equality Act 2010, 5, 39, 98, 108–12; direct discrimination, 109; due regard, meaning of, 110–11; harassment, 110; indirect discrimination, 109; legitimate aim, 109; meaning of religion or belief, under, 108–9; objective justification, 109; occupational requirement, 133, 143n69; protected act, 110; protected characteristic, 4–5, 39–41, 98, 116–17; provision, practice, or criterion, 109; public functions, 111; Public Sector Equality Duty, 110–11; tackling prejudice and promoting understanding, 111; victimization, 110
Equality and Human Rights Commission, 1, 51, 68, 112, 113; Draft Code of Practice, and, 4, 54, 59, 68, 186
Equal Rights Trust, the, 117
Estonia, 74n38, 147
European Convention on Human Rights, 2, 9, 78, 96, 98
European Court of Human Rights, 2, 9, 59, 78, 90, 92, 93, 95–97, 108, 148, 151, 152, 188;
Every Child Matters, 31–32, 128

Finland, 74n38
Food and Drink Federation, 140n28
Food Safety Act 1990, 139n27
Food Standards Agency, the, 120, 121
France, 115, 155
Francione, Gary, 185
freedom of thought, conscience, religion, 2, 53, 59, 60; interference, with, 2–3, 53, 57, 71, 81, 84, 86, 89, 91, 92, 103n42
Friedman, Jerry, 53, 72n12
Friedman v. Southern California Permanente Medical Group, 72n12
Fuller, Sarah, 180n16

Gadenne, Donelle, 35, 40, 46nn47–50, 47n62
Germany, 2, 60, 69

Giudice Del Lavoro – Tribunale Di Bologna – Sentenza, 183n58
G.K. and A.S. v. Switzerland, 183n55
Gove, Michael, 15n8
Grainger plc and others v. Nicholson, 96, 97, 108, 131, 132, 149, 150, 182n39
Greece, 74n38
Gregson, Rebecca, 15n6

Handyside v. United Kingdom, 143n78
Hashman v. Milton Park (Dorset) Ltd. (t/a Orchard Park), 36–37, 97–98, 107, 123, 131–32, 137
Hass, Michael, 78, 102n22
Herrmann v. Germany, 81–82
Hodson, Gordon, 15n7
Horta, Oscar, 180n15
human rights: campaign for vegan rights, narrative of, 12; critique, 50, 61, 62; dignity importance of, 12, 62–63, 73n34, 83–84, 104n48, 108, 110, 117–18, 137, 154, 155, 193; exclusive, nature of, 12, 54, 58, 61, 62, 193; relationship to animal rights, 78, 79, 81–83. *See also* Judge Pinto de Albuquerque; reorientation of, 62–63; research, 61; suffering narrative of, 61, 63

India, 74n38
International Covenant on Civil and Political Rights, 85–86, 89–94
International Vegan Rights Alliance: Declaration, 70, 74n38; early manifesto, 68; first symposium, 49, 69–70; function, mission, and strategy, 64–66, 68, 75, 114, 45n33; gifted to The Vegan Society, 70, 147; logo, 67; professional legal activism, 65, 192; representatives, 65, 68, 69, 74, 115, 145, 146; statistics, 70, 151, 179n1; strapline, 14n1, 67, 68
Issues faced by vegans, 17–48; accessing vegan milk in nursery and school, when, 29–31, 76, 100, 126–28, 147, 148, 190; accused of extremism, 38, 133–34, 191; banter, 18, 36, 149, 186; bullying, 18, 33, 34, 129; consumers of goods, facilities, and services, as, 19–28; denial of service, 23, 119; education, in, 28–36, 76, 84, 125–30; employment, in, 36–42; excursions, access to, 21, 113; forced to handle and cook animal products, 26–27; hatred/hostility, 4, 15n7; jokes, 36, 56, 149; kill nonhuman animals, requirement to, 35; military service, in, 134, 151–53; pension, access to ethical, 39, 59, 134; PPE, provision of, 36, 38, 132–33, 142n68; prison, in, 27–28, 58, 92, 103n42, 125, 148, 152, 186; recruitment, in, 38, 133; ridicule, 3, 4, 18, 19, 186; silencing, 186; veganophobia, 4, 157; verbal abuse, 20, 112; veterinary education, in, 35–36;
Italy, 3, 73n28, 137, 152

Jakóbski v. Poland, 73n27
Jenkins, Ruth, 33
Judge Pinto de Albuquerque, 81–82

Kearns, Alicia, 15n17
Knauff, Adam, 13, 145, 156–79
Knauff v. Ontario (Natural Resources and Forestry), 14n2
Knight, Andrew, 35
Kudelka, Petr, 69, 179n4

Labchuk, Camille, 60, 169, 170, 184n71, 187
Laffineur-Pauchet, Marie, 115, 155
Law v. Canada (Minister of Employment and Immigration), 139n21
London Dungeon, The, 22, 115–18
Lugassy, Hayley, 34, 129
Luxembourg, 74n38

MacInnis, Cara, C., 15n7
Marshall, John, 4
McCarthy, Kerry, 4
McClintock v. Department of Constitutional Affairs, 104n58
McGuire, Luke, 34, 129
M Forstater v. CGD Europe and others, 140n35
Ministry of Defence Vegan and Vegetarian Network, 134
Morgan, Karen, xvin5, 15n7
Mr E McClung v. Doosan Babcock Ltd and others, 182n47
Mr M Ali v. Indian Cuisine Limited, 24, 121
Ms K Reilly v. RT Management Bridgeton Limited, 42, 136–37
Ms T Owen v. Willow Tower Opco 1 Ltd, 41–42, 135–36
Müller-Amenitsch, Ralf, 69, 115, 153, 155, 188; *Vegan im Recht*, 69; *Weltanschauung*, explanation of, 60, 115, 153, 188

NatWest Bank, 20, 112–13, 138n2
Netherlands, the, 74n38
Nursery Milk Scheme, the, 29, 126, 141n47

O'Connor, Graeme, 180n16
Ontario Human Rights Tribunal, 3, 13
O'Sullivan Maureen, 138n3

philosophical belief, 3–5, 36–37, 39, 41, 51, 53–54, 60, 90–98, 109, 116, 129, 132, 136, 150; climate change, in, 96–97; hunting, against, 36–38; legal test, *Grainger* UK, 47n59, 60, 108, 131–32, 149, 150, 182n39; legal test ECtHR 90–92; legal test Ontario, 156–58, 187
Piazza, Jared, 15n6, 34, 129
Prevost, Astrid, 155
Prisco, Carlo, 73n28, 152, 183n56

R (Williamson) v. Secretary of State for Education and Employment, 34, 94, 104n62, 107
Rea, Lord, 4
Religion or belief, protection for, 45n43, 52–54, 72n13, 83–100, 107–9, 187
Rights of the Child, 148, 192
Romania, 74n38
Roussel, Krystal-Anne, 184n71
Russell, Heather, 180n16

Scotland, 10, 74n38, 146, 148
Scottish Government, 100
Seeds of Change…explanation of, 1, 2, 11–12
Simpson, Victoria, 46n43
Soifer, Sarah, 73n26
South Africa, 74n38
Sparks, Tom, 78
Swallow, Jess, 191

Taylor, Paul, 103n36
trading standards, 121

United Nations Human Rights Committee, 54, 72nn17–18, 86, 92
United States of America, 74n38, 146, 182n52
Universal Declaration on Human Rights, 61, 83–85, 89, 93

Vartic v. Romania, 73n27
Vavřička and Others v. The Czech Republic, 143n79
vegan: belief, 53, 146, 150; equality survey, 9, 10, 18, 19, 27, 28, 36, 54, 56–57, 69, 72n22; identity, 34
Vegan Equality Non-Discrimination (VEND), 49, 54, 63, 147; logo, 64; strapline, 64
Vegan Inclusive Education, 32–33, 141n55
veganism: anthropocentric culture and, 3, 12, 16n24, 61, 62, 153; anti-vegan attitude, 3–4, 12, 14, 36,

157; defending, 2, 58, 59, 63, 77, 100–101, 179n1, 188; definition, 7, 149; Parliament, United Kingdom, views in, 4–5; social, political and legal landscape and, 3, 13, 54, 76; trivialised, 60

vegan rights: advocating for, 31, 54, 55, 63, 68, 69, 71, 100, 142n62; animal rights, and. *See* "human rights, relationship to animal rights", above; appeal to law, rationale for, 1, 2, 75–77; campaign for, rationale and mission, of the, 2, 50, 56, 60–61, 100, 147; celebrating, 1, 11, 12, 16n27, 134, 191, 194; defending. *See* "veganism, defending", above; grounded by *belief*, objection to, 57; human dignity, and. *See* "human rights, dignity, importance of" above; individual, 3, 9–12, 54, 61–63, 92, 94, 99, 113, 135, 149, 189–90; justice, and, 1, 3, 6, 8, 12, 13, 18, 19, 63, 65, 67–68, 71, 75, 99, 137, 157; legal framework for protection, of, 83–100; limitation, 13, 62; paradigm shift and, 8, 135; policy change, and, 58, 78, 188, 190, 191; representation of duty to respond to suffering, and, 62; representation of "others", and, 194; representation of primary mission of rights enterprise, and, 62; research objectives, 52–55; revolution, 1, 2, 11, 194; strategy, 1, 58, 190;

Vegan Rights: Questions and Answers, 9, 10

Vegan Society, The: International Rights Network, xiv, xv, 14, 141n47, 142n59, 147, 181n25, 192; Research Network, 182n35; rights-based advocacy, 142n62

Veganuary, 22, 115–16

Vegconomist, 146, 180n11, 73n36

Vegetarian for Life, 124, 140n39, 180n14

VG Münster [Verwaltungsgericht Münster], 183nn60–65

W. v. the United Kingdom, 71n3, 72n10, 102n12, 103n42, 138n1, 140n32, 148

Warsi, Baroness, 4–5

Welfare Food Regulations 1996, the, 126

Winters, Ed, 45n40, 195n7

Wisconsin v. Yoder, 103n37

X. v. Germany, 103n40

About the Author

Jeanette Rowley (PhD) established the global campaign for vegan rights over a decade ago. She founded the International Vegan Rights Alliance in 2012, is a consultant to The Vegan Society, and chairs the International Vegan Rights Network. She is the author of *Vegan Rights: Questions and Answers* (2014), *Towards a Vegan Jurisprudence: The Need for a Reorientation of Human Rights* (2020), and co-editor of *Law and Veganism: International Perspectives on the Human Right to Freedom of Conscience* (2022).

www.ingramcontent.com/pod-product-compliance
Ingram Content Group UK Ltd.
Pitfield, Milton Keynes, MK11 3LW, UK
UKHW041836031026
15587UKWH00002B/803